So you'd like to buy an airplane!

SO YOU'D LIKE TO

BUY AN AIRPLANE!

A handbook for prospective owners

by AL GRIFFIN

THE MACMILLAN COMPANY

Library of Congress Catalog Card Number: 77-75393

First Printing

The Macmillan Company
866 Third Avenue, New York, N.Y. 10022
Collier-Macmillan Canada Ltd., Toronto, Ontario

Printed in the United States of America

To A. F. GUTZMER
who was an early pioneer in
transportation and communications
when they really counted most

Acknowledgments

Among the editors and publishers who have printed the author's magazine articles on transportation and communications, he is especially indebted to the following, who have extended permission to reprint excerpts and for the use of industry figures covering the use of aircraft in their respective specialized fields:

ADVERTISING & SALES PROMOTION	Agency management
AMERICAN DAIRY REVIEW	Milk distribution
AMERICAN PAINTING CONTRACTOR	Field supervision
AMERICAN SALESMAN	Sales management
AUTHOR & JOURNALIST	Assignment coverage
BOAT & MOTOR DEALER	Marine distribution
BOATING INDUSTRY	Manufacturing
BUILDING MATERIALS DEALER	Lumber retailing
BURROUGHS CLEARING HOUSE	Banking and finance
BUYER'S GUIDE	Aircraft acquisition
CANDY INDUSTRY	Manufacturing
CANDY MARKETER	Wholesale, retail
CARTE BLANCHE	Private aviation
CONSTRUCTION EQUIPMENT & MATERIALS	Heavy construction
DEPARTMENT STORE JOURNAL	Retail merchandising
DOMESTIC ENGINEERING	Heating, air conditioning

ELECTRONIC TECHNICIAN	TV, radio
ELKS	Fraternal
ESCAPADE	Chances/odds
FUELOIL & OIL HEAT	Heating contractors
GENTLEMEN'S QUARTERLY	Private planes
GEYER'S DEALER TOPICS	Office efficiency
GIFT & ART BUYER	Purchasing
HOBBY/MODELS	Crafts retailing
HOTEL & MOTEL JOURNAL	Operations
HORIZON	Travel
IMPLEMENT & TRACTOR	Farm equipment dealers
INDEPENDENT PETROLEUM MONTHLY	Field production
INDUSTRIAL DISTRIBUTOR NEWS	Mill supplies
INGENUE	Women
INVESTMENT DEALERS DIGEST	Securities
JUVENILE MERCHANDISING	Retailing
LP GAS	Distribution
LAWN EQUIPMENT JOURNAL	Wholesale, retail
MAN'S MAGAZINE	Low-cost flying
MAN'S WORLD	Test piloting
MEN'S MAGAZINE	Aerobatics
MOBILHOME DEALER	Retail distribution
MODERN CONVERTER	Paper and packaging
MODERN MAN	Flying circus
MODERN STATIONER	National distribution
MOTOR AGE	Automotive distribution
N.A.D.A. JOURNAL	Automobile dealers
N.A.H.B. MONTHLY	Home builders
NATIONAL BOTTLERS GAZETTE	Plant administration
NATIONAL JEWELER	Merchandising
NATIONAL PETROLEUM NEWS	Consumer distribution
NATIONAL PROVISIONER	Frozen foods
OFFICE PRODUCTS DEALER	Commercial distribution
OMNIBUS	Communications
PAPER SALES	Wholesale merchants
PANORAMA	Americana
PHOTO DEALER	Retail sales
PHOTO TRADE NEWS	Administration

PLAYBOY	Recreational
PLYWOOD INDUSTRY	Forestry
PRINTING IMPRESSIONS	Publishing
PUBLIC UTILITIES FORTNIGHTLY	Aerial patrol
QUALIFIED ELECTRICAL CONTRACTOR	Major construction
RETAIL LUMBERMAN	Materials distribution
ROGUE	Weekend flying
RUBBER WORLD	Plant administration
SAGA	Transportation
SHOOTING INDUSTRY	Arms distribution
SIGNATURE	Diners' Club
SPORTING GOODS DEALER	Equipment retailing
SPORTSMAN & GUNS	Collecting
TEXTILES	Multiplant operations
TRUCKING INDUSTRY	Expediting
WELDING DISTRIBUTOR	Field service

Contents

xi

geoning Experimental Aircraft Association, Rockford Show, Unorthodox powerplants, EAA biplane, Stits Skycoupe, Do-it-yourself costs, Midget Mustang racer, Bushby's two-seat MM-II, Beckham Taylor monoplane, Bowers and Nesmith/Cougar folding wings, Frey and Astlund Stardusters, Volmer Jensen/Chapeskie Sportsman amphib, Wicker Nieuport fighter, Plans; standard biplanes from EAA, Meyer, Mung; Aerobatic biplanes from Pitts, Smith, Stolp; Parasol wings with open cockpit from Ace, Woods; Folding wing from Bowers, Eaves, Stits; High-wing "box" construction from Wittman; Low-wing standards from Bushby, Cvjetkovic, Falconar, Stits, Taylor, Thorp, Turner; Amphibian from Volmer; Midget racers (within definition) from Bushby, Cassutt, Styles, Taylor

Illustrations

Introduction

Have you heard stories about how you can solo for a pilot's license after only eight hours of instruction? How a private plane gets better mileage per gallon of gas than an automobile? Or how the most dangerous part of any flight is driving to and from the airport?

All true . . . but with reservations. Manufacturers' claims aside, private flying today has plenty of limitations as well as advantages. But there are many reasons why it now represents one of the fastest-growing industries in the country.

In many ways, the year 1968 marked a milestone in private aviation. Unlike the better-organized automobile industry, which so efficiently showcases its new products every year at automobile shows, the airplane industry had never had anything comparable until 1967, when the first annual Exposition of Flight was held in April in Las Vegas. Like many firsts, there were a lot of bugs in it, but by the following year the organizers had a smoothly running "Airplane Show," as slick as anything sponsored by Detroit.

For one thing, the date was moved up to the end of May, when flying weather is better for anybody coming in from the east. Expanded indoor facilities allowed for 40 general aviation aircraft displays with space for 500 exhibit booths, and even a

"Queen of Flight" was chosen, complete with bathing suit. Manufacturers displayed their wares in the air as well as on exhibit, and the United States Aerobatic team put on performances, as did the Air Force Thunderbirds and the Golden Knights. The advisory committee included Barry Goldwater, Arthur Godfrey, Roscoe Turner, and Cliff Henderson. In short: big time.

The show did much to put the industry solidly into the mainstream of transportation merchandising. Business surged accordingly as private aviation took on the tone of full-fledged business instead of what had often seemed to be just an expensive sport in the past.

With a history strewn with hundreds of defunct manufacturers, the industry finally shook down in 1968 to the point that the manufacturing picture solidified into something almost resembling the automobile industry for production efficiency. As of 1968 the Cessna Aircraft Company, of Wichita, Kansas, was the undisputed General Motors of private aviation, building almost as many planes as the rest of the airplane manufacturers put together.

Bill Lear brought Detroit technology and technique to the industry by concentrating engineering, design, purchasing, and production on a single model (yes, in one color). By 1968 Lear Jet was getting the lion's share of the lucrative corporate-jet business accordingly, with a 500 mph-plus airplane (now admittedly modified) that sells for little more than half of what half a dozen competitive makes cost.

Champion Aircraft Corporation did the same basic thing with its sports plane, bringing the price down to under $6,000. Piper Aircraft Corporation cracked the price barrier for a plane with automatic retractable landing gear and brought out the new Cherokee Arrow for 1968 at $16,900. Mooney Aircraft lowered the price on *its* low-line retrac to $16,600 to get in on the action.

In 1968, too, opposition to turbocharging gave up the lost cause, and the now-proven blowers were embraced by manufacturers all down the line. This advance enables dozens of new models, formerly limited to relatively low ceilings because of thin air, to fly above the weather at high altitudes with the same operating efficiency an unaspirated engine gets at sea level.

Cessna assembly-line operations turn out planes at the rate of one every 17 minutes at Wichita Commercial Division plant.

Taking a big step ahead of the pack, the Ted Smith organization began marketing the first of the Aerostar line, where the same basic design—using the same parts—can be built as anything from a two-seater with a small piston engine to an eight-passenger twin jet, in what many authorities consider the opening gun in a genuine revolution to standardize production.

The present range of private aviation is tremendous. By the spring of 1968, inventory ranged from do-it-yourself glider kits for a few hundred dollars to LeRoi Grumman's breathtaking new Gulfstream II, carrying a basic price tag of $2,525,000 (FOB Bethpage, Long Island . . . with 53 on firm order as of the finish of the Las Vegas Airplane Show).

The Year of the Big Change can also be called the Year When the Numbers Were Rounded Out. For the first time, there were over 100,000 civilian planes operating in the United States ·

(not counting about 2,000 commercial airliners). The 10,000th airport was built (and there are also 5,000 golf courses now where almost any par 5 hole makes an excellent landing strip for a light plane, not to mention innumerable open fields, country roads, deserts, strip mines, sandy beaches, frozen lakes, and so on, which are often pressed into emergency service). Some 50,000 flight instructors are now registered, and over a million prospective airplane owners have now soloed, too. This book is an attempt to combine and condense some of their practical experiences.

Much of the industry's impetus comes from business aviation, which is growing so fast that corporate aircraft already account for more than half of all civilian flying. An odd note: the number of professional pilots who fly company planes is dwindling steadily as rapidly increasing numbers of businessmen do their own flying.

In fact, many businessmen buy a plane before they even know how to fly the thing. One consideration is the fact that using a plane of your own costs about a third as much as learning to fly in an airplane owned by the flight school.

Many people do indeed start to solo after only a few hours of dual instruction, and the only basic requirement for the standard VFR (Visual Flight Rules) license has long been a mere 40 hours of flight time before certification. Even this may change in the next year or so, to make it easier than ever to get a license that will allow a Basic Pilot to fly anywhere in the United States, with or without passengers, in uncomplicated aircraft during daylight hours.

However, the executive whose company has tied up perhaps $100,000 in a company plane usually makes sure of what he's doing before he takes any chances with such expensive hardware. The average independent flyer who has invested his own savings in a light $12,000 plane (or $3,500 in a second-hand one) is even more chary of risking his investment. Only a limited number of shortcuts are safe enough to be considered seriously.

The overwhelming majority of private planes really are operated for about 10 cents a mile, including depreciation, insurance, hangar rent, and engine overhauls, as well as gas and oil—but only because there are so many more little ones. The cost of operating many private planes can be so high that the only justifiable cost has to be considered in relation to the seat-cost per mile flown, with operating costs running all the way up to $850 an hour for some of the big corporation planes. Over-buying is one of private aviation's most common characteristics.

Flying a light plane is not yet quite foolproof . . . but it's getting comfortably close. Unless he flies into power lines or dives straight into the ground, the light-plane pilot has to really try hard to kill himself these days. Manufacturers now build in a margin for error so that their planes are far more "forgiving" than they used to be, and flying has never been safer for those who stay within the rules.

Modern aerodynamic design eliminating the possibility of a spin, bigger ailerons for more positive control, tricycle landing gear to correct even sloppy landings, and more dependable powerplants all help make flying easier as well as safer.

Actually, flying is much easier than driving an automobile. Except for the fact that an airborne plane eventually has to get back onto the ground, a student pilot could learn practically everything he needs to know about actually flying a plane in half an hour. There are no stop lights, no blind corners, no railroad crossings, no schoolchildren to watch out for, no tail-gaters, and not even any gear shifting.

Once it is trimmed out, a modern plane will literally fly itself, and a well-designed airplane can actually take off by itself as well. Flight training is about 90 percent concerned with the fact that the aircraft must eventually return to earth.

Kicking the tires on an airplane is not quite enough for the prospective buyer, though. If he wants to use it for recreation, his first problem is to decide what he wants to get out of it (he'll be putting a lot into it, including his family). If the prospective purchaser is a businessman, his biggest immediate problem is to figure out if his company really needs it (he might be investing anything up to a couple of million dollars of the stockholders' money). And in most cases, an airplane is not something the prospective buyer has grown up with, like an automobile; he is in uncharted territory in the area of aircraft acquisition.

At this moment of writing, there are over 250 different makes of civilian aircraft in the skies of America, with more coming (and going) every year. Almost 200, admittedly, are no longer being manufactured, even though old-but-not-forgotten companies are being revived in some instances (see the Summary of Makes and Models at back of book). But they are all still flying, in a host of models, and many are still on the market. With the care that most planes necessarily get, most of them will remain on the used-plane market for a long time to come.

The anecdotes and case histories in the following chapters are designed to give the prospective buyer of a private plane, whether new or used, some insight into some of the considerations involved. Individual models are starting to change a little every year, almost like automobiles, but the varying specifications for any particular model are more notable for their similarities than for their differences. This book is meant to give a guideline, not to be a catalog. The most popular planes, and the ones that are most "interesting" from the standpoint of problems, are covered in some depth. A serious mistake in private aviation can cost more than mere money; here is how a lot of other airplane owners minimized the possibilities . . .

AL GRIFFIN

Evanston, Illinois

CHAPTER 1

Flying for fun

Smoking tires squealed against protesting bricks, and a quarter of a million Memorial Day racing fans surged to their feet as the big Offie started to fishtail when it blatted into the south turn. Their relief was audible as the driver recovered and roared into the east bank with a burst of confidence. Explosive excitement hung in the air like gasoline fumes.

Fred Hoffman sank back into his grandstand seat and grinned up at Ben Phillips, who was still standing with his binoculars trained on the back straightaway.

"Sit down, pal," Hoffman said. "The race still has a long way to go. And judging by the way it's going so far, they'll be fighting it out like this right down to the last lap."

"Yeah, I know," Phillips said as he picked up his beer. "That's what bugs me . . . I'm going to have to leave pretty soon."

"You mean you're not staying for the finish?"

"I'm afraid not. When I arranged to ride down here with Pete Pappas I didn't realize that he'd have to be back in Chicago by tonight. Getting here took almost five hours of hard driving yesterday, and the traffic getting out of Indianapolis will be even worse after the race is over."

Phillips took a long pull at his beer. "And once we get out of the city," he added, "everybody with an open stretch of road will be trying to do what he saw during the race today. Thousands of people are leaving already to try to beat the traffic. I'm willing to bet that the guys out there on that speedway right now are a lot safer than we'll be on the highway on the way home."

"Then why not ride home with me?" Hoffman offered. "I'm alone, and I'll be glad to have the company."

Phillips raised his eyebrows. "It's not that Pete isn't a good driver," he said. "What makes you think that you could make better time than I could in Pete's car . . . do you know a shortcut or something?"

"Well, yeah, I guess you could call it a shortcut, compared to the zigzagging your route calls for," Hoffman said. "I came by plane."

"What? Go all the way out to Weir Cook Municipal Airport to try to get a plane? Not me, Fred. For one thing, our car is parked way to hell and gone over on Northwestern Avenue, which was the closest parking spot we could find. For another, the flights after a race are always booked solid, with a long waiting list, too."

Hoffman laughed. "Yeah, but this is my own private plane."

"Wha-a-a-a-t?"

"Sure. And it's parked just a couple of blocks north of here, at the old Shank Airport. With the plane, we can stay to see the end of the race and still be back in Chicago before Pete gets there."

Phillips leaned back in his seat and took a long look at his companion. "So you finally got a plane of your own, like you've been talking about for so long, eh?" he said. "When did you get so rich all of a sudden?"

"You don't have to be a millionaire to own a plane these days," Hoffman grinned. "This isn't a four-engine jet, you know . . . it's just a little one-lunger for four people."

"Yeah. Well, thanks, but I think I'd better go back with Pete," Phillips said. "I appreciate the offer, but . . . you know . . ."

Hoffman just kept grinning.

"Well, goddammit, I don't even like to fly in the commercial planes, regardless of how much experience the pilot's got," Phillips blurted. "Gosh, I don't want to hurt your feelings, Fred, but the last time I saw you you were using an automobile like everybody else, and that was only last winter."

"I've had my license for almost two months."

"Oh, great! Look, I'll admit it . . . I've never been up in a private plane. You don't honestly expect me to start by putting on goggles to fly around in some chicken-wire kite, do you?"

"What have you got to lose?"

"My arms and legs! Not to mention my life. No, I think I'll take my chances on the ground."

"Your arms and legs will be a lot safer 3,500 feet above the traffic than they'd be in Pete's car down on that highway. Have you ever seen the statistics?"

"Well, yeah . . . but it's going to take more than facts to convince me! At least you can walk away from a minor automobile accident if your car quits. But you sure can't walk away from that plane 3,500 feet up in the air! What happens if that sewing machine you call an engine ever gives out while you're up there?"

"Ever have an automobile engine quit on you?"

"Well, no, I haven't. Oh, I had a fuel pump act up on me once, but I just got out and fixed it. And that's the whole point!"

"For one thing, there is no fuel pump on the plane, like in your car," Hoffman said patiently. "The gasoline tank is in the wing, and it feeds direct to the carburetor by gravity alone. The potentially troublesome fuel pump is only one example of how a lot of the weak points of a piston engine have been eliminated in aircraft versions.

"For instance, if anything goes wrong with your battery, generator, or voltage regulator, your car quits; but an airplane engine operates independently of the electrical system. It works on a spark generated from crankshaft-geared magnetos. There is no distributor to get out of whack, no points to clog up, and if the battery goes on the fritz, the engine won't even notice.

"Furthermore, for double safety, the engine can operate on either of two sets of components in the dual ignition system, with two mags, two spark plugs, and two sets of wires for each cylinder . . . and if the set you're running on goes bad, you simply switch over to the other one."

Phillips nodded. "All that means to me is that you people are so worried the engines might quit that you go to great lengths to prevent it," he charged. "Just for the sake of argument, what do you do if the engine *does* quit?"

"Nothing."

"Maybe scream a little, eh?"

"Not at all. An airplane depends on its wing for flight, not on its engine. You've got about a mile of gliding capability for every 1,000 feet of altitude, and in thickly populated country like this, you are almost always in sight of some kind of landing field, not even counting more than 10,000 regular airports scattered around the country.

"I had to practice dead-stick landings so much that I was known for a while around my home-base airport as Noiseless Hoffman before I got my license. You don't think that I'd be silly enough to go up there and risk my neck, do you?"

"Well, you got a point, but I dunno, Fred . . . don't snow me now. Is that contraption of yours officially certified as safe?"

"Absolutely. If the parachute fails to open, you get your money back."

"Hey!"

"It's a joke, son. No kidding, private flying is so safe nowadays that nobody ever uses a parachute any more. Well, how about it, do you want to see the finish of the race or not?"

"Golly, I sure don't look forward to that long drive back to Chicago in that highway traffic with Pete," Phillips mused. "Does that thing have a radio in it, in case you get into trouble that you don't know how to handle?"

"Two of 'em. And a stereo tape record player."

"Huh?"

"You bet. We ride in style. Wait'll you see it."

"Well, I guess it wouldn't hurt to take a look at it."

"We'll be home in time for dinner."

At the airport, late afternoon sun glinted from the wing of Hoffman's trim little Cessna 172 standing on the flight line.

Phillips stepped forward nervously and peered inside the cabin.

"Hey, this looks like the inside of an automobile!" He whistled. "I'll admit that I'm impressed. I had visions of an open-cockpit two-seater held together with piano wire through a flapping fabric. This thing's even got ribbed upholstery and wall-to-wall carpeting, even for the passengers in the back seat. And get a load of those picture windows! Are you sure you haven't hit an oil well someplace that you're not telling anybody about, Fred?"

"Nope, I still just run the grocery store," Hoffman said. "But don't let the gloss fool you; this is a businesslike airplane. Just incidently, it probably cost less than that motorboat of yours. I get better mileage per gallon of gas than I get with my Pontiac, too."

He pulled a clipboard from the map compartment and walked to the front of the plane, where he yanked at the propeller and then made a notation. As he made his clockwise circle of the plane, inspecting visually and by hand to check off one item after another against his clipboard list, Phillips trotted alongside.

"What's the matter, Fred, anything wrong?" he asked anxiously.

"No indeed, that's what I'm making sure of," Hoffman said. "Remember what I said about how safe flying is? One reason is because no pilot would consider taking off without going over his check list for a flight line inspection to start with.

"In 99 cases out of 100 it's a waste of time, too, but I always go through the motions anyhow. Sure, I know that this ship has been checked out by the mechanics, but a lot of the training you take to get your pilot's license is concerned with how never to leave anything up to chance."

"Want me to spin the prop for you?" Phillips offered.

"You've been watching too many old movies on TV," Hoffman said. "Just get in the door over there on your side and fasten your seat belt."

The engine caught immediately when Hoffman punched the starter. The plane began to roll sedately down the taxiway.

"How come you push that stick forward when we are still on the ground?" Phillips asked suspiciously.

Editor and publisher Harold E. White checks everything, including
fuel sample drained from carburetor, preparatory to making a flight
in *The Naperville Sun*'s Cessna 172.

"That's to keep the plane from tilting forward when the
wind is behind you, like now. Compared to low-wingers, which
have their advantages as well as disadvantages, these high-wing
planes are somewhat less secure in surface winds when taxiing."

Phillips got a good hold on his arm rest.

"Relax," Hoffman told him. "Once we're in flight, you'll
appreciate the fact that an airplane is designed to be most at
home in the air. All airplanes are a result of compromise, but
very little flight efficiency is sacrificed in the interests of ground
handling for this plane, and I wouldn't have it otherwise."

At the end of the runway, Hoffman turned into the spring
breeze, locked his brakes, and went through the full preflight
check list and power run-up.

"Are you sure this dinky little field is long enough?" Phillips
demanded, eying the nearby end of the airport.

"More than twice as long as we'll need," Hoffman said. "This plane can take off in less than 1,500 feet even when there's a four-story building at the end of the runway."

The engine roared as Hoffman closed the throttle. The plane began to move down the strip and then gained speed rapidly. A gentle shudder swept through the craft and suddenly they were smoothly airborne. The ground rushed by and then slowly dropped away.

The horizon dipped out of sight as the Cessna headed for upstairs, and it passed the end of the field 400 feet above the surface. Hoffman glanced over to see his passenger peering out the window.

"There, that didn't hurt a bit, did it?" he said.

"It wasn't as bad as I thought," Phillips admitted. "It's sure different from taking off in an airliner, the way this thing scoots into the air almost as if it likes it. But aren't we heading in the wrong direction? Chicago is over thataway."

"No turns until you're 1,000 feet past the airport boundary," Hoffman said. "And even at an airport this size, you don't make any turns until you've got more than 600 feet of altitude."

"What, even when there's nobody else around?"

"It's that precaution factor again," Hoffman said. "You know, like 'what if the engine quits' and you need enough altitude to get down again when you might be losing lift in a turn. Just about everything connected with private aviation allows for a big margin of safety. Now, as we swing around look down there for the IC railroad tracks. We're flying our first leg on the Iron Beam."

"Iron Beam . . . you mean to say that a little thing like this follows a directional guidance system with an automatic pilot?"

"Not quite," Hoffman laughed. "This plane isn't equipped for complicated instrument flying of any kind. And I couldn't use hardware like that even if I had it; so far, I've only got a VFR license."

"VFR?"

"A Visual Flight Rules license only entitles me to fly during daylight hours during good weather, piloting by ground identification. Didn't you notice that the plane doesn't even have any lighting system? It's designed strictly for guys like me who fly only in ideal conditions.

"No, the 'Iron Beam' is a much more fundamental 'guidance system' than an electronic one. It simply means that we follow railroad tracks. But even airline pilots often fly the Iron Beam. The railroads were laid out by some of the best engineers this country has ever seen, and they followed straight lines as much as possible while still being consistent with covering the flattest possible terrain. The compromise between these two considerations is what the doctor ordered for VFR flying.

"Furthermore, a busy line like the Illinois Central gets so much traffic that the rails are kept polished enough by wheel friction so that they reflect sunlight and are easy to follow. See 'em down there?'"

Phillips pressed his nose to the window to see the arrowlike ribbon of steel heading out straight northwest of the city.

"That's the Iron Beam that will lead us home," Hoffman said. "But first I want to show you something. Look off there to your right."

The plane swept into a gentle banking turn. Below, the speedway was a massive platter of spent excitement. The parking lots surrounding it were still clogged with thousands of cars trying to funnel into the traffic arteries, and racing fans heading north on Route 52 inched along bumper to bumper in ugly snarls as far as the city limits.

"One of those immobilized bugs down there could be Pete's car," Phillips chortled. "From up here, the mess down there looks even worse than I thought it would be."

"Now you're getting the idea," Hoffman said. "Let's do a little sightseeing to get our money's worth."

"Hey, I thought we were in a hurry."

"In a plane you don't *have* to hurrry, and a swing over the city will take less than a minute. Look at the 16th Street bridge crossing the White River down there. It always reminds me of an Erector Set."

At 4,500 feet they were high enough so that they could see the entire metropolitan area, but not so high that they couldn't appreciate the details below them.

The needle of the Soldiers and Sailors Monument at the heart of town cast a finger of shadow up crowded Meredian Street. As the plane banked over the campus of Indiana University they could see sunbathers on the roofs of some of the buildings, and when they passed over Riverside Amusement Park they could clearly spot workmen putting in overtime to ready the rides with finishing touches for the impending season opening.

From the southwest, a hint of shadow flicked across the Cessna, and far off to their left they saw the silver of a four-engine fan jet swing in a giant bank for its approach to the municipal airport. Plumes of feathery vapor trailed the four jet pods majestically limned against the late afternoon sky.

Hoffman switched his radio to the tower frequency and called in to report his altitude and direction.

"Another requirement?" Phillips asked.

"Not really," Hoffman said. "It just makes good sense. The crew on that fan jet probably knows I'm here, but I want the tower to know that I'm moving out of the area. What with Sky Harbor's light planes behind us, and the military aircraft using the Fort Harrison airport to the northeast, this is a high-density air-traffic area and there are usually a lot of planes in the air.

"When you let the tower know where you are and where you're going, they can keep the commercial pilots posted accordingly. Even though it's not mandatory, it's an extra measure of safety, like when we filed that flight plan in the operations office before we took off."

"You mean you took the trouble to fill out that form even if you didn't have to?" Phillips asked incredulously.

"Sure. The flight-plan system is actually designed for instrument-rated pilots who fly when visibility is less than a mile, so their flights can be spaced out by the Air Traffic Controllers in order to minimize the chance for an air collision. But most VFR pilots like me, flying only in good weather when visibility is better than three miles, get in on the system too, simply because it's there.

"Filling out the form isn't all that complicated, either. In fact, I could have filed a flight plan by radio after we were in flight if I'd wanted to. However, the circuits are usually pretty busy around big cities and it's bad manners to tie them up for the time it takes to radio in information like time of departure, cruising altitude and speed, estimated time of flight duration, point of first intended landing and estimated time of arrival, the amount of fuel on board, and so on."

"When I was looking over your shoulder back there in the flight office, I noticed that the form you filled out even called for the colors of the plane," Phillips said. "What was that all about?"

"That's to make it easy for the Search and Rescue boys to find us," Hoffman said laconically.

"What!"

"Sure, that's what a VFR pilot uses the flight-plan system for, like insurance. About halfway home, you'll even hear me radio our progress to the Lafayette area Air Traffic Control center with an 'on course, on time' report. Lafayette will then get the Indianapolis ATC man on their direct line to advise of our progress, and our flight plan will be marked accordingly. When we get to Chicago, Indianapolis will be notified to close out the flight plan and everything will be Jake.

"On the other hand, suppose that we are half an hour overdue in Chicago and haven't been heard from. For example, we left Shank at 5:05 and estimated our time of arrival in Chicago at 6:25. It is now hypothetically 7. Indianapolis will know from the chart that we went past Lafayette's ATC at, say, 5:43, and will phone Chicago to see if anything has been called in.

"If we haven't been heard from by the time we're an hour overdue, Search and Rescue is alerted. Our entire course will be combed by phone from the last point that heard from us. And once a plane is three hours overdue, a tremendous organization moves into action to send out search parties on foot, Civil Air Patrol planes, and service helicopters. If you are ever lying out in an isolated field someplace where you got a broken leg in a forced landing, you'll want the S&R people to know you're in trouble so they can do something about it.

"And that, my friend, is why the FAA flight-plan form calls for the make, model, and colors of your plane—so that it can be recognized from the air."

"Broken leg, eh?" Phillips shakily lit another cigarette.

"That's about the worst thing that can happen if you rack up a modern light plane in a forced landing, even when you rip off the landing gear on rough ground," Hoffman said. "VFR pilots seldom manage to kill themselves unless they dive or spin straight in, and this plane is virtually spinproof. Look, it even flies itself." Hoffman took his hands off the wheel and stretched luxuriously.

"Hey, don't do that!"

"Don't be an old lady. Once a plane like this is trimmed out at the right power setting in relation to stabilizer fix, there is no need to keep monkeying with the controls to maintain steady flight at the right altitude on a smooth day like this. A plane in flight is so much easier to operate than an automobile that all you have to do is keep your eyes open, and you can sit back and enjoy the scenery."

The Indiana flatlands rolled by beneath them, with immaculate farms checkerboarding both sides of the gleaming railroad track. The town of Lebanon slid by under their flitting shadow like a storybook illustration, and 15 minutes later even the haze of industrial Lafayette looked picturesque from 7,500 feet.

"One of the many things I like about flying is that the earth looks so clean and well-ordered from up here," Hoffman pointed out. "Altitude is like a fresh snowfall in the winter—it hides all the dirt and ugliness and renews your faith in the world at large with a new perspective that you just can't otherwise appreciate.

"Do you see that little covered bridge down there on that side road? From here you will never know if the paint is scaling off, or if there's a board missing here and there; all you see is the little bridge itself. The air is a world of purity and clarity, and this is the best of all possible ways that I know of to see the country for what it really is."

"I'll admit that it beats traveling by car," Phillips said. "It doesn't even seem like we're moving . . . it feels more as if the earth itself is doing the moving, like some kind of panorama rolling out down there."

"That's because there is no direct relationship between the plane and the ground," Hoffman said. He touched the wheel and sunlight flooded the cabin as the plane swung in a soft banking turn. "The controls seem to make the earth wheel or rise, while the plane 'stays steady' as far as we are concerned inside it. It's all part of the sense of remoteness that contributes so much to flying's total satisfaction."

"There certainly isn't any sensation of speed," Phillips noted.

"Oh, we're moving, all right," Hoffman said. "Look, I'll show you."

He opened the window at his left, and the drone inside the cabin suddenly became a roar of sound as the airstream tore at the glass.

"Okay, okay, you proved your point . . . shut the window," Phillips yelled. "What's our airspeed anyhow?"

"About 130 miles an hour," Hoffman said. "That's really not a whale of a lot faster than you can make an automobile go, but it's a steadily maintained speed for the entire trip . . . which is about 25 miles shorter in a relatively straight line by air, incidently, compared to highway mileage."

"That's still pretty slow compared to the speeds by jet," Phillips observed.

"I can still beat their total elapsed time on a flight like this," Hoffman averred. "The airlines have mostly moved to the big new fields farther out from downtown, where the real estate is less costly for the long runways some of the goliath jets have to have, and where the racket from the jet engines won't rile so many residents.

"From the neighborhood where I live, getting out to O'Hare Field, at the west of the city limits, is almost an hour's drive. Checking in with the airline clerks and having the luggage weighed and processed means that you usually have to get to the airport maybe half an hour before flight time, too.

"But *this* baby operates out of a close-in airport 10 minutes from the house.

"However, I didn't buy the plane to try to beat the airlines' time; I bought it for personal enjoyment. The difference between taking a commercial plane and flying yourself is like the difference between watching a golf tournament on TV and playing in it yourself. Or if you want to get poetic about it, like the difference between listening to a song and singing.

"Mainly, it's the freedom I enjoy, Ben, a freedom that only starts with the fact that I take off when *I* feel like it, not when some printed schedule says that I have to be waiting around at an airport someplace. The plane gives me not only freedom of movement but freedom of decision, too. After the rat race all week, a little plane like this gives you the ultimate in 'getting away from it all.' There just isn't any better combination of exhilaration and relaxation."

"You sound like an old-time Sunday driver," Phillips laughed.

"You know, you're right," Hoffman admitted. "The automobile at one time did provide a comparable freedom of movement. But how many people do you know who still take a ride on Sunday afternoons for the fun of it? It's not fun any more; it's work. And dangerous work, besides; two cars approaching each other at 65 miles an hour have a combined speed of 130 when they meet . . . with the opposing fenders maybe three or four feet apart when they pass each other. Man, any pilot who gets within 500 feet of another plane gets called on the carpet by the FAA but fast!

"No, Sunday driving is pretty much a thing of the past as far as pleasure is concerned. And its freedom is still confined to that narrow ribbon of concrete. That's the real reason why so many people have turned to boating for recreation."

"Ah, now you're talking my language," Phillips said. "Heading a good power boat for open water is my idea of real freedom. You've got speed for sport and sun for relaxation, and you can get out where there's nobody around for as far as you can see if that's what you want, too."

"It's the next best thing to flying," Hoffman conceded. "But it's still a two-dimensional freedom. It's only when you expand to a three-dimensional freedom that you can really feel 'as free as a bird.' Up here we've got a whole ocean of air to maneuver in, with a flexibility that no earthbound traveler can even come close to."

Above them and off to their left, they watched a fast twin-engine Aztec flow by and pull ahead. The Piper pilot waggled his wings.

"He seems to know you," Phillips said.

"Only as another flyer," Hoffman said. "The flying fraternity

Fred Hoffman's Cessna 172 gives him a sense of three-dimensional freedom—four-dimensional when he counts the way his plane can expand his time.

is a breed apart. Once you fly a plane you will never be the same man again, and you know that every other flyer feels the same way. That comradeship is almost universal, too, whether the pilot flies corporate aircraft for a living or he's a weekend pilot just out joy-riding. It's a mutual sharing of one of the few challenges left to modern man."

"Wouldn't you call that attitude a hangover from the old days of barnstorming?" Phillips asked. "From what I can see of the way you fellows operate today, none of you could exactly be called daredevils."

"No, there's a closer bond than that," Hoffman said. "Flying is demanding in that it is intolerant of stupidity or carelessness. But the thing that all flyers share is the fact that they participate in one of the most fullfilling activities for any man, with a downright beautiful balance of considerations. Maybe the word 'spiritual' is too big a word for a boat owner, but that's one of the factors in flying nevertheless. Balance that with the practical and utilitarian, and you've got a world of both sunsets and spark plugs."

"Or 'angels and engines'?"

"Why not? As you may have surmised, I *like* flying."

"You've got it bad all right," Phillips agreed. "Do you get the chance to travel around like this very often?"

"Almost every weekend," Hoffman said proudly. "Using a plane can even be four-dimensional, when you think of it in terms of the way it can expand your time. For example, I would never have been able to get away to see the race today if it hadn't been for the plane. In fact, I really didn't even decide to come until this morning.

"Last Sunday I played golf in Iowa, and next weekend I'm taking the family to St. Louis for my niece's wedding. I'm getting in a lot of hunting and fishing trips that I could never make before, too; some of the best spots in Wisconsin and over in Michigan are pretty remote, and I have never been able to afford to take the time off work that I'd need to drive there. Inasmuch as most of them are in areas not served by the airlines, I've just had to forgo them until now.

"The plane enables me to have capsuled vacation trips almost any weekend, where before I had to cram a whole year's recreation into a couple of weeks during the summer vacation season. And not just me; my kids are seeing as much of the country every month, and in a meaningful way, as they ordinarily could see in years of ordinary summer vacationing. The wife is even beginning to be a pretty good navigator.

"Which reminds me," Hoffman said. "That's the town of Fowler up ahead, where we leave the Iron Beam and head straight north by open navigation."

He pulled a chart from the map compartment and handed it to Phillips. "I've marked our course from Fowler to Midway Airport in Chicago," he said. "The landmarks we have to spot are penciled in red. As we fly over each one, the successive one will be in sight. That drive-in movie down there is our take-off point, and our next checkpoint is that water tower ten miles north, which will mark Goodland as we pass it off to our right. When we cross the Iroquois River, start looking for small planes using the Lake Village Airport just this side of the Kankakee River. From there on in, our route will be clearly marked with lakes, ballparks, transmission lines, bridges, and industrial complexes."

The Cessna flew over the Lake Village Airport at 6:01, four minutes ahead of schedule, thanks to a tail wind. Touch down was now less than half an hour away.

Farmland gave way to thick scatterings of towns, and by the time the plane crossed the Indiana state line at Hammond, the area below was a vast sea of buildings. Haze from the steel mills in Gary hung over the lower edge of Lake Michigan like a dirty shroud, and the refineries in Whiting stabbed flaming burn-off into the gritty sky off to the east.

Then they were over Chicago itself, the densely packed area stretching for almost thirty miles ahead. Housing tracts shouldered high-rise apartment buildings on the lake shore, and rows of bungalows and two-flats by the thousands crouched on wary plots while the slums edged in from the west.

The green oasis of Marquette Park was the last checkpoint on the chart, and Phillips could see the towers at Midway Airport two miles to the northwest. Hoffman circled the field at 2,000 feet, checked in by radio, and entered the traffic pattern at a 45-degree angle on the downwind leg. As he slipped out of the base leg into the final approach, he touched the throttle for enough power to maintain an 80 mph airspeed as he crossed the airport fence. Without using the flaps, Hoffman floated the Cessna in for minimal flare out, with no noticeable change in the level attitude, until he heard the squeak of the wheels touching down.

"To tell the truth, the landing was the only thing I was really worried about," Phillips kidded as they taxied over to the operations building. "But this one was certainly slow enough to be safe."

"And with plenty of moxie in reserve," Hoffman said. "This thing can land under full control at less than 50 miles an hour if it has to."

Phillips stretched luxuriously as he looked at his watch. "Fred, this has been a real eye-opener," he said. "We spent less than an hour and a half for the whole trip! I didn't think you really meant it when you said that we'd be back in time for dinner, but I'd sure like to buy you a steak on it."

"Fine with me. Where do you want to go?"

"Let's go to Pete's restaurant. I can hardly wait to see his face when he finally walks in and sees us sitting there with some of his good after-dinner brandy under our belts.

"Besides, he owes me on that Indy bet. Unless he was listening to his car radio on the way home, he still probably doesn't know that I won it."

Ben Phillips is only one of millions of Americans who get their first ride in a private plane "by accident." Thousands of them, like Phillips as it turned out, never do recover; today, Ben goes out to the local airport almost every weekend to work on his Student Pilot's Certificate, and he is shopping for a plane of his own.

Although the airplane manufacturers would have the public believe that anybody who earns $8,000 a year can afford to own an airplane, Ben is more realistic about his moderate means. He is checking not only the low-cost new single-engine fixed-gear planes but the used-plane market, too. He is also considering going into a partnership to share the costs of mutual ownership.

The selling job was easier than he thought on his first partner: his wife. This can be a serious block for many first-plane buyers, but Ben eased his Frau into the idea by having her drive him to the airport to wait while he goes up for his flying lessons.

The atmosphere of enthusiasm around an airport is catching —especially for somebody down on the ground watching somebody else drifting around up above. The boredom of waiting may have had something to do with Mrs. Phillips' impatience, too, but whatever the reason, she began asking to be taken up by Ben's third trip.

His "shocked" refusal only whetted her flying appetite. In any case, she is now almost as anxious as Ben is for the license to come through so he can fly his family himself.

He has also conned her into going along when he goes around to look over planes for sale. He nods his head a lot when she offers opinions.

"She has good taste in fabrics," he says privately.

Even the kids go along on these inspection trips. Children, incidentally, take to flying readily. Although they have fewer fears to unlearn than adults, the main reason that they are good flyers

Aviation is such a taken-for-granted part of the modern child's world that kids not only readily accept flying but can be downright bored with it.

is because they are simply growing up in an age of aviation and accept it as a matter of course. Although boys usually like planes more than girls do because of the machinery involved, one normal reaction of almost all moppets is to become downright bored with the whole business once the novelty has worn off. This can even be a source of chagrin to the occasional father who might have harbored wistful hopes that his kids might even regard him as something of a hero type instead of just as a flying chauffeur.

Because Ben owns a vacation cabin in Minnesota with the property on lake frontage, he is toying with the idea of getting a plane equipped with floats.

"There are a lot more lakes and rivers than there are airports," he says. "Even some of the smallest planes can be rigged as seaplanes. With that kind of a setup, I could take my boys fishing maybe once a week instead of once a month."

He smiles as he fingers his flight log. "I'll have my VFR license by the end of the month," he says confidently. "My first passenger is going to be Fred Hoffman."

CHAPTER 2

Corporate aviation

The dusty taxi crouched to a halt at Chicago's O'Hare Field and the sales manager of one of the city's major paper companies flipped a bill to the cab driver and sprinted for the loading ramp. He didn't make it. Panting, he stood at the closed gate and watched his flight take off without him. Damn! There would be a three-hour wait until the next plane . . . if he could still book passage on it. And there would be a stopover at Springfield to make a connecting flight to the final destination.

From the corner of his eye, he noticed the sun glint from the cowl of a sleek twin-engine Cessna 310 flying across the field high overhead. The identification number on the fuselage—111Q—meant nothing to him. But it meant plenty to the five people in the little plane; the 220 mph aircraft was owned by the Martin-Brower Corporation . . . on the way to beat out the competition for another new account.

Mel Schneider, head of the Chicago-based paper company, had left his office on the near South Side a full hour after his competitor had hailed a cab. After a relatively short drive down Archer Avenue to Midway Airport, Schneider had taken off with a Martin-Brower sales team and a vice-president of the client company, which was opening a new warehouse 400 miles away. There was even an empty seat.

The flight in the 310 would take more air time than a commercial airliner for the trip, but the paper merchant's flight would be direct, and the plane would land at a close-in airport near the customer's headquarters. Martin-Brower would be making its sales presentation while its competitor was still working crossword puzzles at Springfield, waiting for his connection between the "faster" commercial craft.

Rip Fry, Martin-Brower's full-time professional pilot, logged one of the heaviest schedules in business aviation during 1967— well over 1,000 air hours on company business. Martin-Brower executives still fly the scheduled airlines on most flights of over 500 miles between major cities where service is frequent enough to be convenient, but their 310 is being used more often all the time. Before the 310, the company had operated a single-engine 190 mph Cessna 210, but when its use rose to close to 100 hours a month, the paper firm traded it in for the bigger, more dependable, and faster twin.

With the opening of a new Ohio branch in 1966, Martin-Brower found itself with 11 scattered branches, many of them

Mel Schneider (left), head of Martin-Brower Paper Corp., debarks from company's twin-engine Cessna 310.

in towns were airline service was either poor or nonexistent. Although it handles comprehensive lines of paper goods in general, the company concentrates on supplying chains of supermarkets, department stores, and franchise operations with their packaging requirements. Many such headquarters offices are also off the airlines' beaten paths, and the company-owned plane is used for executive transport in visiting customers throughout the Middle West.

"A company plane is not only an efficient administrative tool but also a remarkably effective competitive weapon," Schneider says. "Inasmuch as we take off at *our* convenience, we waste a minimum of time waiting around airports with a mindless printed schedule dictating our activity. Our plane enables us to do things which would otherwise be impossible.

"For example, we use the 310 a lot for spot market checks, and we have covered as many as four different points in as many different states in a single day, a job which would ordinarily take two or three times as long by car."

Stories like Schneider's abound not only around every airport but at most business conventions as well. One businessman who finally listened to one too many, for example, was a Southwesterner named George Hollis. His situation was complicated by other factors, but he was by no means unique.

One day recently he slammed the door of his car and strode across the parking lot toward a building marked "Aircraft Sales & Service." A glint of sunlight flashing from the sky caught his attention, and he glanced up at a sleek 707 streaking majestically overhead at 30,000 feet. Within moments, even the proud vapor trails had feathered into nothingness. George cursed and yanked open the door of the airport's sales office with renewed determination.

"Good morning!" a man in a golf shirt said from behind a desk. "Can I help you?"

"You can if you can sell me an airplane," Hollis said.

"Got a pilot's license?"

"No, I haven't," Hollis admitted. "But I understand that most guys start to solo after 8 or 10 hours of instruction, and that only 40 hours of flight time is required to qualify for a license."

"It'll be less than that if we get the new FAA rules," the man said as he stood up to shake hands. "My name is Phil Weintraub and I sell as many airplanes as anybody else in the state . . . to people who can afford them. What have you got in mind—a sports plane?"

"Hell no," George said. "I want a plane I can use for business. When I built my plant in this burg I got a good deal on taxes, real estate, and a labor pool, but I didn't realize that I'd be so isolated from my markets and suppliers. Public transportation out of here has dwindled to the point where it's almost useless for my needs. What will a plane of my own cost me?"

"Well, if you want to travel at around 130 mph, your new single-engine planes average around $12,000," Weintraub said. "That's plus instrumentation, of course."

"That much?" Hollis said. "And that's pretty slow, isn't it?"

"If you want more speed, you'll have to go to retractable landing gear," the salesman said. "That adds about 50 mph to your air speed . . . and about doubles your price."

Hollis whistled. "Twenty-five grand!" he said, "I'm not so sure that a single-engine plane is what I'd be satisfied with, either, what with all the lakes and mountains that I'd be flying over. How much is an extra engine?"

Weintraub chuckled amiably. "Twin-engine planes average around $50,000," he said. "And you can add anything up to $20,000 or $30,000 for navigation and communications equipment besides, if you want all-weather capabilities. Maintenance isn't cheap, either.

"Aircraft manufacturers like to estimate the total operating costs at under $30 an hour for a twin, but I'll be honest with you . . . plenty of companies using corporate aircraft figure as high as $65 an hour for a professionally piloted twin—even a light one."

Hollis threw up his hands in resignation. "I've got a good business, but not that good," he said. "A company plane would be literally over my head. It looks like I'll just have to be satisfied with a lot more nighttime driving on those goddam toll roads."

George Hollis represents a growing number of peculiarly "underprivileged" Americans who are being caught in a unique pinch in the expanding economy: an increasing lack of public transportation in many areas of the United States. And the very expressways and toll roads Hollis detests so much have as much to do with the worsening situation as any other single factor.

Over 85 percent of all interstate travel is now by automobile. As the network of superhighways developed, the railroads began to curtail passenger service as the demand dwindled. Because time is the most valuable thing an executive has, the railroads lost almost all their business travel to the airlines.

The more service the railroads eliminated, the faster the highway system had to grow. The continuing spiral resulted in a situation where many railroads are now frankly trying to discontinue their unprofitable passenger service altogether.

In the late 1950s, the railroads' floundering attempts at economy measures caught the attention of the increasingly cost-conscious airlines themselves. The airlines, too, are now cutting back on less profitable schedules and are concentrating on the long nonstop flights between major cities. With the cost of bigger and bigger jet aircraft getting pretty high into the millions per plane, they didn't have much of an alternative.

However, this now leaves countless cities with poor or even nonexistent public transportation (unless you count the buses . . . and most businessmen don't). These hapless towns are left in a virtual travel vacuum, with the railroads pulling out of the market and the aviation industry not yet mature enough to enter it wholeheartedly while there is still so much cream to skim off the top.

As of the summer of 1968, the airlines provided service to only 550 out of more than 10,000 airports in the United States. However, only 62 airports are presently receiving jet service— and 85 percent of all airline miles are by jet aircraft. Over 45 percent of all the airline traffic is at only 10 metropolitan areas, and in fact, more than 90 percent of all passengers are enplaned at fewer than 100 hub areas.

Furthermore, in the three years 1964, 1965, and 1966, 46 cities lost scheduled airline service altogether, but only two gained any.

Another 53 communities now receiving scheduled airline service are up for "use it or lose it" decisions. Almost 100 "airline" airports now have an average of less than two flights a day.

With this concentration of flight operations, an airline passenger can get reasonably good service only if he is traveling between two of the ten major metropolitan areas. Outside of the hub areas, the infrequency and odd hours of service are only a little worse than the dog-leg routes so often encountered. From these complications arose the need for private aviation, which now has a fleet that outnumbers the 2,000 airline planes by 50 times.

Private planes now fly more than two and one-half times as many passenger miles as the domestic airlines. With the airlines doing so much to popularize air travel—and at the same time making it so hard for so many people to use—well over half of all business flying today is done in corporate aircraft. And no wonder.

Of the 211 cities with over 50,000 population, 14 are not even certified for scheduled air service. There are 176 cities with a population between 25,000 and 50,000—and 43 of them are not served by the airlines. Only 60 cities with a population of less than 10,000 are certified for air carrier service, even though more than 75 million people live in cities of less than 10,000.

George Hollis, whose plant is located in a town more than 40 miles from the nearest airport served by even a small airline, has good cause to be disgruntled.

Chicago's Midway Airport, used by hundreds of flying businessmen like Mel Schneider, was once the busiest airport in the world, with a commercial flight taking off or landing on the average of once a minute. But along with many similar metropolitan airports across the country, Midway has been largely abandoned by most of the airlines in favor of the bigger new airports farther out in the outskirts, where building them is "more practical" than within the built-up sections of the city itself. In fact, many irate citizens *demanded* that the jets get out of town when the noise got too bad.

Business planes have largely inherited most such close-in

airports. There are half-hearted attempts to revive some of them once in a while, as when some of the airlines once again began using Midway in the spring of 1968 with piston-powered planes, which could still use the in-city runways. But companies like Martin-Brower often have such airfields practically to themselves to minimize downtown-to-downtown travel time. Private planes make so much economic good sense that there are now over 40,000 airplanes registered for private business use in the United States.

A good example of a small-scale operation is the four-passenger single-engine Bonanza owned by Dellekamp's Department Store, of Crawfordsville, Indiana. The Beech is usually piloted personally by W. Emerson Dellekamp, president of his company.

"Flying time to Chicago, for example, is about an hour in our 180 mile an hour plane," he says. "While the airlines make the flight in much less flying time, they land out at O'Hare Field out on the western city limits. By the time you collect your luggage and get downtown in a cab—unless you want to save a few dollars and wait for the airport limousine/bus—you have shot better than an hour. We land either at in-city Midway or, if we have business right downtown, at Meigs Field right on the lake front in sight of the Loop.

"Traveling to Detroit provides even more spectacular time savings. If you fly by commercial jet you not only have to go out to O'Hare to get the plane, but if it lands at Willow Run Airport, you are still about 35 miles from downtown Detroit. In our little ol' Bonanza, we take off from Midway or Meigs and land at Detroit City Airport, right on Gratiot Avenue, just a few minutes from Woodward Avenue and practically everything else in town."

Dellekamp claims that when he and his staff make a buying trip to Chicago, they can get to their destination in less time than it takes many buyers for Chicago/suburban stores to get downtown. He credits the mobility and flexibility of his personal transport facilities as an important factor in keeping the store's inventory in Crawfordsville "as up-to-the-minute as any in the country." Dellekamp holds an instrument rating, which enables him to operate the fully equipped 1960 Bonanza as an all-weather plane, and he makes as many as 100 flights a year.

Another instrument-rated Bonanza owner is Leonard Aldridge, head of a Lake Forest, Illinois, electrical contracting firm.

"Considering the salaries in this industry," he says, "time is worth a lot of money . . . and our company plane makes the most of it. Our plane is nicknamed 'The Time Machine,' the way it really does manufacture usable time.

"One thing that makes a man good in this business is experience. With the extra time provided by a plane of our own, some of us can visit as many as ten points a week, whereas we could cover maybe five by car or by scheduled airline . . . and by the end of a year, this adds up to what would otherwise be two years' experience."

Aldridge logs over 400 hours of air time a year.

Sam Dean, president of the Dean Milk Company, considers the company plane a downright money machine. "It has demonstrably increased the productivity of some of our key personnel by as much as 40 percent a year," he avers. "Every one-day trip in the plane represents a two- or three-day trip by automobile, and when you multiply that kind of time by the number of people who use the plane, we can only consider the plane as a machine to get the most out of every last minute.

"In some of our operations, one man can serve half a dozen plants by using the plane, whereas we would otherwise have to have half a dozen men in as many individual jobs. Our plane enables us to get maximal utilization of our facilities, and it is as much of a modern administration tool as a long-distance phone or a computer."

Dean Milk owns a Douglas A-26, a converted Army bomber that carries 8 people. It is used over 500 hours a year, and the average number of passengers per trip last year was 4.8, including Dean's production, plant engineering, and merchandising people. The $100,000 conversion can hit 360 mph, which is faster than any commercially manufactured plane on the market for corporate use, except for the jets.

"Our plane is a morale booster, too," says Dean. "Our people can visit as many as three or four points hundreds of miles apart in a single day and still be home with their families the same evening. We have a network of dealers, customers, and suppliers throughout the Middle West, not to mention 17 plants of our own scattered as far south as the Gulf. Our personnel people regard use of the plane as one of our most meaningful fringe benefits."

One day last spring a blue and white airplane approached rapidly from the Missouri horizon as a paving crew prepared the slab for an emergency landing.

"Here comes the boss!" one of the men shouted over the full-throated roar of the banking single-engine Beechcraft. Gunnar Jenson, of the Orr Construction Company, Chicago Heights, Illinois, touched down on the semifinished highway and taxied to a stop alongside an idled Euclid roadscraper.

"Here's the spare parts," he said to the grinning men who crowded up to the cabin. "I brought Harold along, too, just in case you need an expert hand with the installation."

The time: 11:45 A.M. Less than two hours before, Jenson had taken off in the company-owned plane from a Chicago-suburban airstrip 300 miles away, in response to a long-distance phone call reporting a mechanical breakdown and resultant work stoppage. The no-longer-worried field foreman had the crew back at work by the time the lunch hour was over.

"Without our plane, that crew would have been idle for a whole day instead of a couple of hours," Jenson says. "The only commercial airline flight to the area leaves Chicago in the late afternoon and lands at Quincy, which is more than an hour's drive from the job site in a rented car. But as it was, I was back at my desk by four o'clock . . . after stopping on the way back to visit a bridge job near Clinton, Iowa."

Orr Construction Company is a relatively small ($5 million per year) road, sewer, and bridge builder covering a sizable part of the Middle West out of its Chicago-area headquarters, which is only a few minutes from a local airport. Jenson has been flying the 155 mph plane since 1959 to facilitate bidding, for field supervision, and for executive transport in general as well as for emergency deliveries.

"Our volume has increased almost 50 percent since we bought the plane," Jenson says. "We are seriously thinking of trading in the single-engine Beechcraft on a bigger and faster twin-engine Baron, and the main reason we are now holding back is because the lighter one-lunger can land in, and take off from, the smaller airfields, which are often closest to the jobs. We land not only on unpaved airports and open fields, but sometimes even on beaches, strip mines, and abandoned roads."

The construction industry in general is one of the most enthusiastic users of corporate aircraft, primarily because so much of the out-of-town work is being done in relatively underdeveloped areas where conventional airline service is minimal.

Another typical contractor is William E. Schweitzer, head of the northern Illinois construction company that bears his name.

"Our plane is a regular workhorse," he says. "Right now we have major jobs in Peoria, Springfield, and Danville, including a 33-story building, which entails a tremendous amount of detail work. We have sometimes found it necessary to visit all three of these projects in a single day, which are 155, 194, and 132 miles from our home base, respectively. The time savings we achieve with our Sky Knight impress even our auditors."

The Schweitzer plane is an $80,000 twin-engine Cessna, which carries five people at 190 mph. Del Campbell, the company's full-time professional pilot, logs between 400 and 500 hours a year on company business to points as far as Toledo and Minneapolis.

"Our people never have to rush an out-of-town conference to make a plane schedule," he says. "Regardless of how long a conference lasts, the plane is always waiting and ready."

Schweitzer's travel philosophy is fundamental. "We use a plane to get around the country in exactly the same way we use an automobile to get around town," he says. "Sure, we could use a bus or a taxicab to get around town, but only at the sacrifice of a lot of valuable flexibility. Same with our plane . . . just stretched out a little."

Gunnar Jenson likes to talk in terms of money. "We made 82 trips last year, averaging three people per trip," he says. "Our par log was two and one-half hours per trip, with each one-day trip representing the usual two- or three-day trip by car. That figures out to be a time savings of around 5,000 man-hours, mostly management personnel. Add that up any way you want and the plane comes out to be a matter of economy."

John Glatz, Dean Milk's full-time pilot, looks at it another way. "Even from the standpoint of pure dollars and cents in immediate outlay, a company plane is a good investment," he claims. "We made a trip to Memphis with seven people aboard last week —where the round-trip airline fares would have totaled better than $550—and we beat their downtown-to-downtown travel time by almost an hour, too. But multiply savings like that on airline tickets by a couple of hundred times a year and you come up with a pretty impressive figure."

When a private plane logs, say, 600 hours a year (some company planes are used over 1,200 hours a year), a seven-passenger plane used on a scheduled basis can account for better than 4,000 air hours by the seats—roughly, $200,000 worth of travel by commercial jets. Even a little 180 mph four-passenger plane used for 400 hours a year will fly almost 300,000 seat-miles, or about $30,000 worth of airline travel.

Sexton Printing Company, Kansas City, Missouri, is a good example of a small operation that figures mileage on cost per seat-mile. Their single-engine Piper can carry six people, and any time it takes off with more than two people, it flies at a lower cost per seat-mile than airline passenger fares for the group would cost.

But unless the airplane owner is kidding himself, this kind of thinking applies only (1) when the plane is a small and therefore slow model, (2) when it's second hand, like Dean Milk's converted bomber, or (3) when it's both. Dave Fox, who operates a flying service in upstate New York, claims that the total cost of operating his Piper J-3 is $3.78 an hour, including fuel, oil, engine maintenance, airframe and prop maintenance, and tiedown fees.

Compare this with the cost of operating the 10-passenger, 575 mph Gulfstream II—$850 per hour as figured by Don Douglas, chief pilot for the Home Oil Company. Douglas, of course, is figuring depreciation on an original $2,325,000 investment. Fox's aerial rowboat not only is *not* depreciating but is actually *ap*preciating . . . he bought it second hand 10 years ago for a modest $600 (that's right: a six and only two zeroes).

The average businessman gets quite a way from both those extremes. Regardless of his costs, he still has to justify them to his auditors.

"We consider our $60,000 Beech Baron one of the best investments we have ever made," says John Brock, of the Quintana Petroleum Corporation, Houston. "At current bank rates, that $60,000 is actually worth about $3,600 a year, or $300 a month . . . and we save more than that on motel bills alone."

That airy "$300 a month" does not, of course, include anything but the bare cost of the money. Although it is true that most light planes really do get better mileage per gallon of gas than the average company car, the cost of gas and oil account for only a fraction of the realistic operating costs.

Reserves for mandatory inspections and overhaul of engine and props come to $4 or $5 an hour even for smaller planes. Insurance for corporate aircraft can amount to a pretty hefty per hour figure, too.

When the average auditor starts trying to figure depreciation, though, he is often in trouble. On off-brand models or on planes built for specific purposes where there is no mass market for resale, the cost of depreciation can be bigger than all other costs combined.

One complicating factor that throws off a good many accountants is the fact that airplanes, with few exceptions, do not depreciate like automobiles. For one thing, a mechanical failure in a plane can be deadly serious, and airplanes get meticulous maintenance accordingly. As a result, the average airplane depreciates slowly, and there are thousands of planes 15 and 20 years old still providing dependable service. Many of them are actually worth more in today's market than when they were originally built.

In fact, *most* planes in use today are more than 10 years old. One of them is the elderly Twin Beech operated by Vaughn Petroleum, Inc., of Dallas. Vintage 1946, the eight-passenger plane delivers a heavier work load today than it ever did.

"This plane is now old enough to vote," said Vaughn's secretary-treasurer, W. C. Longquist, a couple of years ago. "But the way it's operating, it should be good for another 20 years. Tearing down the engines every 100 hours and replacing them every 1,000 could theoretically keep an airplane flying practically forever." His must have taken a second lease on life, because it is going stronger than ever.

The tax collectors are not unmindful of this situation, and one of the first things an airplane owner finds out is that an aircraft ownership certificate draws IRS agents like a picnic draws ants. The official government position is to encourage civil aviation in all its aspects, but there is cause to wonder if Internal Revenue has ever received the message.

Many tax men have the attitude that the primary purpose of any private plane is for joy-riding and is only registered in the company name so it can be written off against income taxes. As a result, aviation expense vouchers are closely scrutinized.

The supposedly affluent airplane owner who blithely writes up a flight ticket for "entertaining a customer" had damn well better be able to prove that he didn't have a couple of fishing buddies or relatives along for the ride if he wants to get the deduction allowed.

Thus, an airplane cannot be depreciated as easily as some accountants would like to believe. The company that tries to write off a plane in less than 10 years is usually asking for trouble.

No two tax agents think alike either. The civil aviation industry, headed by the manufacturers, is trying to get the IRS to codify its standards to make some of the sometimes confusing bookkeeping easier. This can be particularly difficult when a plane is sometimes admittedly used for personal use . . . why *not* use a plane for recreation on weekends after it has been used all week for business? But as of now, many aircraft owners complain vehemently that the accounting problem is the single toughest thing about flying.

The "flying for fun and profit" angle is, without much doubt, a real factor in aircraft acquisition for many small companies. Regardless of how much a flying businessman might talk about the time he saves in flying straight over the winding roads in hilly country, in about three cases out of five he just *likes* to fly. He often devotes more time to it than would really be necessary if he were actually interested only in transportation as such. Regardless of his initial motives for buying the plane, he can often become deeply involved on a personal basis, too, whether he admits it or not.

Why else does "working" often include hanging around the

airport with cronies and talking aviation with almost anybody who will listen? And even studying. Learning radio procedures, instrument flying (whether he needs it or not, as in "good weather" areas in the Southwest), and how to read charts and radio facility books can become pretty absorbing. Practically all businessmen/flyers subscribe to the myriad aviation magazines. Moving up from a secondhand Piper or Cessna to a twin-engine rig is often motivated by additional anticipated pleasure almost as much as by practical reasons.

Small wonder then, that the 1,400-page *Civil Aircraft Register* is happy hunting grounds for IRS agents. But they are not the only ones who take a long look at corporate aviation. Stockholders often get nervous when they find out that the corporation executives have taken to flying around in private airplanes. On more than one occasion corporate aircraft has been sold off to smooth the ruffled feathers of irate groundling investor/voters.

This is one reason why so few corporate aircraft carry any insignia identifying them as company planes. Another reason why even trademarks seldom embellish the fuselage or tail of a company plane is because some companies feel that when they transport customer/executives there might be some reluctance to travel "in an ad."

"I don't think I should be expected to accept a ride in one of their milk wagons, either," one such customer of an eastern milk processor huffed. That was one cow that got scraped off the aluminum fast.

But there's another side to this coin, closely related to the sheer satisfaction of flying: pride of ownership. This is a factor in aircraft acquisition that applies to some of the biggest hardware as well as the smallest. Does Joan Crawford really need all that room in the Pepsi-Cola Fairchild F-27? Could Arnold Palmer or Frank Sinatra get along without their $600,000 or $700,000 500 mph jets? Probably not. But there is no doubt whatever about any business associate being favorably impressed when somebody flies in to see him by private plane.

The cash value of creating that kind of an impression—and not just in the various phases of show business—is hard to figure. But it definitely exists.

Luxurious interior of a corporate configuration of the Fairchild F27 (transport configuration: 30 passengers), like the one operated by Pepsi-Cola, provides all the comforts of an airliner, with the possible exception of a hostess—(unless you count Joan Crawford).

"When I tell a customer that I'm flying in to meet him," says the sales manager of a Georgia textile mill, "he invariably has somebody on hand to meet me at the airport, if indeed he isn't there himself. What's meaningful about this, of course, is that he treats the visit as a matter of some importance.

"Our Super Skylane has not only enabled us to open up new markets which were heretofore out of our reach, but has made them more responsive. Since we bought the plane two years ago, our volume has increased by almost another third. This is with the same line of products, the same price structure, the same sales staff, the same competition, and the same everything else with one exception: we now make our calls in our own private plane. We have even added a belly pod to carry a cargo of samples."

Among the most deeply impressed customers for a company using private aircraft, albeit on a more immediately practical basis, are farmers and ranchers in outlying areas. Many, of course, use planes of their own to cover widespread operations.

Taylor Implement Company's 160 mph Super Skywagon, flying out of Ipswich, South Dakota, can service distant emergency calls in a matter of minutes.

Many of them depend increasingly on suppliers who can give them fast service for emergencies. Taylor Implement Company, Ipswich, South Dakota, has answered many a call to fix a broken-down windmill with the help of its own *Wind Mill*, a 160 mph Super Skywagon.

Although company planes are used mostly as "people carriers," their use for emergency cargo transport is increasing. By taking out the passenger seats, owners of many light planes can convert them to "flying station wagons" in a matter of a few minutes. Three- and four-door models are particularly adaptable for this purpose. Among the heaviest users of such "AC-DC" planes are distributors of such vital equipment as truck parts and electronic components and even florists, who can carry a high-dollar payload without a lot of weight.

Ken Broda, of Chicago, is an undertaker who uses the company Cessna as a flying hearse. There are so many morticians using planes for this purpose that they have a flight association of their own.

Light, single-engine plane converted to cargo use carries profitable payload for florist with perishable, lightweight cargo.

Ken Broda, a Chicago undertaker, uses his company plane as a flying hearse for service covering the entire Middle West.

Until private planes are a lot more commonplace than they are now, they will still be good for publicity for a long time to come, too. Herman Miller, of Bayside Electronics, Stockton, California, made a lot of headlines recently when he flew the company Piper Aztec, *The Yankee Trader*, on an around-the-world tour "in quest of business."

Wes Larson, president of the Beverly Bank, Chicago, startled South Side neighbors one morning when they found a single-engine plane parked in the bank's front yard just off a busy intersection . . . to promote the bank's airplane loan business, after the plane had been hauled through the city streets in the dead of night.

"That stunt, which resulted in space in all the metropolitan newspapers, is one of the reasons why our relatively small bank is one of the biggest in the field of aircraft financing," Larson says. "And naturally, we fly aircraft of our own on company business, too."

The corporate airplane is so versatile in its many uses that users feel unnaturally constricted when their "basic transportation tools" are hangared for overhaul work. To minimize this handicap, many companies now own two or more planes. Some companies like Shell Oil, J. P. Stevens, Pepperell, Burlington Industries, and General Motors operate entire fleets of planes, some of them bigger than the fleets operated by some of the smaller airlines.

"The company plane today is what the company car used to be," says Martin-Brower's Mel Schneider. "Competition being what it is, there just isn't any good reason not to use every modern facility offered by today's technology. I just don't know anybody who still uses a horse and wagon to get around in . . . and it's only a matter of comparative efficiencies between oats and octane. The company car is to public bus lines what the company plane is to the airlines."

And this is just one good reason why there are now more than 500,000 people qualified to fly corporate aircraft in the United States, from blacksmiths to movie stars and from corporation presidents to their secretaries.

CHAPTER 3

How to get
a pilot's license

"Where's the flight school around this airport?" Barry Wilson asked a grease-stained man crawling out from under an airplane.

The mechanic stood up and wiped his hands on the side of his coveralls as he looked Wilson over speculatively. "Want to learn how to fly, eh?" he asked.

"You betcha."

"You came to the right man, pal," the mechanic said. "A friend of mine who is a real good pilot is in the coffee shop right now, and he's already forgot more about flying than most of those punks in the flight school will ever know. You're in luck, too, because this guy just got in town and he can use a couple of students and he won't rob you blind on what he charges, either. Come on . . . I'll introduce you."

At the small field's refreshment counter, Wilson was led up to a dapper man sipping coffee out of a fly-specked mug.

"Hiya, Ace," the mechanic greeted. "I want you to meet a pal of mine who wants to learn how to fly. This is Barry Wilson."

Ace pushed back the visor of his pilot's cap and looked up. "Have you ever had any flying lessons?" he asked. He didn't smile.

"No, but I figure that it's about time," Wilson said. "I've been an aviation buff ever since I was building model airplanes out of balsa wood on my mother's dining room table. I just got a promotion from the plant to the office and I'm finally in a position where I've got the time and money for flying lessons."

Ace stood up and shook hands. "Sit down and have a cup of coffee," he offered.

"Gee, thanks."

"I assume that you haven't checked with the flight school, right?" Ace asked. "Okay then, here's the pitch. I'll level with you, Barry . . . I'm new in town and I'm anxious to get started, so I can make you a good deal. How does $12 an hour sound?"

"What's the catch?" Wilson asked warily. "I heard that flying lessons cost a lot more than that."

"No catch, no catch!" Ace said, arching his eyebrows. "You're right . . . flight schools, for example, have to charge a lot because they have a lot of overhead they have to cover. But I'm strictly on my own, and I can afford to work for a lot less. And I'm giving you a break because you'll be my first student in this area. Okay?"

"What kind of a trainer will we be flying?" Wilson wanted to know.

"The best, nothing but the best," Ace said. "I got an Alon with full dual controls that's worth close to ten grand with all the equipment in it. Ever ride in a plane with all the visibility you get in an Alon?"

"Well, no," Wilson said, but his eyes brightened.

"Come on then, we'll go for a hop," Ace said. "Once you get used to it after we're up, I'll let you take over the controls yourself to see how you like it."

"Well, I don't know, I've been kinda figuring . . ."

"No charge."

Wilson grinned. "I guess it wouldn't hurt to take a ride, would it?" he said.

"Let's go."

There's something almost hypnotic about taking over the controls of a light plane for the first time. By the time the little Alon landed 20 minutes later, Wilson was a convert. After the way he saw how Ace handled the plane so expertly . . . almost casually . . . he decided that he was lucky to find such a good pilot for an instructor.

"Okay, you got a deal," Wilson said, back in the coffee shop. "When do we start?"

"Hold on there," said Ace. "Have you got a medical certificate?"

"Certificate?"

"Yeah, that's right; a medical certificate. You have to pass a physical before you can start flying. Didn't you know that?"

"No, I didn't," Wilson said. "But I'll sure get one. You know, Ace, you sure know all the ropes!"

"Thats what I'm getting paid for," the pilot said laconically. "You get yourself checked out by a pill-pusher and I'll see to it that you get your student pilot's certificate automatically. Let me check with the airport manager for a list of authorized medical examiners in the area. I'll be right back."

When he returned from the phone, Ace handed Wilson a short list of doctors. "Go to see whichever one is most convenient for you," he said. "Just tell him that you want to get a third-class medical certificate for a student pilot."

"Is the exam tough to pass?" Wilson asked.

"Gosh no," Ace laughed. "It's just to meet the minimum requirements set up by the FAA, which has also designated about 5,500 doctors around the country as authorized examiners. About all the doc will check is to see if you are in good general health. Do you have any heart trouble or problems with your nervous system?"

"Nope."

"Well, those are the main reasons for rejection. Along with diseases that require the intake of drugs. You're not a junkie, are you?"

"Heck no!"

"Then you should breeze through the exam in a few minutes," Ace said. "If all the grandfathers and grandmothers in their 60s and 70s and even 80s can pass the exam, *you* shouldn't have any trouble passing it. Even physical handicaps don't automatically bar anybody from becoming a pilot. As a matter of fact, there are hundreds of private pilots with lesser disorders and physical defects of one kind or another. All anybody has to do is show that his ability to handle an airplane isn't impaired."

"How about my glasses?"

"No problem, assuming that your vision is corrected to the FAA standard of 20/30 or better. Even color blindness is tolerated, although that would restrict you to certain kinds of flying. No, I don't think you have any worries. You look to me like a pretty healthy guy, and that's really all that counts."

Ace was right. Wilson passed the simple medical exam with flying colors and was given a heart-warming paper that proved to be not just a third-class medical certificate but a combination student pilot's certificate as well. Wilson was delighted to learn that it was valid for two years to the last day in the month of issue. It cost no more than any other visit to a doctor's office.

Wilson began taking flying lessons from Ace on a twice-a-week schedule and got what the mechanic told him was "prime time" . . . Saturday and Sunday mornings. By the second weekend he was shooting touch-and-go landings with the arms-crossed Ace at his side with almost a bored look on his face. He'd get a "watch it, Barry," when he'd come in too fast or too high, but otherwise the pilot took it for granted that Wilson was learning fast.

Upstairs, the instruction was thorough even though it did allow a wide margin for error. Wilson learned to bank the hard way, he was deliberately forced into stall situations to learn recovery, and he had the engine shut off on him unexpectedly after briefly being told what to do in case of such an emergency. For one harrowing five minutes he was flown into a cloud and put on his own to see if he had absorbed *that* lesson. After working with altitude problems, which Ace seemed to concentrate on, grasping the knack of take-offs and landings seemed relatively simple.

After eight hours of dual instruction, Wilson got the yen to start logging solo time. "Why not?" he demanded. "There are plenty of guys who start to solo after less dual time than I've had, and you said yourself that I'm a better-than-average student."

"Quit complaining," Ace told him. "I'm not charging you any more for dual time than I am for solo time, am I? You'll solo when *I* think that you're ready to solo."

Wilson wasn't finally handed the keys on his own until he had better than 12 hours of dual instruction under his belt. And then he was still controlled tightly by radio, with the main difference being that Ace was putting him through his paces from the ground instead of in the seat next to him. For all practical purposes, he was on an electronic leash that kept him in sight of the little county airport, and Ace wouldn't let him get within miles of a cloud.

More weeks went by. Wilson circled the field so many times, and made so many practice take-offs and landings on command that he was beginning to feel as if he was almost a part of the Alon's upholstery.

"That's the way you're *supposed* to feel," Ace said.

"But this has been going on for a month of Sundays—and Saturdays, too," Wilson beefed. "According to the FAA regulations I've been reading about, I already have the 20 hours of solo time out of the 40 hours' minimum necessary to qualify for a license, but I need at least 10 hours of solo time on cross-country flights of more than 25 miles with landings made away from base."

"Oh, you've been reading up on the regulations, have you?" Ace said. "For your information, one of the requirements is for at least one solo flight of *100* miles or more with a landing, too; next thing I know, you'll be belly-aching to do *that* one right off the bat.

"Tell you what. Next Saturday I'll go with you . . . just to be along . . . while you fly over to the Springfield airport, which is 32 miles. If you take me over there for a cup of coffee and bring me back alive, I'll get out of the plane and let you go right back and make the same trip on your own."

"I can do it, Ace, you'll see."

"Not so fast . . . there's a catch to it. Between now and next Saturday, I want to have you start boning up on the bookwork."

"B-b-b-b-bookwork?"

"That's right. All you know so far is something about how

to fly the plane, but you don't know how to get it anywhere by yourself. You will need to know something about navigation, like how to plot a course, how to figure fuel consumption and en route time with wind-drift correction, how to read a chart, and so on. How's your math?"

"So-so."

"Mine too, but you'll need to know something about angles and triangulation. I've already filled you in on preflight inspections and loading a plane per center of gravity and things like that, but you can stand some brushing up on powerplants and airframes. And when it comes to that radio you think you know all about, you know from nothing about using flight service stations."

"Oh, I've read about omni."

"Great. Read something about meteorology, too."

"Meteorology?"

Ace laughed. "It's not as awesome as it sounds," he said. "As far as you're concerned, it just means a basic understanding of weather symbols, so you'll know what the weatherman is talking about when you call in for a forecast.

"These are only the highlights of the book larnin' a pilot needs. Tell you what . . . stop by the house on the way home tomorrow after work and I'll have a set of complete Jeppesons for you. That's not the only correspondence course by a long shot, but I know where I can get the books second hand and they will only cost you about half as much as they would new. For another $20 I can pick up a computer and course plotter for you, too. Do you think you're ready for 'em?"

"You betcha!"

As a result of doing his homework assiduously every night, Wilson was able to make his 32-mile touch-out successfully the following Saturday and spent the next half-dozen weekends doing nothing but cross-country work. He was building up his solo time more rapidly now, and the Sunday he made his "long distance" flight he marked down his three hours' air time with smug satisfaction. Only a few more hours to go to pass The Magic Forty!

But on the very next lesson, Ace chewed him out royally for the way he made his preflight.

"You're getting sloppy," he snarled. "I better go up with you today to see if your airmanship in general is getting as slipshod as your ground work."

He had something to criticize about almost everything Wilson did or didn't do. The entire next four hours were spent in dual instruction, on trips to rural airports all over the map.

"You are a long way from being a competent pilot," Ace told him flatly. "I want you to keep soloing until you can bring me back flight tickets that have some relationship to your plotted courses."

Wilson doggedly followed instructions. The hours piled up as the weeks went by. Ace still kept telling him that he wasn't good enough, even after he had a total of 55 hours, 29 of them solo.

One Saturday morning he showed up at the airport to find the little Alon nowhere in sight. He noticed the mechanic lounging in the shade of the hangar and ambled on over.

"Where's Ace?" Wilson asked. "Still up on dual instruction with that paving contractor?"

"Why no, hadn't you heard?" the mechanic sounded surprised. "Ace isn't here any more. He got a job down in the Rio Grande Valley, and he left for Texas the day before yesterday."

Wilson was stunned. "Holy cow," he groaned. "*Now* what am I going to do? According to Ace I need plenty more work, but I sure don't like the idea of changing instructors at this late date."

"Ah, you're as good a pilot now as most of the guys around here who *own* airplanes," the mechanic said. "If I was you, I'd go into town and arrange with the FAA office for a written exam without any more lessons."

"But doesn't Ace have to endorse my certificate?"

"Naah, who told you that? Nowadays a student can take the written any time he feels that he's ready for it. Go take it!"

The first thing Monday morning, Wilson got on the phone and arranged with the area office of the FAA for his written exam. Two days later he took a day off work and made the trek to show the United States government how good a pilot he was, on paper.

After filling out a simple form, Wilson was ushered into a quiet room with several other student pilot applicants. After the examiner made sure that he had nothing with him except a computer and a plotter, he was given a pencil, two sheets of scratch paper, reference maps and charts, and the test itself.

"Keerist!" Wilson muttered under his breath as he riffled through the closely printed sheets. "I'll be lucky if I can finish this within the four-hour limit."

Basically, the test was in the form of about five dozen questions, with four or five multiple answers for each—only a 20 to 25 percent chance of guessing a right answer. Wilson also quickly saw that the real test was not a test of what he had stored in his head, but a test of his knowing how to use the reference material.

This included a sectional map, portions of airport directories, federal aviation guides, and so on. He noted, however, that no reference data was included on the FAA regulations for pilots . . . after finding that the test did include a heavy emphasis on that knowledge.

Wilson soon found himself involved in a hypothetical flight, for which he had to chart his course. To do so, he had to interpret a host of signs and symbols used in FAA and other flying communications as well as those used on the maps, dealing in the specifics of a flight of several legs.

His "aircraft" was spelled out as a four-seat single-engine plane with fixed tricycle landing gear and equipped with the usual simple instruments, two-way radio and VHF omni receiver. The flight was designated as normal for Visual Flight Regulations. Wilson grinned when he saw that he had "two passengers," too.

Descriptive data covering the aircraft were nothing that couldn't be found in the average owner's manual, but the weather data were something else again; although the data for a VFR day even included a weather map showing fronts, most of it was in teletype form, which had given him trouble in the secondhand books he had pored over so many nights (but which Ace told him was seldom used by the average pilot anyhow).

The airport directory extracts were simple enough, with specific data for each one involved in the flight, including radio communications information and the Koch chart showing take-off and landing distances at all temperature and altitude ranges likely to be encountered in the area.

The test was tough, but not too tough for a man who had done his homework as well as Wilson had. The alternate use of miles and knots per hour was a little troublesome, as were the temperatures sometimes given in Fahrenheit and sometimes in Centigrade. The FAA's use of Greenwich Mean Time (which Ace called Zulu) wasn't as bad as he thought it would be. When Wilson finally stretched with the test completed, he was surprised to see that he had done it in less than three hours.

The suspense over the outcome didn't take long. He was pretty sure that he had gotten better than the 70 percent passing grade and was only mildly surprised when he found that his grading mark was an 85.

He decided that one of the things that made the test easier than he thought it might be was the lack of real pressure, from the knowledge that anybody who flunked the written test could take it over again within 30 days. Nevertheless, he felt a great sense of relief at having passed one of the really big hurdles toward getting his pilot's license.

"It sure feels great," Wilson told the FAA examiner. "And now for the final hurdle . . . with the written exam out of the way, I'm ready for my flight examination, right?"

"Well, I hope so," the examiner said. "You know you have to have 40 hours of flight time for the final air exam, with the right amounts of minimum solo and cross-country time, don't you?"

"Oh, sure, I got all that and more," Wilson said.

"Okay, fill out this form with the data and the name of your flight instructor."

Wilson did so, and whistled cheerfully while the FAA man checked his files. Wilson's whistle trailed off when he saw the look on the man's face.

"I'm sorry, fella," the FAA man said. "But we don't have any instructor by that name registered."

"What's that mean?" Wilson faltered.

"Well, putting it bluntly, it means that the only instruction that can be credited to certified flight time is by an instructor who has a government-recognized instructor's rating. Did this man tell you he was a certified instructor?"

"Well, no . . . I didn't ask . . . but . . ."

"In that case, I'm afraid that you are still 40 hours of air time away from your pilot's license," the FAA man said. "The flight examiner can act only on the okay of your student's certificate by a certified instructor. Judging by the results of your written test I would say that your instructor did a pretty good job for you, but if he's not an official instructor, well . . ."

"That sonofabitch!" Wilson blurted. "I've spent over $700 learning to fly, and now it's all down the drain!"

"Well, maybe not all of it," the FAA man soothed. "The time you do put in with a certified instructor will certainly be easier for you."

"Easy, schmeasy!" Wilson cried. "Starting with a new instructor will be like starting all over again."

"Well, a lot of people do it when the instructor they start with quits teaching for a better-paying job," the government man pointed out. "Flight instruction is one of the poorest-paying jobs in the industry, and a lot of them move around quite a bit."

"Oh boy, that's fine consolation!"

"From what you tell me, this guy Ace was really trying his best to teach you to fly properly," the FAA man persisted. "Maybe he had hoped to get a certification of his instructor's rating, or maybe he even thought that you would drop out before you finished, like so many people do."

"That's still taking money under false pretenses," Wilson said. "Come to think of it, though, he did get so nasty at one point that I wondered at the time if he was trying to discourage me. And to think the way he milked me out of all those extra hours over and beyond the requirements . . ."

"That probably wasn't a milking operation as such," the office examiner said. "In the first place, any instructor wants to be pretty sure that the student won't smash up his airplane before he lets anybody use it for solo flight. Plenty of students get more dual instruction than you did before they are allowed to solo. And the way he held you to the airport before letting you try cross-country flying was probably just more for the investment he's got in his plane.

"The twice-a-week schedule he put you on is a far safer, faster, and thus more economical way to learn to fly than just once a week, too. As for that dual instruction you put in after your 100-mile cross-country, that's part of FAA requirements for *certified* instruction, too . . . three hours minimum.

"No, he wasn't just milking you for more air time; at the end there I think maybe he was just plain scared to let you loose because of the exposure he knew was inevitable once you took your written exams."

Wilson drummed his fingers in disgust. "Well, thanks anyhow," he said. "I guess I'll go find another flight instructor."

"You do that," the FAA man said. "But this time, don't just ask the first guy you see around an airport, like that mechanic who undoubtedly gets paid for steering prospective students in the right direction." He handed Wilson a mimeographed sheet. "Here, take this list of authorized instructors who hold certified instructors' ratings, and pick one you can get along with after talking with two or three of them . . . and after talking with some of their students and ex-students, too, if possible."

"Thanks."

"Happy landings!"

All the flight instruction Wilson got had been correct with only one exception . . . it wasn't official. There are a lot of good pilots around almost any airport who are not recognized by the FAA as certified instructors, and an instructor's rating is not easy to come by. Many good pilots moonlight with flying lessons, although the only honest way to do so is with the student's knowledge that the instruction is strictly for brush-up work.

Some pilots (like Ace) are crop sprayers between seasonal jobs. Others are skywriters waiting for good weather or corporate pilots while the boss is on vacation. These men have demanding jobs and are often better operational pilots than the average ground instructor in many smaller fixed-base operations. They lack only one thing: that all-important "sheepskin."

Barry Wilson did finally go on to get his private pilot's license, and he did it in two weeks by using his summer vacation for the purpose. After putting in the required types of hours, his final flight examination was easier than many sessions he had put in with Ace, and Wilson smiled wryly when the FAA flight examiner commended him for his proficiency.

Basically, that's the way almost half a million Americans have earned their pilots' licenses. And their numbers are increasing rapidly. During 1967 the FAA issued over 160,000 student pilot's certificates, which is well over 100 percent more than in 1965. The FAA believes that by 1970 as many as 300,000 student pilot's certificates will be issued annually.

All pilot training and certification in the United States is under the control of that august Federal Aviation Agency. There is no minimum age limitation for dual instruction, and a youngster can legally solo on his 16th birthday. He can get a pilot's license when he's 17—if he can read, write, and understand the English language like any other applicant.

In fact, teen-agers make up 12 percent of the nation's student pilots and almost 5 percent of the licensed pilots. FAA-approved flight-training schools are operated by 122 colleges, and 107 of them even have active flying clubs for students, including several that operate fleets of more than 10 airplanes.

There is no upper age limit for the private flyer. As long as he can prove to an Authorized Medical Examiner that he is in good general health, an octogenarian has as much right to earn a pilot's license as anybody else.

Sex is no factor at all. Last summer Marion Rice Hart, age 76 (she got her license when she was a relative youngster of 55), flew alone across the Atlantic and back again in a single-engine Bonanza and raised hardly a news report. There's a burgeoning "Grandmothers' Flying Club" in Los Angeles, too, complete with a training school for "fledgling" members.

There are literally thousands of airports, aircraft dealers, and fixed-base operators of all kinds offering flight training. Hundreds of well-equipped flight schools and flying clubs have everything from formal classrooms with audio/visual equipment up to and including ground-bound Link trainers (as well as the new low-cost Frasca simulated flight trainers and other brands and rigs, all working on the theory that the cockpit of an airplane makes one of the poorest classrooms ever devised).

Typical of the modern flight school is the one operated by

the Spartan School of Aeronautics in Tulsa, which opened in 1928 and has since trained over 12,000 students. The latest complete private pilot's course at Spartan costs students an average of a little over $900, including ground school. Spartan's training planes can be rented at $18 an hour for dual instruction or at $13.50 an hour for solo. Training at the comprehensive ground school costs $2.50 an hour for the bookwork, for a total that's been averaging $50 for complete ground instruction (less for students who do not need as much as 20 hours of such training).

A list of certified flight and ground schools, which meet government standards for physical facilities as well as for flight and classroom equipment, is available from the FAA, Dept. FS-446, Washington, D.C. 20553. The list covers only *combination* schools and does not include the thousands of recognized instructors with ratings accordingly who specialize only in *flight* instruction.

For the student pilot who prefers not to take a classroom course for the bookwork, packaged correspondence courses are available in profusion, some better than others. For the student who doesn't have *any* money except for the actual flight instruction, a good public library has all the books necessary (and more besides, which is the main trouble in digging out the right reference material on a strictly do-it-yourself basis).

Some particularly apt students have started to solo after as little as a single hour of dual instruction. An okay for something like this is strictly the responsibility of the individual flight instructor. It pays to be bright. A student pilot can also save a lot of money on the cost of getting his license by buying his plane *before* he starts putting in all that solo time, too, instead of renting a plane from the instructor.

Once the student has an okay to solo in the instructor's property, all he needs is The Man's approval to fly just about anywhere as long as he doesn't take any passengers. He can even fly on business trips as long as he gets the instructor's okay for each particular trip.

Generally, a student pilot can fly only the make and model of the plane on which he has been tested. However, if he can prove to the instructor's satisfaction that he can fly another type, it is possible to have his student's certificate endorsed to include the different airplane accordingly. It's not advised.

Although piloting skills are developed most quickly with regular and frequent practice (say, two or three lessons a week), there are plenty of pilots who have spent a year or more in earning their private licenses. Many spend 60 or 70 hours in the air, too, before their instructors feel that they are ready for the FAA flight examinations.

Naturally, there has been plenty of grousing about this. A student pilot whose only ambition is to fly his family or friends in a simple plane during good weather has always had good cause to gripe about being forced to learn a lot more than he will ever use. He didn't need to learn how to drive a Greyhound bus before he got a driver's license for his first Chevy, and there really isn't any good reason why he should have to meet the same standards as the man who will use high-performance aircraft 400 or 500 hours a year flying on business all over the United States.

Like most rigid rules, the FAA regulations can't please everybody. But the mandatory 40-hour requirement for license qualification has been an outstanding example of a compromise that pleases nobody. A fair-weather weekend pilot doesn't need to be that good (and there is also a growing shortage of FAA examiners).

On the other hand, a real honest-to-gosh private pilot needs to be better than that. In effect, the first-planned requirements for serious pilots were watered down so the little guy could get in on the deal. The result has been that a number of private licenses have been issued to serious pilots who were not yet really ready for them. These are the guys who make the newspaper headlines and obituary columns.

There is now a new set of rules under consideration. Barry Wilson may have gone to get his flyer's license about a year too soon.

If industry pressure groups get their way, the eased rulings will open the field enormously by the end of 1970. Under the new rules, beginners will be able to start flying on their own sooner—and thus at less expense. The changes, incidentally, also call for an improvement in the skills and proficiency for the regular private-pilot category.

The new ticket called the Basic Pilot's Certificate is an intermediate step between first solo and the issuance of an upgraded Private Pilot's Certificate. A Basic Pilot's license, which does allow for passengers, can be earned after as little as five hours of cross-country time after the first solo.

This new Basic Certificate is intended to satisfy the modest needs of pilots who want to fly primarily for pleasure. Many basic pilots will never need to progress beyond this stage, if they are satisfied with flying relatively simple types of planes with fixed landing gear, fixed-pitch propellers, and minimum stalling speeds of not more than 60 mph.

The basic pilot will be permitted to fly only during daylight hours, when clouds and ceiling are at least 1,000 feet above the ground and visibility is not less than three miles. He will be permitted to fly more sophisticated aircraft only after having been checked out on each particular type . . . and never with passengers in any type of plane other than the one he used to get his Basic Certificate.

Except for the five hours of cross-country, no minimum amount of flight time is called for to qualify for a Basic Pilot's Certificate. No FAA examinations, either, written or flight. The responsibility for issuing the Basic license is shifted directly to the individual student's instructor after he is satisfied that the student can handle an elementary plane safely through the basic flight maneuvers.

Under the old system, ground schools averaged 20 hours of class time, with double or triple that time spent in studying homework. For the new Basic Certificate, a *total* of 30 hours should be enough for almost anybody but the rankest boob to qualify, including not only the necessary bookwork but also the dual instruction, solo instruction, and cross-country time.

Ah, but the new Private Pilot requirements! To start with, there is an increase of flight-time experience from 40 hours to 75 hours. The additional 35 hours is for more inflight training, tailored for more experience with night flying and longer cross-country flights in more sophisticated aircraft with retractable landing gear, controllable-pitch props, and the rest of the esoteric hardware now on the market. In fact, the changed rulings would be in large part due directly to the increasing complexity of today's modern light aircraft.

The upgrading of the Private Pilot's license enables such a pilot to be eligible for instrument rating without the expense of so much more additional flight time (private pilots have had to have at least 200 hours before they could hope for an instrument ticket). New minimums for a Private Pilot's Certificate would also call for 20 hours of ground instruction, including 15 hours in a flight simulator, from a certified instructor. This makes a lot more sense than the way a man has been able to get a private license with *no* ground instruction beyond whatever self-study he found he needed to put into passing the written FAA exam.

In theory, the new rules for FAA pilot certification could practically eliminate most air accidents. The overwhelming percentage of crack-ups have always been caused by intermediate private pilots who think that they know more than they really do. A pilot who has progressed to a commercial license or better *does* know what he's doing, and most beginners are so careful that they seldom run into trouble.

Unless they ask mechanics for advice about training.

CHAPTER 4

Single-engine
planes, fixed gear

Except for a fellow like comedian Danny
Kaye, who went after . . . and got . . . his IFR license (Instrument Flight Rating) in one big gulp starting from scratch, the
average man who decides to take up flying usually starts with a
student (or VFR) license. This entitles him to fly only single-
engine planes with fixed landing gear, without any of the more
sophisticated gear such as variable-pitch propellers, auto-pilots,
and similar equipment that makes flying so much safer and more
efficient for seasoned pilots but that might take a beginner's mind
off the more basic fundamentals.

With private aviation growing as fast as it is, there are understandably many more VFR pilots than all the rest combined.
Because this is the basic airplane market, single-engine fixed-gear
aircraft account for the overwhelming majority of all planes in
use. Not counting the home-builts, one-shots, and planes hope-
fully advertised by manufacturers who are still trying to get
companies off the ground, there are dozens of makes and models
being built today by the recognized manufacturers. Cessna leads
the pack by a wide margin, but there is plenty of stiff competition.

One of the first things a prospective airplane buyer has to consider is whether he prefers a high-wing or a low-wing plane. The subject is good for a heated argument at almost any airport. In fact, companies have even been broken up over this difference of opinion; Clyde Cessna and Walter Beech were once partners, along with Lloyd Stearman, in the Travel Air Manufacturing Company, where the arguments over basic airframe design got so rancorous that Beech's partners pulled out to start shops of their own.

Beech never did view the high wing with any marked degree of enthusiasm. But his detractors, today as then, point out that the high wing tends to be more stable in the air. The fuselage hangs from the wing as from an open umbrella, and the plane is easier to control in flight—particularly at slow speeds, where most trouble develops. Visibility of the ground can be important, too.

"Who can underrate control?" one high-wing advocate declaims. "There's a good reason why stunt flyers stick to the umbrellas. Any aerobatics pilot knows that the airframe design is the most important part of a plane, and if they depend on a high-wing for precision and flyability, their opinion is good enough for me."

One admitted limitation of many high-wing planes, though, is relative instability on the ground. On low-wing planes, the landing gear can be spaced farther apart with the wheels attached directly to the wing for a broader base. The bigger the "landing triangle" in relation to the size of the plane, the harder it is to tip over.

A low wing can be stronger, too, because it is directly anchored more solidly to the fuselage. The struts used to secure a high wing to the fuselage can create enough drag to slow down a plane appreciably.

Unless the high wing sits on top of a lofty cabin, it can create turbulence that interferes with the efficiency of the tail surfaces, a fact that complicates the job of the aircraft designer. This particular problem is minimized with low-wing models, with the troublesome turbulence going over the tail.

Even the ground crews are heard from in the high-wing/

low-wing argument, although they prefer low-wing models almost to the man: a low-winger is easier to refuel. However, the fuel supply in a high wing is in the wing itself and the gas is fed to the engine by gravity, which practically anybody will admit is more reliable than even the best fuel pump.

It all boils down to a matter of what particular characteristics are most important to the individual buyer. The phrase "You can't have everything" applies to aviation even more than to many other fields. Almost any given feature on an airplane is achieved at the sacrifice of some other feature.

The man who puts economy first has to forgo speed, and vice versa. The man who dotes on fuel consumption has to forget about power. Pilots who insist on safety as a primary consideration have to sacrifice weight. Just about any feature on an airplane, from visibility to cargo capacity, exists at the sacrifice of something else.

The requirements, needs, and preferences of so many pilots differ so widely that an airplane almost becomes a tailor-made purchase. There is no such thing as "a good all-around airplane."

A sports plane may be no good for a businessman who needs to carry a lot of equipment, and a big plane for the man with a big family might not do for the fisherman who needs a plane with a lot of range for trips up into Canada. The dependability of twin engines might be deemed necessary for somebody who does a lot of flying over mountainous terrain but unnecessarily expensive for a Midwesterner who seldom gets out of sight of an airport somewhere below him.

But all planes start with one thing: weight. As a rule of thumb, the lighter the plane, the better it flies. The extra weight of any additional equipment or facilities over the basic airframe can be justified only in their relative value compared to the airworthiness that they inexorably cost.

The FAA certifies planes according to their gross weight, which is the combination of the empty weight plus the allowable useful load. The planes covered in the following chapters are listed in that order accordingly, from lightest gross weight on up, rather than in progressive order of prices or empty weights.

Listings cover every basic model currently being manufactured on a production basis for distribution in the United States. Prices, specification figures, and performance scores are constantly changing but have been pegged at mid-1968, aviation's "Year of the Big Change." Basic characteristics for the various categories remain constant, though, and many manufacturers' roseate puff figures have been made more realistic through pilot checks by the author.

AA-1 Yankee
1,430 pounds gross weight

Weighing in at 885 pounds stripped, this Cleveland contender is a 1968 challenger with a lot of ambition. The tricycle-geared two-seater sells for $6,495, and although the first one wasn't delivered until April, director of marketing Larry Kelly vowed to see the delivery of the 175th by the end of the year, with 700 units scheduled for 1969 and—get this—1,500 in 1970.

That's more airplanes than were sold in 1967 by Mooney, Hawker-Siddeley, Champion, Grumman, Lake, Dassault, Maule, Lockheed-Georgia, Swearingen, Alon, Lear, North American Aviation, and Bellanca—all put together.

If the Yankee is going to be outselling the entire output of Beech Aircraft by 1970 (19 models in the Beech line in 1967), the little plane deserves a close look. And you have to look pretty closely, because it's pretty small.

Except for the new Palomino (which see), the Yankee undersells the next-lowest price low-wing plane by about $2,500. But even that little Piper Cherokee 140 trainer is 720 pounds heavier in gross weight. The Yankee's useful weight capacity is 545 pounds, including gas, oil, and instrumentation.

It's a gutsy little boat, though. Its airspeeds are faster than any standard competition under the $11,000 class. With only a 108 hp Lycoming 00235-C2A engine, it can hit a top speed of 144 mph at sea level, cruise on 75 percent power at 133 mph at 8,000 feet, and travel on 65 percent power at that altitude at 125 mph. Stall speed is high, though, for such a small plane: 64 mph.

After a 790-foot ground run, it can clear a 50-foot obstacle

American Aviation Corporation's Model AA-1 Yankee

in a total of 1,440 feet. It climbs at 900 feet per minute (for the first minute at sea level), and its service ceiling is 12,200 feet. Coming down over a 50-foot obstacle, the Yankee lands in 1,185 feet, including a 442-foot ground roll, with indicated airspeed at 50 feet coming in at a safe 77 mph.

Cruising on 75 percent power at 8,000 feet, it will use 22 of the 24 gallons of fuel in the tank in 3 hours and 20 minutes, for a distance of 435 miles. Optimum range is achieved at a 10,000-foot altitude and is 512 miles. These figures include climb fuel allowance, with a rich mixture during climb, leaned out only after cross-country altitude, but depend to some extent on the optional wheel skirts.

American Aviation Corporation, builder of the Yankee, has cut surprisingly few corners to achieve the low price. For example, standards include a 40-amp alternator, metal prop and spinner, complete electrical system, navigation lights, electric flaps, toe and parking brakes, and adjustable bucket seats.

"Howja do it?" this author asked Kelly.

"Jet-age materials and manufacturing techniques," he replied blandly. "For example, lightweight aluminum honeycomb, bonded together . . . no rivets, just like on the SST. The smooth skin is one of the secrets of the Yankee's speed, too."

Another cost-cutting secret: the Yankee is basically the Bede BD-1 design, and American Aviation was spared the costs of engineering and design, which were covered by some of the other people who have tried to get it on the market from time to time. The AA-1 Yankee is a much refined version, though.

This Yankee doodles along just dandy.

Mooney Cadet
1,450 pounds gross weight

Weighing only a little more than the Yankee at gross, the Cadet is to other light planes what a Thunderbird is to the rest of the Fords. The accent is on sporty features, leaning toward flash.

Manufacture of the design has a long history of fitful starts and painful stops, going back to the 1930s. Over the years, more than 5,000 units have been marketed under such trademarks as Fornaire and Ercoupe. The guaranteed spinproof, split-tail (and mush-ruddered) two-seater made a pretty good comeback in Mc-Pherson, Kansas, where over 200 were built until Mooney came along and gobbled up the outfit in 1967. The Cadet was still known as the Alon A-2 well into 1968 before Mooney put its own corporation stamp on it officially.

The Alon A-2 was one of the very, very few planes on which the price had been lowered in recent years—from $8,395 to the 1967 price of $7,975. However, Mooney took care of that little nonconformity, and the price of the Cadet is now $9,295.

Even as did the Alon A-2, the Cadet sports a lot of gloss. The interior is genuinely handsome, with "sports car styling" on the beautifully upholstered two-tone bucket seats, wall-to-wall wool carpeting, fiberglass soundproofing, and sculptured side panels to set off a high-style instrument panel—all with quality and finish as good as or better than that in many planes costing twice as much.

Stepping over the side onto that high-class seat can be almost embarrassing for anybody with dirty feet, but that's the only way to get in. Seat flaps are provided as upholstery protection for the fastidious.

The C-90-16F Continental engine puts out 90 horses at 2,475 rpm. The fixed-pitch propeller is a McCauley, and the 930-pound EW (empty weight) low-winger lifts a useful load of 520 pounds with ease. Once it's in the air, that is; many pilots claim that the wheels are so far aft that a hefty yank on the yoke is needed to get the Cadet airborne and that when the main gear lifts first, the nose pitches up even more.

The insensitive rudder is mushy at all speeds, and plenty of leg stretching is required when landing with a slip or in cross-winds. For an extra $95, the buyer can get a model without any rudder pedal at all, for a two-control lash-up that allows the plane to be steered like an automobile.

According to Mooney, the canopy can be pushed back for inflight speeds under 100 mph, as well as for taxiing on the ground. Sporty indeed. Noisy, too. With the bubble canopy closed, an overhead panel minimizes the risk of sunburn (or eliminates it with a tinted canopy for an extra $80).

Take-off distance is 540 feet on the flat (1,100 feet over a 50-foot obstacle). Rate of climb is 640 feet per minute at sea level, and service ceiling is 17,300 feet. Maximum speed is 129 mph, cruising speed at 75 percent power is 124 mph, and "economy cruise speed" is 117 mph. Range, with 24 gallons of gas burning at 4.6 gallons per hour, is 615 miles. Landing roll is 350 feet; coming in over a 50-footer, the Cadet needs 1,200 feet. Stall speed is 42 mph.

Not sporty enough? For only $25, a tasteful Naugahyde cover is available as an option for the cockpit—just like a TR3 convertible.

Lark 95

1,500 pounds gross weight

This little airplane is *not* in production as of this writing. However, it's been in production several times in the past, and there isn't much doubt but that it will be in production again— but perhaps not under the name of "Lark," which Aero Commander is now using on a revamp of what it called the model 100 until 1968—nor by the name it was once known as . . . the Cadet; Mooney's got that one sewed up. How about the Phoenix?

The airframe is basically a 30-year-old design—a reincarnated Culver Cadet, which was designed back in the 1930's by Al Mooney for the ill-fated Culver Aircraft Corporation. That company started to build the Cadet at a bad time: 1941.

The scattered assets were accumulated by Homer H. Helton, a retired Air Force lieutenant colonel who got the design back in business in 1966. Its certification was still good, thereby saving the new manufacturer perhaps a million dollars or so that a new design might cost to get through all the stages for a new FAA certificate. One result was Helton's price for the Lark 95: $7,600.

Basically, the Lark was still a Cadet using some of the oldest ideas in the industry—a wooden fuselage, for example. Helton covered the plywood skin over the low-wing two-seater with Dacron, but that's still considered fabric.

The short and chunky design has gliding characteristics about like that of a brick. In any but the smoothest air, it is a good reminder that light planes don't ride bumps well, and never did (or ever will). And like most old-time planes, the design's seats are a tight fit for any relatively well-fed flyers.

But within his certificate limitations, Helton made literally hundreds of improvements. Biggest changes were a wider fixed-gear tricycle landing gear, a bubble canopy, and a bigger engine. He had still more changes for the Lark in the hopper. An important one was an enlarged tail design; when used for aerobatics, entry speeds had been critical due to elevator and rudder deficiencies. The plane did not fall under the contemporary aerobatic certification regulations because it was built as the Culver Cadet before they came into effect!

Access to the Lark . . . strike that; to the *Helton* . . . is from either side of the 26-foot 11-inch wingspread, but like the old Alon (now Mooney Cadet) the only way to get in is to step on the seat before sitting down.

The 70-inch fixed-pitch metal propeller is churned by a Continental C-90-16F engine, which is rated for 95 hp at 2,625 for take-off. The plane is airborne in about 500 feet and climbs at almost 1,000 feet per minute toward its service ceiling of 16,250 feet, figures that a lot of bigger planes would like to match.

Maximum speed is 142 mph, and the "Helton" cruises at 130 mph with 75 percent power for a 500-mile range. The 19-gallon tank has an all-usable gravity feed with an auxiliary pump. Useful load leaves something to be desired at 550 pounds. Stall speed is at a 57 mph clip. Landing roll-out is a relatively long 700 feet, and a new pilot may have a tendency to oversteer the nose wheel, almost like on a sports car.

About that wood. "It's stronger and safer," Helton avers. "Use of wood also eliminates rivet drag, which means better airspeed and improved performance all around. This is a good airplane because it's wood, not in spite of it."

Wood also costs less to set up for.

Cessna 150
1,600 pounds gross weight

This lightweight two-seater (four, if you cram a couple of small children into the back) is doing to the aviation industry what the compact car did to the automobile industry, only more so. The 150 outsells any other new plane on the market by a wide, wide margin.

One of the things the public likes about the 150 is the fact that it's another one of the few planes that carries a lower price today than when it was first put on the market. It's up $300 over the 1967 price, but the current $7,295 price tag represents better than a 10 percent price drop from where it started for the 975-

Cessna Model 150

pound EW product, with no sacrifice in performance, equipment, or features.

Many buyers are also impressed with the idea that the 150 can be serviced by the biggest dealer/service network in the aviation world. The ship even carries a six-month warranty— almost as if it had been made in Detroit.

Many of the bugs in the first models have been remedied since the current series came on the market in 1964. Width of the once shoulder-lapping cabin has been increased to 40 inches where it counts, at elbow level. New rubber isolators now cushion the entire power system for a lower noise level. The nose-gear strut has been shortened by more than 40 percent to cut drag. The former erratic generator has been replaced with a gear-driven 60-amp alternator for a dependable electrical output at all speeds rather than just at some.

Complaints about the old heating and ventilating system have resulted in an efficient revamp, and there is now a windshield defrost outlet on the cowl deck. "Open view" control wheels allow the pilot to see the new quick-scan instrument panel without obstruction. New stall-warning indicators are free of the electrical system.

The former "slam-'em-again" doors (on which both windows can now be opened for cross ventilation) have been reengineered for a firm latch with light pressure, and the carpeted floor is now completely flat; no more humps or ridges to impede foot room. The new swept-back vertical tail adds nothing to performance, but the 150 now looks better . . . and thus is more salable. There's even a needle-nosed spinner.

In short, Cessna is doing everything possible to make sure that the 150 maintains its lion's share of the existing market as well as to prod the awakening but still nonflying public out of their cars and into an airplane.

The Cessna 150 makes the most of a high-wing airplane's stability potential (the center of gravity well below the center of lift). The tapering, flexible Cessna wing has a "twist" in the outboard sections that provides aileron control long after the inboard sections of the wing have stopped producing lift. The outsized, electrically controlled flaps, with slotted design like on an airliner, are positively positioned from zero degrees through 40 degrees in a wide range of settings.

The easily controllable 150 has more rudder than most Wichita products and has FAA clearance for spins. The little plane is huskier than it looks, too; it is certified for the utility category, which has more rigorous standards than the normal category.

The engine is a 100 hp Continental 0-200A, which can burn economical 80-octane fuel. There are no tank switches to remember, for the gas is automatically fed by gravity into a single line from two overhead fuel cells holding a total of 26 gallons.

The 150 comes in three versions: Standard, Trainer, and Commuter. Top speeds on the Standard and Trainer are 122 mph, and cruising speeds are 95 to 100 mph at comfortable power settings of 2,300 to 2,600 rpm. They take off in 1,385 feet after a ground roll of 735 feet. Sea-level rate of climb is 670 feet per minute, and service ceiling is 12,650 feet. Landing over the same 50-foot obstacle it took off over, total distance is 1,075 feet, including a 445-foot ground roll. Stall speed: 48 mph. Range: 565 miles with maximum payload.

The Trainer is a couple of inches longer than the Standard

and weighs 30 pounds more when empty. The $8,995 price includes dual controls, rate of climb and turn/bank indicators, a 90-channel nav/com radio, a more sensitive altimeter, an electric clock, and sun visors.

The Commuter, weighing 85 pounds more than the Standard for a 1,060-pound EW total, costs $10,195. Useful load is down to 540 pounds, compared to the 625 and 605 pounds on the Standard and Trainer, respectively, due to added gadgetry. Aside from all the additional equipment in the Trainer, the Commuter also sports individually adjustable bucket seats, an omni-flash beacon light, horizon and directional gyros with a suction gauge and vacuum system, speed fairings, a tow bar, and many more pieces of hardware that the dealers love to recite.

The Cessna 150 is also floatplane certified. The wet version weighs 50 pounds more than the land plane and carries a 515-pound payload. Top speed is just over 100 mph, and its cruising range is 375 miles at 75 percent power flying at 7,000 feet—with no reserve. Rate of climb at sea level is 550 feet per minute, service ceiling is 10,500 feet, and at that altitude it can keep going for 8.6 hours at 78 mph with an optional 38-gallon tank.

Because the floatplane has more clearance, it can utilize a big 75-inch propeller (compared to 69 inches on the land planes). All or any of the equipment used in the land-locked versions is available on option in the floatplane 150. Water run distance for take-off is over 1,300 feet, and a total distance of 2,100 feet is needed to clear a 50-foot obstacle. The 150 will land on 415 feet of water, or a total distance of 850 feet over a 50-foot obstacle.

With an estimated 175,000 student pilots taking flying lessons at this writing, the odds are good that a big percentage of them will learn to fly in a model 150. If there's anything wrong with that, it's the possibility that they might not learn enough about flying from the 150 . . . it's just too easy to fly.

"You don't have to 'fly' a marshmallow like that, you just drive it," snorts one grizzled old home-built veteran. "With all these women and school kids getting pilots' licenses, I don't know what the aviation world is coming to."

Cessna knows.

Beagle B 121-100
1,600 pounds gross weight

The British pound sterling may have been devalued, but not the British idea of what their airplanes are worth. This London-based manufacturer first entered the American market seriously in 1967 with a really good (but expensive) twin and liked the looks of the market so much that it decided to move in where the action is with a light single-engine plane us Colonists could appreciate.

However, $9,800 is a lot of money for a two-seater with an empty weight of only 970 pounds, a 100 hp engine, and a cruising speed on 75 percent power of 117 mph. Nine lower-priced competitive models weigh more, have more powerful engines, and have faster 75 percent-power speeds.

The B 121-100 boasts a Rolls-Royce 0-200A engine but still has a top speed of a modest 129 mph. On a 65 percent power setting, this dog ambles along sedately at 112 mph, although the stall speed is 57 mph. Under ideal sea-level conditions, it climbs at 500 feet per minute and has a service ceiling of 12,500 feet.

It will clear a 50-foot obstacle in 1,150 feet, including a 700-foot ground run. Carrying maximum useful load of 630 pounds, it has a range of 350 miles and burns 6 gallons of gas per hour from its 26.5 gallon tank. It uses well over 1,000 feet of landing distance to come in over a 50-foot obstacle to a full stop.

It would take Sherlock Holmes himself to detect this plane's competitive advantages that make it worth almost ten grand.

Champion
1,650 pounds gross weight

This lightweight is the lowest-priced production plane on the market: $5,795. Even that's $500 more than the price just a year ago, and *that* was up over $400 from the year before that.

Until 1968, the Champion was called the Champion Citabria, but nobody could pronounce it. "Citabria" is "airbatic" spelled backward. And well it might be, because that's about as close as this tandem two-seat high-wing 980-pound plane is going to get to being seriously aerobatic. Fun to fly? Absolutely. Strong? Assuredly. This little bugger has a six G design (withstands stresses six times the force of gravity) and although it's among the slowest fastbacks on the market, it can really scat around the corners. But for aerobatics? Nyet. The Champion . . . nee Citabria . . . just doesn't live up to its designers' expectations or its salesmen's claims.

In a loop the pilot tends to fall out of his seat regardless of how hard he's pulling back. In an attempted spin, the unwilling Champion quits spinning after about two turns even with the elevator and rudder pushed all the way in. With the large fixed vertical stabilizer opposing rudder attempts, an attempted snap roll becomes a mushy gyration that tends to stop altogther as soon as the plane is upside down. When it does flop through, it usually has the nose well below the horizon when the "snap" stops.

If a hammerhead roll is taken too slowly, the undoctored engine quits as soon as the plane is inverted and the rudder is too weak to hold up the nose without the slipstream. Dish-out.

Aerobatic (?) Tandem Champion

But the company did sell 274 planes last year, and one reason is because the Champion is outstanding in another area that the designers may have never even thought of: it's an almost ideal plane for aerial photography. It flies beautifully even at 60 mph and can go all day on a single 39-gallon tank of gas in the upper three versions.

The big sliding window admits very little draft, and a ledge close at hand under the panel is ideal for film packs, lens filters, and other small gear. The hands-off stability is exceptional, or the pilot/photographer can fly the plane by his knees with the stick control.

In 1968 Champion switched to model numbers that are as confusing as any designations in the industry. All five of the "different" models are basically the same plane, though, and all five simply work around within the limitations of the single FAA certification at 1,650 pounds gross weight.

The basic "model" is the 7ECA, powered by a 115 hp Lycoming 0-235-C1 engine, which provides a top speed of 117 mph and a cruise speed of 112 mph with 75 percent power. Useful load is 670 pounds for a 12,000-foot service ceiling. Stall speed is 50 mph. Of the 890 feet needed to take off over a 50-foot obstacle, it uses 400 for ground run. On landing, ground roll is 400 feet out of a total 755 feet needed to come in over a 50-foot obstacle. Rate of climb is 725 feet per minute.

For another $935, the Wisconsin manufacturer will substitute a utility wing with 35-degree flaps, which cuts the total take-off distance over a 50-foot obstacle to 860 feet, including a mere 310-foot ground run, despite the fact that the modification adds 45 pounds to the empty weight. This, then, becomes the model 7GCBC. Both use 6 gallons of gas from the standard 26-gallon tank per hour, for a maximum 728-mile range. 7GCBC climbs at 775 feet per minute.

If you're good at remembering model numbers, try this one: the 7GCAA is the standard Champion with a 150 hp Lycoming 320-A2B engine. This brings the empty weight up to 1,038 pounds and cuts the useful load to 612 pounds. Service ceiling is upped to 17,000 feet, climb rate goes to 1,120 feet per minute, and top speed is 130 mph. Cruise on 75 percent power is 125 mph, gas consumption is 9 gallons per hour, and range is 537 miles. Take-off over a 50-foot obstacle is 630 feet, including a 400-foot ground run. Price is $6,985.

To compound the confusion in model numbers, the company also uses the same 7GCBC designation for the *150* hp model when the utility wing is substituted for the standard wing. *This* 7GCBC has an empty weight of 1,075 pounds, but clears a 50-foot obstacle in 525 feet, including the 310-foot ground run, and climbs at 1,145 feet per minute. Other specs are the same as the standard 150 hp 7GCAA.

There is also a 7KCAB, with the 150 horses coming from a Lycoming IO-320-E219 engine, which gives it a top speed of 133 mph. Although the empty weight is now up to 1,100 pounds, it still has the same take-off characteristics as the 7GCAA and uses only 8.5 gallons of fuel per hour. Price of the 7KCAB is $8,350, but it includes an inverted fuel- and oil-injection system and a greenhouse roof for aerobatic playing around—which was the whole idea of the Champion to start with.

Price of the 150 hp 7GCBC is $7,675. See if you can find it! It's in that numbered text *some*where.

Piper Super Cub
1,750 pounds gross weight

More people have learned to fly in Piper Cubs than in any other airplane, and it is still favored as a training plane by many instructors. For one thing, it is not the easiest plane to fly by a long shot. The controls are surprisingly stiff for so small a plane, and it's tricky to land (one reason the bounce-back wheels are placed so well forward). But the student who learns to fly in a Cub becomes a better-than-ordinary pilot accordingly.

The modern Cub has come a long way from the J-3, starting with the price: $9,925 compared to the first $1,325 price tag. Although it is only two inches bigger in any dimension, it can now carry 820 pounds of useful load, can hit 130 mph, and has a more respectable range of over 400 miles. At sea level it can

Piper Super Cub

climb at 960 feet per minute, and it holds a world's record for unaspirated piston-engine light aircraft: 30,203 feet.

The Super Cub also outperforms some of the best STOL (Short Take-Off and Landing) planes specifically built for "steep gradient" operation. It takes off in 200 feet, and needs only 500 feet from a dead start to clear a 50-foot obstacle. Landing over a 50-foot obstacle, it needs only 725 feet, including 350 feet of rollway.

However, it is still quite obviously a descendant of the J-3. The Super is still hard to climb into or out of, it is one of the noisiest of all two-seaters, and visibility for the passenger in the back seat is practically nil.

Unlike the amazingly reluctant-to-stall J-3, the now heavier Super Cub *can* stall. However, air handling is still excellent, and pitch response is particularly impressive. Lateral, longitudinal, and spiral stabilities are better than good. Stall speed: 43 mph.

The Lycoming 0-320 engine develops 150 hp and uses a modest 8.5 gallons of gas per hour at its 115 mph cruising speed on 75 percent power. The Super Cub is like the Volkswagen in that it is constantly being improved without many outward changes; that cruising speed, for example, is 10 mph faster in the 1968 model than in the 1967. Rated service ceiling is up to 19,000 feet.

The Super Cub is one of the last fabric-covered planes still being built. Its days on the production line are probably numbered. In the meantime, it is available from the onetime silk mill in New Haven in several versions, including a deluxe model that sports such features as a complete electrical system, a more sensative altimeter than the one supplied as standard equipment, a parking brake, and a metal nose spinner. Buyers other than pasture pilots can get it equipped with either skiis or floats.

Even the seaplane version gets a four-hour cruising range out of the 36-gallon fuel capacity, although with the floats an airspeed of over 100 mph is seldom reached with the standard 75 percent power setting. The floats, of course, make a hash of the Super Cub's STOL characteristics even with the same air-grabbing flaps extended.

"The Cub's pedigree goes back better than 30 years," says owner Anthony Barone, of Wurtsboro, New York. "I like the idea that Piper had a chance to get the bugs out of the design in the 27,000 Cubs they built before they built mine."

Maule M-4C Jetasen and M-4-210C Rocket
2,100 pounds gross weight

The Maule fellows up in Jackson, Michigan, know more about building good airplanes than they do about selling them. If they knew (or cared) as much about merchandising as they do about engineering, they could give the Big Five a good run for their money. Belford D. Maule, who is not only the president of his company but the chief engineer as well, sold 48 planes during 1967. Maule airplanes do not fool around with new-fangled notions like tricycle landing gear, and the design is one of the few left still using a tail wheel.

The high-wing four-seat M-4C Jetasen, weighing only 1,100 pounds EW, carries a useful load of 1,000 pounds and cruises at 150 mph on 75 percent power at its 12,000-foot service ceiling. Priced at $11,498 bare (ah there, get that "discount-store pricing"!), it costs about $12,500 equipped—with plenty of room in the 42-inch-wide cabin for even more hardware. It converts handily to a two-seat cargo ship that can travel up to 700 miles on its 42-gallon tank feeding 8 gallons of gas per hour to a 145 hp Continental 0-300-A engine.

Rate of climb with gross weight is nothing to brag about at 700 feet per minute, but that modest figure shoots up to 1,000 with one person and half a fuel load aboard. With full flaps, stall speed is an eminently satisfactory 40 mph. Take-off and landing distances over a 50-foot obstacle are 900 feet and 600 feet, respectively, with a 700-foot ground run going up and a 600-foot roll coming in. Top speed is an eye-opening 180 mph, and the Jetasen cruises at 145 mph on 65 percent power.

With the substitution of a 210 hp Continental I0-360-A engine, the plane becomes the M-4-210C Rocket, which is outstanding in its class. This son-of-a-gun can take off in 150 feet.

Among single-engine, fixed-gear planes with unaspirated engines, the Maules have the fastest top airspeed, and the Rocket also has the fastest speed at 65 percent power: 160 mph. Along with its lighter sister ship (the Rocket's empty weight is 1,250 pounds), it has the slowest stall speed at 40 mph. For good measure, it matches the fastest rate of climb: 1,250 feet per minute. Service ceiling is 18,000 feet.

Naturally, there's a slight catch to that 150-foot take-off. That's with just the pilot and half a load of gas. But the regular figures are still pretty good. Take-off over a 50-foot obstacle requires a 585-foot total after a 380-foot ground run, and total landing distance is 600 feet with a ground roll taking up 450 feet of that. The engine uses 9.5 gallons of gas per hour for a 680-mile maximum range with a 45-minute reserve.

Useful load of the Rocket is 850 pounds. The four-place configuration is priced at $14,998 and built as the Cargo Rocket the ticket is $14,595.

The plane is ugly, but with its own special qualities, it's lovable.

Piper Cherokee 140
2,150 pounds gross weight

Piper built 4,302 airplanes during 1967, and the Cherokee design is one reason why the company can truthfully say that it has built more airplanes than any other manufacturer in the world. The Cherokee, with its various powerplants, has long been the world's largest-selling low-wing sport/business plane.

Its history is one of expansion and reduction. Engines have been added and subtracted, and the fuselage has been stretched to accommodate everything up to the big six-seater. In the latest version even the wheels have been knocked off to produce the retrac Arrow (which see). The famous 150 and 160 models are no longer in production, but the design remains a classic.

The model 140 is *the* low-wing trainer. Ground stability is remarkable for handling even in high, gusty winds, as the main wheels are a full 10 feet apart on the tricycle landing gear—

Piper Cherokee 140

a full third of the wing span with the wing tips extending just 10 feet beyond each main wheel.

The nose wheel is as big as the main wheels, on the theory that the bigger the nose wheel, the more punishment it can take on rough landings. The big nose wheel not only minimizes tire maintenance costs but makes for smoother roll on all surfaces as well. Unfortunately, it also increases drag in flight. But it is "hunch-up retractable" and can be used in take-offs as a jump assist.

The unique Cherokee "stabilator" is the entire horizontal tail section, which moves as one piece (rather than the more common elevator trailing a fixed horizontal stabilizer). With a small additionally movable surface on the rear of the stabilator, almost like a "tail flap," trim is simple and the Cherokee becomes one of the easiest of all airplanes to fly—or to drive, as some would say. Rudder movement and aileron action (or vice versa) are coordinated for "one-piece control." Some instructors believe that this can be a drawback in a trainer; learning to fly in a plane that turns itself, the student never does learn how to properly coordinate the control surfaces by himself.

The foot-pedal-operated rudder also works in conjunction with the steerable nose wheel. The landing gear has single-disc hydraulic brakes, and the Cherokee can ground-turn in a 15-foot radius: half a wing span. Line checks are simplified by cowlings running the full length of the engine, both sides, for powerplant inspection. The 150 hp Lycoming 0-320 engine is economical with low-octane fuel, and gas consumption is rated at just 7.2 gallons per hour.

The Cherokee's thick, stubby-looking wing is blamed for slow speeds at cruise altitude, but the drag created by the fat wing is offset by its stubbiness. Actually, the thickness is an integral part of an excellent design structure that creates an air foil for high lift.

Piper wistfully advertises the 1,180-pound EW model 140 as a "two- to four-seat" airplane and offers a modification kit with "family seats" for the back. But in this case "family" means "children" . . . small ones. The flying public still considers the 140 primarily as a trainer.

One of the reasons the 140 is such a good training plane is because it has the control and power characteristics of the upper-line Cherokees. The 140 graduate can move steadily up the line to the big 300 hp Cherokee six before he runs out of "simple" single-engine planes, without moving out of Piper's Cherokee family at all.

Priced at $8,990, the model 140 carries a useful load of 970 pounds. Once it is equipped with speed fairings (the more elegant term for "wheel pants"), it can hit a top speed of 142 mph, a 75 percent power cruise of 133 mph, and 125 mph on 65 percent power. Stall speed is rated at 54 mph, but this figure (as well as most others) is effected in direct ratio to the load carried.

Take-off over a 50-foot obstacle is 1,700 feet, including an 800-foot ground run. It climbs at 660 feet per minute from sea level to a service ceiling of 14,300 feet. Landing over a 50-foot obstacle takes an 890-foot minimum, including a 535-foot ground roll. Maximum range is 850 miles from the 50-gallon tanks, but 14 gallons of this is in wing-tip auxiliary tanks; pilots have to remember to switch back and forth to use wing-tip gas evenly unless they enjoy constantly adjusting trim controls.

Otherwise, the Cherokee 140 almost flies itself.

Darter Commander
2,250 pounds gross weight

Aero Commander entered the year of 1968 as a reorganized and consolidated operation. Merging with North American Aviation, the former Aircraft Divisions of the Rockwell Standard Corporation became the Aero Commander Division of the Commercial Products Group of the North American Rockwell Corporation.

Got all that straight? That's more than some of the hapless dealers can do.

Aero Commander divisions have built the most categorically comprehensive line of aircraft of all manufacturers, covering just about everything from jets on down. Their bid for the "flying flivver" market is the Darter, which was known as model 100 until 1968 (with only one exception, all the Aero Commander planes are now named after birds). The Darter is the lowest-price four-place all-metal plane in production today that's really designed for four people. Price: $8,950.

The Darter has a useful load of 970 pounds, it climbs at 785 feet per minute, and its service ceiling is 13,000 feet. By grunting a bit, it can achieve almost 135 mph, but more realistically it travels at 128 mph or 110 mph at 75 percent and 65 percent settings. Stall speed is 48 mph. It holds 44 gallons of fuel, which it uses sparingly at 5.5 gallons per hour; and range is a modest 510 miles. Operations at upper power settings, it should be noted, are apt to consume up to 18 gallons per hour. Total landing distance over a 50-foot obstacle is a mere 650 feet. On take-off, after a 750-foot ground run, it can get over a 50-foot obstacle in another 200 feet for a total of 950.

The back of the high cabin on earlier models created more drag than was desirable, but current production has a better aerodynamic design with a bigger back window to boot. Visibility wasn't too good, either, and the Darter now has a bigger windshield. The visibility is better, but the bigger windshield has unfortunately resulted in a smaller instrument panel.

The interior is rather Spartan, perhaps because of former price cuts, but there are new ram's-horn control wheels in the 1968 model. All windows are sealed, and ventilation is minimal. The metal vane on the nose wheel, designed to "aim" the gear for landing, is as ugly as ever.

The high-wing Darter has a Lycoming 0-320-A series horizontally opposed, four-cylinder engine producing 150 hp at 2,700 rpm. The cabin section of the fuselage is built of welded steel alloy tubing, and the appearance suggests the roll bar of a racing car. The fuel tanks in each wing butt are baffled to prevent sloshing, "just like on the big planes." The tough little bird is genuinely hard to damage.

The Darter really means it when it claims that it was really designed for four people (note: narrow-shouldered passengers required for the back seats). It features bucket seats fore and aft, with the front seats mounted on tracks so they can be moved forward for access to the ones in the back.

Naturally, it has tricycle landing gear, with a tail skid, just in case.

What was formerly known as the model 100 has also been modified as the Lark Commander, which has a swept tail, two large cabin doors, and added pilot and passenger conveniences. It also has a 180 hp Lycoming engine, and the base price for the Lark version is $12,995. Maximum cruise speed is 138 mph and it carries a useful load of 1,000 pounds, compared to the Darter's 970.

Which is plenty for *any* trainer.

Cessna 172 and Skyhawk

2,300 pounds gross weight

Do you drive a Chevy? Then you'll like the 172. It's the fastest-selling full-size four-place plane on the market.

The model has had a longer period of development and refinement than any other plane in its class. Its immediate ancestor was the tail-gear 170, made from 1948 until the tricycle-gear 172 was evolved in 1955 along with the renowned 175, which in turn was discontinued when the Skyhawk was developed in 1961. There are now more 172/Skyhawk airplanes flying than any other plane ever made.

The new engine used in the 1968 models represents the biggest change since the rear window appeared in 1963. The six-cylinder Continental engine formerly used, with 145 hp, has been replaced with a four-cylinder Lycoming rated at 150 hp. This is the same engine used in the revolutionary new Cardinal (which see). It reduces maintenance costs, burns 80-octane fuel, and has a 1,500-hour service life.

The 1,230-pound 172 is strictly a stripped-down airplane, with nothing in it except what it needs to be functional . . . and only for daytime flying at that. Price: $11,700. With an extra $1,550 worth of equipment, it's called the Skyhawk, which means interior and exterior lights, panel instrumentation for night flight, emergency IFR on gyro horizon and compass, altimeter, a rate of climb indicator and one for turn-and-bank gauging. The new panel, too, on the 172/Skyhawk is similar to that of the Cardinal.

The Skyhawk is also dolled up with additional considerations for comfort, convenience, and appearance. For example, it's available in 17 different three-color combinations, compared to the eight two-color choices for the 172. The Skyhawk, considered by most flyers a better value at $13,250 than the 172, now outsells it by a good healthy margin.

Fairings on the Skyhawk's landing gear and wing struts give it a shade more speed, but otherwise its performance characteristics are identical to those of the 172. Neither is renowned for carrying capacity, but the 70-pound-heavier Skyhawk carries even that much less weight than the 172—a useful load of 1,000 pounds, compared to the 1,070 pounds out of the 2,300 gross weight.

Nevertheless, the 172 is the biggest plane in its class: two feet longer and with wings a good six feet wider (36 feet 2 inches) than its low-wing competitor. It also has a 76-inch prop. The long fuselage coupled with the high vertical tail causes the 172 to have less tendency to respond unfavorably to air turbulence. With less weight per square foot on the wings than the low-winger, the 172 comes in for a landing less steeply, without any substantial change in attitude close to the ground.

One aerodynamic advantage of the 172's high wing is the absence of air wake at low speeds. The big advantage, of course, is the lateral stability that comes from having the center of gravity below the center of lift. In a bank, the 172 tends to pull so that the ship is restored to original attitude (whereas the forces tend to increase the roll of a bank in a low-wing plane).

"One thing I like about my Skyhawk is that the big wing shelters the cabin from the sun," says Filepe Ramirez, of Cabo Rojo, Puerto Rico. "That gravity feed from the overhead fuel tanks is comforting when flying over the ocean, too."

When the plane is taxiing, the big wing is so high that it can pass over ordinary obstructions like bushes, runway and ramp signs, service drums, and even parked cars. It is also so high that the preflight inspection for gas load, cap security, and so on is vexsome on these Cessnas; most pilots would welcome some kind of foot support for stepping up as a genuine improvement.

Cessna Skyhawk

Ease of entry is surpassed only by the 177/Cardinal. The wide doors on each side are so big that the passenger entering the back seats steps in behind the front seats, instead of clambering on or over them as in most light four-seaters—a more dignified and graceful entrance for those who put store by such considerations.

The doors utilize a new rotary latch (but even if they do happen to be left ajar, they won't interfere with the flow of air over the lifting surface on a plane like the 172, as would happen on a low-wing plane). The 172 even has an access door to the good-sized baggage compartment. The latest models have a quieter cabin due to rubber engine mounts and cowl isolators, with a revamped ventilation system to reduce air noise.

The 172/Skyhawk uses 8.5 gallons of fuel an hour from a 42-gallon capacity. Top speed is 139 mph, 75 percent power speed is 131 mph for cruising, and stall speed is 49 mph. Service ceiling is limited to 13,100 feet, with a 645 foot per minute rate of climb. Range: with no reserve under optimum conditions, 640 miles with maximum payload at cruising speed. Over a 50-foot obstacle, take-off and landing distances are 1,525 feet and 1,250 feet, respectively, with an 865-foot ground run and a 520-foot roll.

The 172/Skyhawk is one of the biggest reasons why Cessna led the industry in 1967, producing a total of 6,185 airplanes.

Maule M-4-220C Strata Rocket
2,300 pounds gross weight

Getting an FAA certification for an extra 200 pounds in gross weight over the basic design wasn't easy, but Maule pushed it through to accommodate the 220 hp Franklin 6A-350-C1 engine for the bush market. The airframe is basically the same as the other Maules, but the four-seat Strata Rocket can cruise at 180 mph on 75 percent power.

It weighs 1,280 pounds empty, for a useful load of 1,020 pounds. It can climb from sea level at 1,250 feet per minute, and service ceiling is 19,000 feet. Top speed is 182 mph, it travels even on 65 percent power at 175 mph, and the stall speed is still that remarkable 40 mph. It uses 10 gallons of gas per hour from the 42-gallon tank capacity, and range is 680 miles with maximum fuel. Price is $15,498 (nobody knows who Maule is attracting by knocking off that $2).

The Strata Rocket lands over a 50-foot obstacle in 650 feet, including a 500-foot roll. After a ground run of 400 feet, it can clear a 50-foot obstacle in a total of 600 feet.

Just use plenty of carb heat when you try it.

Mooney/Alon A-4
2,350 pounds gross weight

The toughest thing about building a light plane (toughest for the engineers, not for the entrepreneurs) is designing and proving out a good airframe. Once that's accomplished with the originally planned-for engine, substituting a bigger and more powerful engine—and even stretching out the fuselage a little —is relatively simple. That's what Alon did with the 90 hp two-seat Aircoupe. With a 150 hp Lycoming 0-320-P engine, it now rolls out of the shop as the four-seat, 1,150-pound EW A-4.

It can carry more than its empty weight, 1,200 pounds in useful load. The low-wing, tricycle-geared bubble-topped sportster climbs at a satisfying 880 feet per minute, and once up in the blue can hit a top speed of 150 mph without undue strain. With a 75 percent power setting, it cruises at 140 mph for a practical range of 800 miles, using 7 gallons of gas per hour from a 40-gallon capacity. Stall speed is 47 mph, and when the A-4 is deliberately flown into a power-stall it almost literally hangs in the air by the prop for a startlingly long time before it reluctantly lets go.

Although the plane was advertised as being one of the half-dozen lowest-priced planes before the former makers sold out in 1967, Mooney now has it priced at a flat $11,000. There are now 14 competitive models selling with lower price tags. True, it's got two extra seats (small ones), but adding almost $2,000 to the price of its sister ship (the Mooney Cadet, nee Alon A-2) puts the A-4 in a class where it may not be too comfortable, regardless of how much "sports car" styling goes with the bigger engine.

Cessna 177 and Cardinal
2,350 pounds gross weight

The all-new 177/Cardinal was designed primarily for one purpose: to lure the potential buyer who has never before owned an airplane. It is the least like conventional aircraft of any plane that's ever been built and is more like an automobile than anything else in the air.

"The flying fastback" was introduced to the 1968 market with a 150 hp Lycoming 0-320 engine, but there is not much doubt about bigger power options being on the way. The high-wing design is built without wing struts to minimize drag (an idea which is likely to spread throughout the Cessna high-wing line). The far-back wing is actually aft of the pilot, and visibility through the sweeping wrap-around windshield is unexcelled.

Access is the best yet of any light plane, and the doors on both sides are a full 4 feet wide. There are cabin steps, even though the floor is only 23 inches off the ground. The canted instrument panel is downright seductive.

Parking height is only an inch over 9 feet, which makes it

relatively easy for the pilot to drain the sumps and check the undercarriage, as well as to pull the fuel cell caps and wet a finger without getting a leg-up. The fuel strainer knob is also handily mounted next to the oil dipstick, under a little door at the right side of the cowling. Cessna's engineers obviously had in mind the fact that the prime source for power failures has always been inadequate preflight fuel-system inspection.

But they badly muffed engine accessibility. The cowling is a sculptured work of art in fiberglass and metal, but it's tough to get under for the conscientious pilot who wants to check the engine compartment for oil leaks, chafed wire, loose baffles, and other potential causes of trouble . . . like he's supposed to.

Basic specifications and performance figures, which are subject to change without notice, as are *all* aviation figures, are the same for the 177 and the fancied-up version called the Cardinal. Top speed at sea level is 141 mph, and cruise speed at 75 percent power at 9,000 feet is 130 mph (does the 75-pound heavier Cardinal *really* get another 3 mph?). The 48-gallon fuel capacity allows for 5.8 hours of cruising on 75 percent power at 9,000 feet, for a 755-mile distance. Optimum range at 10,000 feet is 825 miles.

Rate of climb at sea level is 670 feet per minute, and service ceiling is 12,700 feet. Ground run is 845 feet, and total take-off distance is 1,575 feet to clear a 50-foot obstacle. Coming in over a 50-foot obstacle, total distance is 1,135 feet, including a 400-foot ground roll.

The propeller is an all-metal, fixed-pitch 76-incher, and the 4-cylinder "Blue Streak" develops its 150 horses at 2,700 rpm. Power loading is 15.7 pounds per horsepower, and wing loading is 13.6 pounds per square foot.

Empty weight of the 177 is 1,340 pounds, for a useful load of 1,010 pounds. The price is $12,995.

The gussied-up Cardinal weighs 1,450 pounds, cutting useful weight to 900 pounds after figuring in all the extra arm rests, wheel fairings, electric clock, sun visors, tow bar, outside air gauge, high-class instrumentation, and other goodies. The price is $14,500.

Cessna Cardinal

The 177/Cardinal just may be the baby that will put the 172/Skyhawk out of business.

Not to mention some of the competition.

Piper Cherokee D-180
2,400 pounds gross weight

The Cherokee D is the big brother of the Cherokee 140. The basic design is so good that only minor changes have been made even in the 1968 model, mostly in the interior.

The D-180 now uses the same beautiful new panel as in the new retractable Arrow, as well as its extra little back window. In fact, the T layout of the instrument panel bears a striking resemblance to the panel used in Cessna's glossy new Cardinal, with everything grouped in front of the pilot. Other features first used in big airplanes include open-yoke control wheels for easier scanning of the office and the throttle and mixture controls in a center console in multiengine style.

Many owners of the 180 (the "C") tended to overload with electronic equipment. For one thing, the 180 makes an excellent instrument trainer with a panel big enough to accommodate, for example, dual nav/com, glidescope, ADF, DME, transponder, and marker receiver. Many pilots flying at night had to remember to switch something off before switching something on, out of respect for the 35-amp alternator. This was replaced in the 1968 D with a 60-amp alternator, and the fuse system has also been replaced with simple circuit breakers.

The four-seat low-wing D-180 has a 180 hp Lycoming 0-320-A3A engine, weighs 1,300 pounds empty, and carries a useful load up to 1,100 pounds. It climbs at 750 feet per minute and the service ceiling is 16,400 feet. Ground run to lift-off is 720 feet, and total take-off distance to clear a 50-foot obstacle is 1,620 feet. Total landing distance over a 50-foot obstacle is 1,150 feet, including a 600-foot ground roll.

Top speed is 152 mph, cruising speed on 75 percent power is 143 mph, and it travels at 135 mph even on 65 percent power. Stall speed is 57 mph. The D-180 holds 50 gallons of gas, uses it at 8.7 gallons per hour, and has a range of 675 miles with full tanks.

The price is $13,900.

Beagle Husky
2,400 pounds gross weight

This $14,000 two-seater has a tail wheel and would like to be known as a sports plane. The high-winger weighs 1,425 pounds empty and carries a 975-pound useful load.

It's powered by a 180 hp Lycoming 0-360-A2A engine, it climbs at 800 feet per minute, and the service ceiling is 14,500 feet. Top speed is 128 mph, and cruising speeds are 114 mph and 109 mph respectively at 75 percent and 65 percent power settings. It uses 9 gallons of gas per hour from the 38.5 gallon fuel capacity, for a range of 580 miles.

The Husky lifts off after a 550-foot ground run and clears a 50-foot barrier in a total of 1,175 feet. It lands in a total of 1,130 feet, including a short ground roll of 350 feet.

The Husky is no dog. Some pilots just think that the Londoners have it a bit overpriced.

Waco M-220-4 Minerva
2,400 pounds gross weight

This is another "fake" Waco (see Waco Meteor). The four-place low-wing is actually a product of Sud Aviation of France, made under "private label."

It has true STOL capabilities, even though it doesn't look it. The Franklin 222 hp 6A350C1 engine churns a constant-speed, variable-pitch prop, which enables the Minerva to clear a 50-foot obstacle in a total of 330 feet. Total landing distance required is even less: a flat 300 feet. Empty weight is 1,260 pounds, useful load limit is 1,140 pounds, and the price is $19,000.

Service ceiling for the tricycle-geared Minerva is 15,000 feet. It carries 45 gallons of gas and has a cruising range of 575 miles (maximum: 625 miles). Maximum speed is 155 mph, and it cruises at 147 mph. Rate of climb is 850 feet per minute and the stall speed is 50 mph.

There is also a lightweight version of the Minerva in the works, to be called the Waco M-125-4 Minerva. There will be absolutely no resemblance to the Waco of yore, and the only similarity is due to the name . . . admittedly used only because of its promotional value.

What a way for Waco to wind up!

Beech Musketeer III
2,400 pounds gross weight for the "Custom"

Of the 19 different airplane models now being built by Beech, the only fixed-gear plane in that big line-up is the Musketeer III. It is also the only fully equipped standard plane in its price class, with adequate flight instruments, engine gauges, and a 100-channel transceiver and 100-channel nav/com radio with omni, localizer and auto-pilot coupler. Other standards: "fighter plane" construction with metal-bonded honeycomb truss-grid wings, a fuel-injection engine that eliminates carburetor icing, and even a tinted-glass windshield.

Welcome options on the 1968 model include a door on the pilot's side and a split rear seat for four-bucket-seat configuration.

The $15,950 tricycle-geared Custom III has a top speed of 146 mph. At a 75 percent power setting, the 1,375-pound low-winger cruises at 138 mph at 7,000 feet. It goes 138 mph at 65 percent power at 10,000 feet, too, where it will do 117 mph with the power cut to 55 percent. Rate of climb at full throttle from sea level is 728 feet per minute at 2,400-pound full gross weight, and service ceiling is 11,870 feet. (Who compiled *those* figures?) With the 1,025-pound useful load, stall speed is 58 mph.

Fuel consumption from the two tanks (30 gallons each) is figured at 8.1 gallons per hour for the 165 hp fuel-injection Continental I0-346-A engine, with a range of 906 miles when traveling on 65 percent power at 10,000 feet. The bonded-skin construction of the all-metal Musketeer helps a lot with its resultant smoother air flow.

Total landing distance over a 50-foot obstacle is 1,260 feet, including a 640-foot ground roll. Take-off: 990-foot ground run or 1,460 feet overtotal. Ground handling is enhanced with the widest wheel tread in the class—11 feet 10 inches—for a broad and stable wheel base.

The souped-up version, known as the Musketeer Super III, has a 200 hp fuel-injection Lycoming I0-360-A engine and weighs 1,410 pounds empty. It carries a useful load of 1,140 pounds at a service ceiling of 14,850 feet, with a gross weight of 2,550 pounds. Speeds: top, 158 mph; at 75 percent power, 150 mph; 65 percent, 141 mph; stall, 61 mph. Range at 65 percent power, with a 54-minute fuel reserve, is 823 miles with a maximum fuel load. Fuel capacity is the same as on the Custom III, and gas consumption is rated at 9.4 gallons per hour with the optional constant-speed prop.

The four-seat Super III climbs at 880 feet per minute from a sea-level take-off of 1,380 feet over a 50-foot obstacle, including a 950-foot ground run. Total landing distance is 1,300 feet over a 50-foot obstacle, with a 660-foot ground roll. Price of the Musketeer Super III is $17,750.

Substituting a bigger engine is usually as far as most aircraft manufacturers go with their basic model in going after market

Beech Musketeer

saturation, but Beech has also substituted a *smaller* engine. A four-cylinder 150 hp Lycoming 0-320 engine makes the Musketeer a Sport III and gets the price down to $13,450.

The Sport III is built with either a 40-gallon or a 60-gallon fuel capacity. With a little straining it can hit 140 mph, and cruise speed is 131 mph. With full flaps, the stall speed is 54 mph. The range of the 2,200-pound GW Sport III is 883 miles, including the usual allowance for warmup, taxiing, and a 45-minute reserve. Empty weight is 1,275 pounds, and useful load limits were upped 50 pounds in the 1968 model to 925 pounds.

Best rate of climb is 900 feet per minute from sea level, and the service ceiling is 14,900 feet compared to the 11,870 feet and 14,850 feet for the Custom III and the Super III respectively. The Sport III uses 1,255 feet to clear a 50-foot obstacle on takeoff, including an 840-foot run. Coming back down the same way, it uses a total landing distance of 1,220 feet including a 590-foot roll, figuring on zero wind at sea level. Using the optional electric trim while up there can make the Sport III an exceptionally easy plane to learn in. When sold as a trainer, the Sport III is all a part of Beech's plot to "Trap 'em and then move 'em up all the way to a Bonanza."

As of 1968, the Musketeer Sport III can be regarded as a lot more than just a trainer, though. With a few modifications, it is certified as aerobatic. All Beech had to do was reinforce the attachment points for the new optional shoulder harness and the quick-release door hinges to meet Part 3 of the Federal Air Regulations. Aerobatic capability is restricted to two-place use, but it can now be legally flown through chandelles, loops, limited inverted flight, rolls, spins, Cuban Eights, and so on. Price for the aerobatic Sport III is $15,450.

Beech would like to see the Musketeer III as the Flying Ford. The company built over 1,300 planes in 1967, and their corporate mouth is watering for the bigger market.

Lark Commander
2,450 pounds gross weight

See Darter Commander.

Reims Rocket
2,500 pounds gross weight

This airplane from France is actually a modified Cessna 172. Reims Aviation is a very, very close affiliate of Cessna, and one reason the Rocket is built in France is because manufacturing it there costs less than shipping it there from Wichita.

The Rocket is different from the 172, though. The single-engine high-wing four-place plane is powered by a big 210 hp fuel-injection engine for the European market. Behind a constant-speed propeller, the Rocket can hit a top speed of 153 mph, and it cruises at 145 mph. Take-off distance at sea level over a 50-foot obstacle is 1,180 feet, and rate of climb is 910 feet per minute. Service ceiling is 17,500 feet.

Total landing distance over a 50-foot barrier is 1,250 feet for the 1,410-pound EW Rocket, and it carries a useful load of 1,090 pounds. The price is $17,500.

The rear seats as well as the ones in the front are reclinable, and an optional two-place "midget" seat can be installed in the

10.5 cubic foot baggage compartment behind the regular rear seats. Ventilators are mounted at the wing roots for the front-seat fresh-air supply, but vents for the back seats are extra-cost options.

Flight instruments are grouped in Cessna's now-standard T, and the Rocket has a 12-volt electrical system powered by a 60-amp, engine-driven alternator charging a 33-amp battery. Radio damage is minimized on the Rocket with a split bus bar, which automatically shuts off electronic equipment during engine startup—a feature that a lot of planes in *this* country could use.

Optimum range, with a normal lean mixture and no reserve, is 750 miles. Only 46 gallons of the 52-gallon gas capacity are usable. Landing gear is strictly "172," and the electrically operated flaps provide an infinite range of settings from zero to 40 degrees.

Quite a few are being imported to the United States.

Beech Musketeer Super III
2,550 pounds gross weight

See Beech Musketeer III.

Cessna 182/Skylane
2,800 pounds gross weight

If the 172/Skyhawk is the Chevy of the line, the 182/Skylane is the Pontiac of the Cessna family. Maybe even the Oldsmobile or the Buick, if you count in the Super Skylane and the turbo-system Super Skylane.

The big, four-seat, high-wing, tricycle-geared model 182 and its deluxe version, the Skylane, have been improved to within an inch of their lives. Incorporating all the rest of Cessna's basic features, the 182/Skylane is as good as the company knows how to make a single-engine, fixed-gear passenger plane in its class. Constant-speed propellers are now standard equipment, a center aisle permits changing seats in flight, the optional oxygen system includes individual ports at each of the four main seats, and up front the engine instruments on the right side of the panel have been canted eight degrees toward the pilot's seat for better viewing.

The 1,560-pound 182 weighs in a useful load of 1,240 pounds. The 60-pound heavier Skylane thus carries 60 pounds less of a payload. Price for the 182 is $17,995, and the Skylane goes for $18,995. For the same reasons affecting the 172/Skyhawk sales ratios, the Skylane outsells the 182—only more so. The Skylane is fully equipped compared to the naked 182.

Except for 3 mph more speed and less than a 2 percent advantage in range (both in favor of the Skylane), performance for the two versions are the same. Rate of climb at sea level is 980 feet per minute and the service ceiling is 18,900 feet. After a 625-foot ground run, total take-off distance over a 50-foot obstacle is 1,205 feet. Total landing distance over a 50-foot obstacle is 1,350 feet, including a 590-foot ground roll. Both use the 230 hp Continental 0-470-R engine.

The Skylane's best power mixture gets a top speed at sea level of 170 mph. Cruising on 75 percent power at 6,500 feet, speed is 162 mph. Stall speed is 55 mph.

With a normal lean mixture at the above-noted cruise speed, the Skylane will cover 695 miles in 4.3 hours, using the 60-gallon gas supply with no reserve. Under the same conditions with 79 gallons used from the main and auxiliary tanks, it will fly 925 miles nonstop in 5.7 hours.

Optimum range at 10,000 feet is 925 miles in 7.6 hours at 121 mph for 60 gallons of gas; with 79 gallons, 1,215 miles in 10 hours. Fuel consumption is rated at 14 gallons per hour.

Tom McLaughlin, of Wyoming-Western Oil Company, Pine Bluffs, Wyoming, knows but doesn't care that his Skylane was exactingly designed as a deluxe "people plane." He carries up to half a ton of freight in it.

Cessna 180 and 185/Skywagon
2,800 pounds (and 3,350 pounds) gross weight

The versatile 180 is variously used as a flying truck and as a six-place people plane. Powered by a six-cylinder 230 hp Continental 0-470-R engine with a 7 to 1 compression ratio, the 1,535-pound high-wing with the tail wheel belies its old-fashioned looks, with a top speed of 170 mph, 1,215-mile maximum range, 1,090 feet per minute climb-out, and 19,600-feet service ceiling. The look-alike 185/Skywagon does even better, with its 300 hp Continental I0-520-D engine; it hits a top speed of 178 mph and is considerably better in useful weight capabilities—although it weighs only 40 pounds more than the model 180, the 185/Skywagon carries a remarkable 1,775 pounds compared to the 180's 1,265-pound payload.

Whether used as flying bus or truck, the model is one of the toughest no-nonsense planes going. Appointments in the cabin are far from lush, but they are designed to last under hard usage. The model 180 is priced at $17,950 and the 185/Skywagon at $21,375. Either version is also available as floatplane, amphibian, or skiplane.

Cruising speed in the 180 at 75 percent power is 162 mph with a stall speed of 58 mph. It slurps 14 gallons of gas per hour from its 65-gallon capacity, and an 84-gallon tank system can be installed as an option. Over a 50-foot obstacle, take-off and landing distances are totals of 1,205 feet going up and 1,365 feet coming down. Ground run to lift-off is 625 feet, and incoming ground run is 480 feet.

Cruising speed in the 185/Skywagon at 75 percent power is 169 mph at 7,500 feet. Service ceiling is 17,150 feet, rate of climb from sea level is 1,010 feet per minute, and stall speed is 59 mph. Optimum range from the 84-gallon optional tanks (standard: 65 gallons) is 1,105 miles at 10,000 feet with no reserve. Take-off and landing distances over a 50-foot obstacle are a respective 1,365 feet and 1,400 feet, with a 770-foot take-off run and a relatively short 480-foot ground roll on landing.

Cessna hands out a whole catalogful of accessory listings. Options for the flying workhorse in either version cover every conceivable requirement for any use from flying hearse to jungle-based transport. One of the handiest for the 185/Skywagon is the belly-pod cargo pack, a lightweight fiberglass "hold" with a carrying capacity of 300 pounds attached beneath the fuselage.

Cessna 185/Skywagon

Since the first models of the 180 and 185/Skywagon made their appearance in general aviation, several meaningful concessions to comfort and convenience have been made (even though grudgingly made). It took until 1966 to get new map pockets added to the left wall, and so many pilots knocked their shins on the interior plumbing that a new, flatter oval-shaped tube is now incorporated into the heater ducting between the firewall and the forward door post for a little more leg room.

The plane is unabashedly built for utility. A beauty it ain't. And there's still that anachronism of a tail wheel.

"So what?" says the field superintendent of an Alabama construction firm who uses the company's model 180 over 100 hours a month, ". . . it's steerable!"

Piper Cherokee 235B
2,900 pounds gross weight

This baby uses the same basic airframe as the rest of the series, but it's a grown-up baby—and not just because the wing span is 2 inches bigger. Most buyers opt for the constant-speed prop, which makes the 235B's performance so outstanding that it stands alone.

For example, it carries a useful load of more than its empty weight. The 1,435-pound EW shell lifts a 1,465-pound payload— 30 pounds more than the empty weight of the plane itself.

To accommodate this truckload, the luggage space in the 235B has been increased by 5 cubic feet, to a 24-cubic-foot total area, which is accessible either through the cabin or through its own large outside door. The cabin has been stretched with contoured window frames and recessed arm rests. What gives the 235B all the guts, of course, is the 235 hp Lycoming 0-540-B2B5 engine, which is actually a derated version of the 250 hp mill used in Piper's Pawnee ag plane. It can use any ag gas from 80 to 145 octane, a real advantage when traveling in remote areas or foreign countries.

All this power in the relatively small airframe resulted in such an uncomfortably high noise level that the earlier 235 had to be quieted with 25 pounds of soundproofing materials for the 235B, used everywhere from the engine mounts to a veritable cocoon around the cabin. Even the windows in the 235B are double-pane glass. Piper was so concerned about noise that the air inlets on the 235B are now near the floor to admit outside air noiselessly.

The result of all this muffling is gratifying, though; the 235B now provides a ride so quiet that passengers can talk in normal conversational tones, and a welcome by-product of Operation Stop/Noise is a virtual absence of vibration—even climbing at 825 feet per minute.

Among all single-engine, fixed-gear planes, the four-seat 235B has the best range at the economical 65 percent power setting: well over 1,000 miles with a maximum load and a 45-minute fuel reserve. Factory test pilots have coaxed up to 1,500 miles out of the 235B nonstop for absolute maximums. The plane holds 84 gallons of gas in its two 25-gallon main tanks and 17-gallon wing-tip auxiliary tanks. The 235 hp engine sucks up 11.5 gallons of gas per hour.

The 166-mph top speed is 10 mph faster than traveling at 75 percent power. At 65 percent power, airspeed is still 148 mph. Service ceiling is 14,500 feet. The 235B stalls at 60 mph.

Take-off distance over a 50-foot obstacle is 1,360 feet, including an 800-foot ground run. The 235B can land in 680 feet, or a total of 1,300 feet over a 50-foot obstacle.

Price is $16,900—three grand more than the price of the 180. Many people thus consider the 235B a special-purpose plane for folks who don't need to consider the extra 365-pound carrying capacity in terms of better than $8 a pound.

Cessna 185/Skywagon
3,350 pounds gross weight

See Cessna 180 and 185/Skywagon.

Cherokee Six (260 and 300)
3,400 pounds gross weight

Providing more room than many light twins, the 260 hp Cherokee Six is still in the same price range as most medium-size four-place aircraft. The Six-260, with six full-size bucket seats, is $19,900.

This is one plane, even more than most others, where almost all buyers take some of the optional equipment as a matter of course—wheel fairings, for one, which provide a couple of more miles per hour in airspeed; and that constant-speed propeller, which is far superior in just about every respect except for about 2 mph more speed with the fixed-pitch prop at top speed.

The 4-foot-wide cabin runs almost 13 feet from the foot pedals in the front to the baggage bulkhead in the rear. Seating

Piper Cherokee Six

arrangement is two by two by two, with a 10-inch aisle between the two center seats. There is even a seventh seat available to utilize that space most efficiently if the three middle passengers don't mind a little shoulder-lapping. There's a door on the left side of the rear of the tricycle-geared low-winger for the rear-seat passengers and one on the right-hand side for the pilot and copilot. Middle-seat passengers can take their pick.

The 110-cubic-foot cabin actually has more room in it than the average family station wagon. When converted to cargo use, the versatile Cherokee Six can stow three 55 gallon drums with a lot of room left over on top. As a flying ambulance, the plane has plenty of room for a full-size stretcher with working space for an attendant. A unique front-end baggage compartment between the engine and the panel provides still more usable space (and with the latest models, an elegant four-piece luggage set that is expressly designed to make maximum use of the nose compartment, is presented as standard equipment to every new Cherokee Six buyer, suitably engraved with the plane's registration number). There's a rear luggage compartment as well.

Empty weight is 1,680 pounds, and useful load is 1,720 pounds. Some pilots consider the 6-260 underpowered for so demanding a job, and under some conditions the climb-out can be pretty flat with the Lycoming 0-540-E4B5 engine. This is one reason why the optional constant-speed prop finds so many ready buyers.

With the adjustable prop, take-off run is cut from 810 feet to 740 feet, and total take-off distance over a 50-foot obstacle from 1,360 feet to 1,240 feet. Top speed is 166 mph; cruising on 75 percent power it's 160 mph, and the 6-260 still goes 152 mph at 65 percent power. Rate of climb at sea level is 850 feet per minute and service ceiling is 14,500 feet. The 6-260 uses 12.2 gallons per hour from the 84-gallon capacity.

Landing roll of 630 feet is the same for the 6-300 as for the 6-260, and total landing distances over a 50-foot obstacle are also the same: 1,000 feet. Both have a stall speed of 63 mph. But from there, the 6-300 takes off on its own.

The 300 Lycoming IO-540K fuel-injection engine has angled valve heads, a tuned induction system, and Bendix gas injection for fuel distribution. Weight of the empty 6-300 is increased to 1,738 pounds, which reduces useful load to 1,662 pounds in the 3,400-pound certification. But what that engine does with the weight allowance is something else.

Top speed in the 6-300 is 174 mph, and at 75 percent power it cruises at 170 mph. It climbs at 1,050 feet per minute and service ceiling is 16,250 feet. This is the plane that seventh seat was really built for.

Using 13.8 gallons of gas per hour, it only has a cruising range of 840 miles compared to 935 for the 6-260 with both at 75 percent power at optimum altitude. But the 6-300's take-off run is cut to 700 feet and total take-off distance over a 50-foot obstacle, to 1,140. Price of the "works like a twin" 6-300 is $22,900, complete with the constant-speed variable-pitch propeller and the set of matched luggage.

As a seaplane with Edo model 3430 floats, the 6-300 cruises at 147 mph at full gross with an optimum range of over 750 miles. Low-wing floatplanes are rare because so many pilots worry about wave-top clearance in rough water, but Cherokee pilots report little trouble, in no small part due to the powerful engine. All versions of the Cherokee Six have a high-sitting nose, too.

In fact, taxiing on the ground is almost like being in a tail dragger. Even a little S work is necessarily resorted to for straight-ahead visibility. That's a small price to pay for flying a vest-pocket airliner, though. The cabin is even equipped with an individual ventilating system over each of the six seats.

Mr. and Mrs. Lloyd Weiser, of Portland, Oregon, recently flew their Cherokee Six on a hunting trip up into Canada, loaded for bear. As it turned out, Mrs. Weiser bagged an 850-pound Canadian moose. They had to take out four of the seats to get him in, but they made it—in air-conditioned style.

Found Centennial 100
3,500 pounds gross weight

This heavy-duty service ship has not been lost . . . it is made by Found Brothers in Ontario. It's one of the few planes still being manufactured with a tail wheel. The high-wing, 2,050-pound Centennial is specifically designed for demanding utility work in rough country, and it incorporates rugged construction accordingly. The changes in the Centennial 100, new for 1968, are quite comprehensive compared to the previous model FBA-2C.

The Canadian plane is refreshingly billed as a five-seater, with an honest single seat in the tapering back of the cabin instead of the abbreviated double seat squeezed in by some American manufacturers in the hopes that their prospective buyers will believe that they are getting six-seat products. The Found Centennial is most often used as a cargo plane, though.

The four large doors open 180 degrees, and the 130-cubic-foot cabin has a flat floor 11 feet 1 inch long by 3 feet 8 inches wide. An 18 by 18–inch hole can be cut in the floor for aerial survey work. The plane has a wide C of G (center of gravity) range, and the problems in weight distribution of the load are minimal. The cantilever wing has excellent ground clearance with its absence of struts, and the plane is available with floats or skis. Found builds two Centennials a month.

The Lycoming IO-540-G1D5 engine develops 290 hp at 2,575 rpm, and useful load is 1,450 pounds. The price is $26,880 in American money.

Top speed of the Centennial is 165 mph, and it cruises either

Found Centennial 100

at 152 mph on 75 percent power or at 135 mph with a 65 percent setting. Service ceiling is 18,500 feet, the gutsy rate of climb is 1,200 feet per minute at sea level, and stall speed without flaps is 56 mph. Fuel capacity is 65 gallons; consumption, 14.5 gallons per hour.

Landing distances are quite impressive for a plane this heavy. Coming in over 50-foot trees, the distance from clearance to touchdown can be as little as 100 feet before the Centennial drops down for a tight 350-foot ground roll, making a 450-foot total landing distance. On take-off over a 50-foot obstacle, total distance is 950 feet after a 490-foot ground run.

Optimum range with maximum gas load for the fuel-injected engine is limited to 685 miles. If you can't find a good Canadian fishing spot in that distance, forget it.

Cessna Super Skywagon
3,600 pounds gross weight

The big brother of the 185/Skywagon is the Super Skywagon, which weighs 1,710 pounds empty. The certified gross weight of 3,600 pounds gives it a useful load capacity of 1,890 pounds, for the most efficient lift/weight ratio of any single-engine, fixed-gear airplane in the business.

The tricycle-geared, high-wing Super makes the most of the fact that there's no heavy main spar through the cabin, as on low-wing aircraft. Even with a full load of fuel and oil, normal radio gear, and a reasonably fat pilot on board, the cargo capacity is still more than 1,200 pounds in the 27 foot 9 inch plane.

The double cargo doors are 42 inches wide. In a "people configuration," the Super easily handles six 170-pound adults in individual seats, and with each one carrying 50 pounds of luggage they can make an 800-mile nonstop trip with no strain. The price for all this capability is $24,995 per copy.

This kind of performance was not possible with the 285 hp engine used in earlier models, and the new Continental I0-520-D is a six-cylinder fuel-injection jobbie with 300 rated take-off horsepower (five minutes) at 2,850 rpm. Bush pilots of the tri-cycle-geared Super who have complained of not enough ground clearance for the prop can now get a three-blade propeller as an option.

Some pilots were formerly bothered by the windshield center strip on earlier models as well as by rare but dangerous wind-shield damage. The windshield is now a clear span for better visibility, and its thickness has been increased to one-quarter inch.

Top speed is 174 mph. Cruise speed, with 75 percent power at 6,000 feet, is 164 mph. The Super stalls at 61 mph. Gas consumption is a thirsty 15.8 gallons per hour. With a lean mixture and cruising at 75 percent power at 6,000 feet, the range is 650 miles from the standard 65-gallon tanks. With the optional 84-gallon capacity, the range is increased to 830 miles. Optimum range is achieved by using the entire bigger tank at 10,000 feet —1,020 miles in 7.5 hours.

Rate of climb at sea level is 920 feet per minute, and the service ceiling is 14,800 feet. Over a 50-foot obstacle, take-off and landing distances are 1,780 feet and 1,395 feet respectively. Ground run to lift-off is 900 feet, and ground roll coming down is 735 feet.

"Our Super Skywagon flew well over 1,600 hours last year," says Pat Covington, founder, president, and general factotum of the Continental Mortuary Air Service in Minnesota.

Covington uses one of Cessna's many options for the Super, a standardized mortuary kit that simplifies loading, a platform with rollers built into its surface that fits into the cargo area. A casket can be loaded directly from a funeral coach through the plane's cargo door onto the rollered platform, where it's secured by cargo straps with plenty of room up front for the pilot and a passenger. Covington utilizes the underslung cargo-pack belly pod, too.

"We use it for luggage," he says, "when we convert to live-passenger services."

Turbosystem Super Skywagon
3,600 pounds gross weight

So far, the Super Skywagon is the only fixed-gear plane (along with its series sister Super Skylane) that has had the engine factory-modified with turbocharging. It makes one helluva difference, too, and the TS/SS can operate at sea-level efficiency at altitudes high over the weather with a service ceiling of 26,300 feet.

Using a 285 hp fuel-injection six-cylinder Continental TSIO-520-C engine, the TS/SS weighs 100 pounds more empty than the customarily powered Super Skywagon. Although it can thus carry 100 pounds less in useful load, the TS/SS carries it at considerably higher speeds.

Naturally, optimum performance is achieved with minimal loads. For the sake of comparison, the following chart starts out with a 605-pound load for flyaway weight of 2,600 pounds as against the top certified gross tonnage. The TS/SS is also available as a floatplane, which carries interesting figures as well:

	Landplane, 2,600 lbs.	Landplane, 3,600 lbs.	Floatplane, 3,600 lbs.
Top speed at 19,000 ft.	206 mph	200 mph	181 mph
Cruising speed, on 75% power @ 24,000 ft.	194 mph	184 mph	164 mph (@ 20,000 ft.)
Sea-level rate of climb	1,660 fpm	1,030 fpm	950 fpm
Empty weight	1,795 lbs.	1,795 lbs.	2,140 lbs.
Useful load	805 lbs.	1,805 lbs.	1,460 lbs.
Wing loading	14.8 lb./ft.²	20.5 lb./ft.²	20.5 lb./ft.²
Fuel capacity, total Standard Optional	65 gals. 84 gals.	65 gals. 84 gals.	65 gals. 84 gals.
Service ceiling	30,800 ft.	26,300 ft.	24,200 ft.

Range:

Normal lean mixture Cruise, on 75% power at 24,000 ft. with 63 gals., no reserve	740 mi. 3.8 hrs. 192 mph	700 mi. 3.8 hrs. 182 mph	620 mi. (@ 20,000 ft.) 3.8 hrs. 162 mph
Cruise, on 75% power at 10,000 ft. with 63 gals., no reserve	670 mi. 3.8 hrs. 174 mph	645 mi. 3.8 hrs. 168 mph	585 mi. 3.8 hrs. 152 mph
Cruise, on 75% power at 24,000 ft. with 80 gals., no reserve	940 mi. 4.9 hrs. 192 mph	890 mi. 4.9 hrs. 182 mph	790 mi. (@ 20,000 ft.) 4.9 hrs. 162 mph
Cruise, on 75% power at 10,000 ft. with 80 gals., no reserve	850 mi. 4.9 hrs. 174 mph	820 mi. 4.9 hrs. 168 mph	745 mi. 4.9 hrs. 152 mph
Optimum range at 15,000 ft., 63 gals., no reserve	910 mi. 6.2 hrs. 147 mph	825 mi. 5.9 hrs. 139 mph	700 mi. 5.5 hrs. 128 mph
Optimum range at 10,000 ft., 63 gals., no reserve	880 mi. 6.4 hrs. 138 mph	750 mi. 5.8 hrs. 129 mph	690 mi. 5.8 hrs. 119 mph

	Landplane, 2,600 lbs.	Landplane, 3,600 lbs.	Floatplane, 3,600 lbs.
Optimum range at 15,000 ft., 80 gals., no reserve	1,150 mi. 7.9 hrs. 147 mph	1,050 mi. 7.6 hrs. 139 mph	885 mi. 6.9 hrs. 128 mph
Optimum range at 10,000 ft., 80 gals., no reserve	1,115 mi. 8.8 hrs. 138 mph	950 mi. 7.4 hrs. 129 mph	875 mi. 7.4 hrs. 119 mph
Take-off			
Ground run	400 ft.	910 ft.	1,400 ft.
Total distance to clear a 50-ft. obstacle	760 ft.	1,810 ft.	2,400 ft.
Landing			
Total distance to clear a 50-ft. obstacle	1,395 ft.	1,395 ft.	1,610 ft.
Ground roll	735 ft.	735 ft.	710 ft.
Propeller: constant-speed variable-pitch 2-blade (3-blade prop optional)	82 in.	82 in.	88 in.
Wing span	36 ft., 7 in.	36 ft., 7 in.	36 ft., 7 in.
Wing area	175.5 sq. ft.	175.5 sq. ft.	175.5 sq. ft.
Length	28 ft.	28 ft.	27 ft., 11 in.
Height (with depressed nose strut)	9 ft., 6½ in.	9 ft., 6½ in.	13 ft., 11½ in.

They don't call this turbocharged Skywagon the "Super" for nothin' . . . the price is $29,245.

Cessna Super Skylane
3,600 pounds gross weight

This high, wide, and handsome airplane is the top-of-the-line flagship of Cessna's single-engine, fixed-gear offerings. It only *starts* with the rest of the Cessna features such as 360-degree omnivision and the almost-foolproof tricycle landing gear. It's only two inches longer than the regular Skylane, but the five-inch-longer high wing supports a much bigger (three windows on each side) cabin, which accommodates six people in roomy luxury. For example, the four front seats are adjustable fore and aft, and all seat backs recline. One of the options has got to be some kind of an ultimate: electrically powered seat adjustment.

With a 285 hp Continental IO-520-A fuel-injection engine, the empty weight is 1,820 pounds, which makes it the heaviest single-engine plane on the market. Useful load is 1,780 pounds for the Super Skylane. This deluxe version of the Super Skywagon has a base cost of $24,995.

Top speed is 174 mph, and with 75 percent power at 6,000 feet the cruising speed is 163 mph. Rate of climb is 920 feet per minute, service ceiling is 14,800 feet, and stall speed is 61 mph. Optimum range at 10,000 feet, using the bigger (nonstandard) 84-gallon tanks, is 1,020 miles at 134 mph. For take-off, ground run is 910 feet and total distance to clear a 50-foot obstacle is 1,810 feet. Total landing distance over a 50-foot obstacle is 1,395 feet, including a 735-foot ground roll.

For another $4,200 the Super Skylane comes equipped with a compressor and becomes the $29,195 turbosystem Super Skylane. The TS model weighs close to 100 pounds more than the unblown version and thus carries that much less of a useful load limit, but it can hit a top speed of 200 mph and it cruises at 184 mph on 75 percent power at 24,000 feet altitude. At that altitude, of course, IFR flying is mandatory, which means more instrumentation accordingly and the added weight thereof.

Although take-off and landing distances are about the same as for the unaspirated version, the turbosystem Super Skylane's rate of climb is 1,030 feet per minute. Service ceiling is way up there at 26,300 feet. A nonstop trip of 820 miles is all that can be expected at 10,000 feet on 80 gallons of gas, where it uses 9.4 gallons per hour at 168 mph. But at 24,000 feet, optimum range on the 80 gallons is 1,015 miles at the same airspeed. At more normal usage on 75 percent power at that altitude, with a speed of 184 mph, range is a 3.8-hour trip of 700 miles with the standard 65-gallon tanks.

One particularly good option is the three-blade prop, designed for additional ground clearance for unimproved field operations. The threesie also provides a quieter ride on the TS Super Skylane, with noticeably less vibration.

It's almost like getting egg in your beer.

BEST OF CLASS

(*Standards*)

LEAST WEIGHT—Piper Super Cub: 930 lbs. empty

MOST SEATS—Piper Cherokee Six 300: 7

BIGGEST PAYLOAD—Cessna Super Skywagon: 1,890 lbs.

BEST LIFT RATIO—Cessna Super Skywagon: 1,890 lbs. of useful load compared to 1,710 lbs. EW

BIGGEST ENGINE—Piper Cherokee Six 300: 300 hp Lycoming (type 10-540-K)

SERVICE CEILING (UNASPIRATED)—Cessna 180: 19,600 ft.

TOP SERVICE CEILING—turbocharged Cessna Super Skylane and Super Skywagon: 26,300 ft.

TAKE-OFF DISTANCE (RUN)—Piper Super Cub: 200 ft.

TAKE-OFF DISTANCE (OVER A 50-FT. OBSTACLE)—Piper Super Cub: 500 ft. total

LANDING DISTANCE (ROLL)—Beagle Husky: 350 ft.

LANDING DISTANCE (OVER A 50-FT. OBSTACLE)—Maule Jetasen: 600 ft. total

RATE OF CLIMB—Maule Rocket: 1,250 fpm (at sea level)

AIRSPEEDS—Maule Rocket, in all categories: top, 180 mph: at 75% power, 175 mph; at 65% power, 165 mph; stall, 40 mph

RANGE, AT 65% POWER—Piper Cherokee 235B: 985 miles (with maximum payload and 45-minute fuel reserve)

FUEL CONSUMPTION—Mooney Cadet: 4.6 gals. per hour

PRICE—Champion 7ECA: $5,795 base cost

CHAPTER 5

Single-engine planes with retractable landing gear

Inasmuch as 75 percent of all people who buy new airplanes have owned planes before, the acquisition of new aircraft models often involves a step up in class. When this represents a yen for more speed, it often means trading up from a fixed-gear plane to one with retractable landing gear. Everything else being equal, retractable gear usually means an increase in airspeed by about another 50 mph.

From the average single-engine fixed-gear plane to an average one with retractable gear usually means about double the price, too. But buyers of new aircraft are usually reasonably well off, with a median income of over $30,000 a year. Time is worth money, and the other side of that particular coin is the fact that speed costs money, too.

"I had been considering a four-seat Aero Commander 100," says Bruce Goodenow, of Los Angeles. "With fixed gear, the price was $8,500. I asked the dealer about the next step up in the line and he showed me a four-seat Aero Commander 200. I got the shock of my life when I found that the price of the retractable-gear 200 model was $29,500. Sure, bigger powerplant and all that, but . . ."

Planes with retractable landing gear not only have bigger engines to make the most of their capabilities, but necessarily have to have an entirely different set of stress structures built into the airframe. The first manufacturer who was able to beat the price differential was Mooney, and there's a slight catch to that.

Until 1968 Mooney tried to compete in the fixed-gear market, but the $13,995 Mooney Master four-seater was actually designed "in reverse." The airframe had originally been designed *for* retractable gear, and the factory simply stuck some fixed gear on it that enabled the company to sell it for $3,000 less than the retrac version. But by spreading the engineering costs over the model range (among other reasons), Mooney was able to market its low-line retrac for $16,950, flyaway Kerrville.

Even that price has now been cut. Piper had been making noises about producing a retractable Cherokee for a long time, and when it was introduced as the Arrow in late 1967, Piper pegged the price at $16,900. But Mooney was laying for 'em. The Texas outfit couldn't stand to see Piper going after the market bracket that Mooney had had all to itself for so long and promptly cut the price of its Ranger to $16,600 "just to be mean about it."

Unless you count the LA-4 and the North Star Riviera, both of which are amphibians, all retractable-gear planes use a low-wing airframe with the sole exception of the 210/Centurion (Cessna just won't give up on that high wing). Absence of the wing struts is only one reason why a low wing performs better aerodynamically at high speeds.

Once an airplane's wheels touch the ground, the lower center of gravity makes a low-winger more stable on the runway, too. So do the more widely spaced main wheels coming out from the bottom of the wings—a welcome safety factor for a high-speed plane.

But the main reason for low-wing design on high-performance aircraft is because it normally goes fast. It even looks faster.

One of the fastest ever, engine for engine, may well turn out to be the plane being built by Windecker Aviation, in Midland, Texas. When the prototype first flew, in October 1967, it did not yet have the retractable gear that the production models will have, but it is undoubtedly the slickest plane yet. The thing is made out of plastic.

Without rivets or seams, the surface is extremely smooth. The use of plastic even allows for the use of aerodynamically perfect compound curves that are either impossible or economically impractical to fabricate with conventional aircraft construction methods.

Epoxy resins and fibers are integrated with high-strength metal alloys to provide a material with a cellular interior and a hard, smooth exterior, almost like bone tissue. The process is the result of eight years' research under contract with Dow Chemical, and the material has a very high strength-to-weight ratio. It is also highly adaptable to mass-production techniques.

As if that no-drag skin isn't enough to worry the competition, the plastic is also a neutral nonconductor. All antennas for communication and navigation equipment can be enclosed inside the fuselage, out of the airstream. The four-seater, already named the Eagle 1, has its eye on a big market.

Standard-production single-engine planes with retractable landing gear range in price from $16,600 to $37,750 and in top speed capabilities from 185 mph to 235 mph. As with almost everything else, there's an exception . . .

Fournier RF-4
840 pounds gross weight

After all the preceding verbiage about high-performance planes, perhaps some mention should be made of the 112 mph Fournier RF-4, just for comic relief before getting into coverage of planes whose prices start at over $16,000 "for the cheap ones." The $5,500 RF-4 might not even belong in this category at all, because it has only *one* retractable wheel.

Empty weight is 562 pounds, with a useful load limit of 278 pounds. The one-seater low-winger (oh yes!) is powered by a 39 hp converted Volkswagen engine. It represents an ultimate in aviation's propensity for compromise: at maximum cruise speed of 112 mph it can travel 450 miles on its 9.5 gallons of gas, as a glider it has a 20-to-1 glide ratio, and it is stressed to normal factors of 11 and —6 Gs, which makes it fully aerobatic in certification.

As a glider it can soar to 35,000 feet. As a cross-country airplane its rate of climb is 787 feet per minute; its service ceiling is 19,600 feet; and loafing along at 60 mph, it uses only about one gallon of gas per hour. As an aerobatic plane, well . . . just how many different airplanes can anybody expect to get for $5,500 anyhow?

The engine has to be hand-swung on the ground, and once it is stopped in flight, the pilot has to dive the RF-4 like a Stuka to get the prop windmilling again. For taxiing, the tail wheel is steerable and there are two hoops of piano wire under the wings for lateral balance. The radio is a little 10-channel cutie powered by flashlight batteries.

They can't make enough of 'em in France to keep up with the demand.

Palomino F-130
1,735 pounds gross weight

Only the "land of fruit and nuts" in California harbors more aircraft manufacturers (14) than Texas, which now has 10 airplane factories. One of them is San Antonio Aviation, Inc., which is out to revolutionize the retractable-aircraft market with the $8,495 two-seat Palomino. It has not yet been considered seriously by the industry.

Bert Wilcut developed the F-130 as the answer to high-priced retracs, but has cut a lot of corners to achieve his price goal. Biggest fault in the tandem two-seater is the fact that the retractable gear has to be cranked up by hand . . . and even worse, cranked *down* by hand. The tricycle gear requires a lot of manual labor to activate: 13 cranks with a handle like an automobile window crank.

The all-metal F-130 has a 130 hp Franklin 0-235 engine, the empty weight is 1,000 pounds, and the useful load is 735 pounds. Rate of climb is 1,200 feet per minute, and the service ceiling is

16,000 feet. From rev to lift-off takes a run of 640 feet, or a total take-off distance of 1,210 feet to clear a 50-foot obstacle. Total distance to land over a 50-foot obstacle is 1,380 feet, including a 660-foot ground roll.

Top speed for the stick-controlled Palomino F-130 is claimed at 172 mph. The Palomino cruises on 75 percent power at 158 mph and on 65 percent power at 142 mph, and the stall speed is 67 mph. It holds 36 gallons of gas, uses it at 5.9 gallons per hour, and has a range of 808 miles with maximum fuel load with a 45-minute reserve on 65 percent power.

Visibility from the canopied cockpit is excellent, but the pilot and his passenger behind him had best wear sun helmets if they don't want to risk sunburn. One of the things San Antonio Aviation most badly needs is a dealer network, as its distribution setup as of mid-1968 is for all practical purposes nil.

Lake LA-4
2,400 pounds gross weight

The four-seat 1,555-pound EW Lake LA-4 is a notable exception to the idea that aircraft with retractable landing gear should be high-performance planes. This one has a top speed of only 148 mph.

Almost $30,000 seems like a lot of money to pay for a 180 hp plane, when you can get another make (with a 185 mph top speed) for little more than half that price. That $30,000 *would* be a lot if such a four-seater . . . if it was a landplane. As a matter of fact, the LA-4 *is* a landplane, but is much more than just that: it's also a water plane that beats most floatplanes all hollow in performance. The LA-4 is a tremendously solidly built boat-hulled amphibian in a class by itself.

For the man who really wants to get away from it all into the isolated areas where unspoiled nature and true peace and quiet are at their best, a water plane's only competition is the pack horse. Hunting and fishing areas that are hardly accessible by other means are within easy reach by air.

Conversely, almost all major cities are located on lakes, rivers, or other navigable water . . . and a plane that can land on water permits flying right to the center of town.

Many pilots enjoy a sense of freedom in being able to operate from "runways" of almost limitless length, and inasmuch as there are a lot more lakes and rivers than there are airports, having a spot to land almost anywhere can be comforting indeed.

The Lake LA-4 is not only America's only single-engine amphibian but also the only single-engine plane of any type with retractable gear that has such short take-off capabilities, as well as the lowest stall speed (51 mph) and lowest per-hour fuel consumption (unless you count the Fournier RF-4). The LA-4 is not a low-wing and not quite a high-wing, either; the wings jut out about midway from the fuselage and the horizontal tail surfaces are about midway up the back-end vertical, too, to make the most of the high-mounted pusher propeller on the top of the plane.

Pilot and passengers ride ahead of the wings and engine, as in a jet. Only 39 LA-4s were sold during 1967, and it's a damned shame. Using only 8.5 gallons of gas per hour, its operating cost per seat-mile is about 2 cents a mile, including oil consumption and 50-hour change, inspection and maintenance, engine and prop overhaul reserves, hangar rent, and insurance.

For the pilot who "doesn't know how to fly a boat" this is a good one to learn in. In fact, the distributors include the flight instruction as part of the deal. For the adept, the LA-4 can do tricks that would fling the average floatplane on its back.

If the lake or river doesn't have a long enough straightaway for take-off in line, the pilot can get the water speed up to 50 mph, swing into a turn sharp enough to jolt a passenger against the cabin wall, and get the rest of his speed for take-off on the dog leg. Or he can build up take-off speed in as little as a 575-foot circle; the floats toward the end of the wing provide amazing stability.

Coming in for a short landing, the pilot can kick the step-high LA-4 into a broadside, for the water equivalent of what a skier calls a Christy—without too alarming a tendency to tip over, either. Lowering the landing gear in the water (slow speeds only, please) can act like brakes, too. The LA-4 makes the most of the fact that water drag can be an advantage as well as a handicap depending on the circumstances.

Another interesting capability is the way the plane can be landed on water and then taxied right up onto the beach. Conversely, the pilot who wants to taxi from land into the water can do so without any trouble, provided that he remembers to retract the wheels once the plane is afloat before he attempts to take off.

The LA-4 has big slotted flaps extending along 80 percent of each wing, and when it takes off it can make a shambles of the rating book with ground runs as short as 250 feet. Officially, it takes off over a 50-foot obstacle in a total distance of 650 feet, but this includes a 450-foot ground run for the anxious-to-climb starter. Total landing distance of 1,275 feet over a 50-foot obstacle is book-listed, including a ground roll (splash?) of 600 feet—but plenty of pilots can stop in 200.

How do you figure take-off and landing distances on water when the LA-4 can be steep-angled almost like a Navion and when a trick-shot pilot is at the controls? Officially, total take-off distance is 1,125 feet, including a 900-foot water run, over a 50-foot obstacle. Landing over a 50-footer, total distance is supposedly 1,575 feet, with a 700-foot water "roll" . . . it says here.

Behind (or in front of) the Lycoming 0-360 engine, the LA-4 climbs at 1,210 feet per minute, and its service ceiling is 13,000 feet. At 6,000 feet it amiably cruises at 130 mph or so on 75 percent power for four hours. To make the most of its 40 gallons of fuel, it can cruise on 65 percent power at 125 mph. Useful weight is certified at 845 pounds.

Base price is $26,580, but inasmuch as even the retractable water rudder is an optional "accessory," the $3,370 deluxe supplementary package is almost a must and seems like a reasonable additional investment, what with the radio and all.

The bugs are minor. The LA-4 is pretty noisy, especially on the water, and when it finally does stall, the shuddering can be pretty violent. The overhead heater doesn't do much for the pilot's feet, and the ceiling lights are ridiculous for their supposedly intended "instrument panel illumination."

But the pilot who might be told to "go jump in the Lake"

need never worry: a wooden paddle is supplied with each LA-4 and can be put to use from the seat at either side hatch.

Piper Cherokee Arrow
2,500 pounds gross weight

Until 1967, the lowest-priced retractable Piper had to offer was the $25,000 Comanche B. However, they have knocked the fixed gear off the much monkeyed-with Cherokee 180, fitted it with the damnedest retractable gear ever seen, added only $3,000 to the price, and now market it as the $16,900 Cherokee Arrow.

In one way, the Arrow is the most dangerous retrac there is. Not for the pilot who flies it, who is babied as no retrac pilot has ever been babied before. But dangerous for the pilot who moves on up in class from the Arrow to a conventionally geared retractable. The Arrow's gear is completely and absolutely automatic. An airflow sensor probe does all the thinking necessary, and the self-activating gear system is as idiot-proof as Piper ingenuity could make it.

When the pilot throttles back and slows down below 110 mph, as for landing, the gear comes down all by itself. On take-

Piper Cherokee Arrow's idiot-proof landing gear

off, the gear automatically comes up when the Arrow reaches 85 mph.

If some clown tries to get the gear up before he accelerates to climb speed (and may still be in danger of sinking back to the runway), the Arrow will refuse to cooperate—the gear stays where it belongs. If he fools around with the controls while the plane is on the runway, a microswitch on one gear leg prevents the gear from rising when there's any weight on it . . . all that happens is that the warning horn goes off.

The automatic system will work even if the master switch is turned off, and even a total electrical failure still won't prevent the gear from extending (although the pilot won't get the benefit of the warning lights and the "three greens" that indicate lock-down).

If the pilot wants to demonstrate stalls or slow-flight gear up, or has to force-land or ditch and needs to belly in with the gear up, there's a toggle he can pull to override the automatics. He will still get the whole battery of blowing horns and flashing lights, though.

Most outstanding feature of the new instrument panel is the power console, with throttle, prop, and mixture controls distinguished by handles of different shape and color to make the pilot feel like an airline captain. The cabin has two new little rear windows, as on the latest-model Comanches, but the back seats are still rather cramped.

The Arrow handles about like any other Cherokee 180 except that it's 20 mph faster. It also taxis a little differently, as the nose wheel has been moved forward so that it can retract backward. The constant-speed, variable-pitch prop is standard, as is the Bendix fuel injection.

The engine is a Lycoming IO-360-B1E, which develops 180 hp at 2,700 rpm. Empty weight of the four-seater is 1,380 pounds, for a certified useful load of 1,120 pounds. Wing span is only 30 feet, with an area of 160 square feet for wing loading of 15.6 pounds per square foot. Power loading is 13.9 pounds per horsepower. Baggage capacity is 200 pounds.

Top speed is 170 mph, and optimum cruising speed on 75 percent power at optimum altitude is 162 mph. A 65 percent power setting produces 157 mph. Stall speed, clean, is 69 mph and with gear and flaps down, 61 mph. Ground run to lift-off is 820 feet, and total distance to clear a 50-foot obstacle is 1,665 feet. Sea-level rate of climb is 875 feet per minute, and the service ceiling is 15,000 feet. The Arrow lands over a 50-foot obstacle in 1,340 feet, including a ground roll of 775 feet with the flaps down.

Cruising range at 75 percent power, using 9.4 gallons of gas per hour, is 860 miles. Optimum range, on 55 percent power, is 995 miles. Fuel capacity is 50 gallons.

After Piper quit making the comparable Comanche 180 in 1964, the company's sales of single-engine retractables was not spectacular. In 1967, for example, only 421 were sold. However, the Arrow is finally giving Mooney some stiff competition.

Mooney Ranger (M20C)
2,575 pounds gross weight

Mooney has come from dead last to fourth place in private-plane sales, right behind Cessna, Piper, and Beech. Furthermore, Mooney sells more single-engine planes with *retractable* gear than *any* other manufacturer. Price has a lot to do with it. Vice-president of engineering Ralph Harmon does wonders in cutting costs without sacrificing quality, and the Ranger sells for $10,000—a base price that was $8,300 less than its next closest fully retractable competitor until the new Cherokee Arrow came along.

The Ranger's basic design is so good that it traces its ancestry all the way back to the Mooney Mite. Many engineers believe that Al Mooney's original Mark 20 concept was brilliant, and it is now used on all three Mooneys in the M20 series.

Until 1967, the smallest one was called the Mark 21, which was spruced up with a dolled-up instrument panel and renamed the Ranger to compete in the 1968 market with Piper's Arrow. Harmon also cut his costs a bit by using fixed cowl flaps and a rigid step instead of the retractable step sported by the Mark 21.

The Ranger is a four-seater, but the back seat looks like it was designed for passengers without legs. The Lycoming 0-360-

Mooney Ranger hunches up for a getaway

A1D engine is 180 hp, empty weight is 1,566 pounds, and useful load is 1,009 pounds. Sea-level rate of climb is 1,000 feet per minute, and the service ceiling is 17,200 feet.

Total take-off distance to clear a 50-foot obstacle is 1,395 feet, including an 815-foot ground run. Top speed is 179 mph, cruising speed on 75 percent power is 172 mph, and stall speed is 57 mph. The Ranger carries 52 gallons of gas, which it uses at 9.4 gallons per hour for a long-haul range of 1,043 miles. The famous Mooney Positive Control is the next best thing to an auto-pilot for flight stability and is handy for a busy pilot in high-density traffic as well as for relaxing on long cross-country trips.

Anybody who takes a long trip in the back seat of a Ranger is liable to be crippled for the rest of the day, though. Its cabin is *considerably* smaller than the inside of a Volkswagen, and pilots who like more space complain about inadequate thigh support, too.

One of the big reasons for Mooney's low prices, of course, is the fact that the retractable landing gear is a manually operated system. The manual gear handle takes some getting used to as well as some muscle power, and the optional electric retraction system for an additional $1,192 gets heavy play. Those rubber but opening all six vents now provided makes the Sirius one of the noisiest single-engine planes imaginable.

The big Franklin 6A-350C1 engine sounds like something from the Indianapolis speedway when idling, and the deep-throated rumbler develops 220 hp at 2,800 rpm. The six-cylinder, air-cooled, horizontally opposed, direct-drive engine uses 100/300 octane fuel.

Empty weight without tip tanks is 1,660 pounds. The certification for maximum useful load has been increased by 220 pounds for a 1,313-pound limit. Rate of climb is 1,050 feet per minute and service ceiling is 18,500 feet. Take-off distance over a 50-foot obstacle is 1,240 feet, including a 720-foot ground run. Total landing distance over a 50-foot obstacle, including a 625-foot ground roll, is 1,540 feet. Stall speed is 59 mph.

Top speed is 180 mph, and maximum cruise at 7,500 feet on 75 percent power is 173 mph. Normal range with standard 55-gallon tanks is 750 miles, but two optional 15-gallon tip tanks are also available. Basic list price is $23,500, including a lot of extras in the all-metal plane that the competition charges for.

The same airframe, with the same engine, also is marketed as the Waco Vela S220-5 for $26,100. Performance characteristics are the same down the line as for the Sirius, despite a minor 10 pounds more in empty weight. The difference is that the Vela has a fifth seat and a second door on the pilot's side.

The Waco TS-250-5 Vega is a 250 hp version of the Vela and carries a base price of $28,995. Passengers who can see around their oxygen masks can watch the world slide by from an altitude of 26,000 feet at a top speed of 225 mph.

One trouble, however: there is apt to be electrical arcing in the radio equipment at high altitudes. That's nothing against the Vega in particular, though. It's a common problem in modified aircraft that are turbocharged for high-altitude flight, and there is no way to get away from it without pressurization.

Likewise, the baggage can sometimes wind up in a mess if it includes cosmetics, fountain pens, or other fluid containers whose contents are likely to leak at high altitudes, or even freeze (and sometimes both, in that order). The cabin of a Waco Vega is certainly no place for a six-pack, either.

Didn't Lockheed have a name like Vega at one time?

Bellanca 260-C

3,000 pounds gross weight

The Bellanca is now just about a semieverything.

Its retractable landing gear retracts only enough so the plane cannot be called fixed-gear; and with the wheels "up," there is still enough wheel area hanging down (close to a foot) to defeat the whole purpose of going to all the trouble of having retractables in the first place. And who ever heard of any other plane with retractable gear (it's to get high performance by reducing drag, you guys!) where the airframe still has supporting struts in the tail?

The Bellanca is semimodern, too, with the sleekest of up-to-the-minute exteriors belied by a rag fuselage and a plank wing. But don't knock it until you try it. The company sold 84 airplanes during 1967, which is no mean feat for a little outfit starting over again in Texas. In some ways, the Bellanca is the most modern of all production planes, in its use of flush plastic windows and molded plastic doors.

The Bellanca is most renowned for its low-speed, high-lift wing with the remarkable lift/drag ratio that's so consistent at so many different angles of attack. But that's mostly at the cambered outboard portion; the inboard portion of the wooden wing has a straight, low-drag *high*-speed section.

There are also two sides to the story concerning Bellanca's use of wood and fabric. Company executives talk at length about the advantages of nonmetal construction such as pound-for-pound strength, flexibility capabilities without risk of material fatigue, and lack of rivet drag. But they talk somewhat defensively, almost as if they know all along that metal is really better.

Fact is, metal construction can be used economically only on a mass-production basis, what with the expensive tooling and the complex machinery it requires. Hand-crafted wooden wings and tubular steel fuselages with fabric covering simply cost less on an amortized basis in relation to investment. When Cessna makes a $50,000 die setup that will be used on 5,000 airplanes, the pro-rated cost is $10 per airplane. If Bellanca would make such an

Bellanca's wood shop

investment for 84 planes, splitting up the $50,000 cost would amount to almost $600 per plane, which would make a difference of perhaps $1,000 a copy at retail. It doesn't take much of a mathematician to come up with the answer to that problem: wood.

This cost saving has a lot to do with Bellanca's relatively low prices, too. The company is trying to do in the single-engine piston field what Bill Lear did with his model 23 jet, by delivering a complete package at a flat price. The $22,950 price of the Bellanca 260-C—remarkably unchanged for several years—includes a full IFR panel with auto-pilot, gyros, and the works.

Tinted glass, too, not to mention the little round throw pillows in the schmaltzy interior (president and general manager Robert Humphries, who left the general managership of Lear Jet to join Bellanca in 1965, didn't learn *that* in Wichita). There's even a headliner that looks and feels like velvet, of all things. Hydraulic gear and flaps, naturally.

That enviable wing design gives the 260 the shortest rated ground roll of any standard single-engine plane with retractable gear—400 feet—and total landing distance over a 50-foot obstacle is only 825 feet. With a 260 hp fuel-injection Continental I0-470-F engine and a constant-speed propeller, the 260 climbs at 1,500 feet per minute. Service ceiling for the four-seater (all nonreclining!) is 22,500 feet; it weighs 1,850 pounds empty and has a 1,150-pound useful load limit.

Bellanca 260-C

Top speed is 208 mph, just 5 mph more than 75 percent-power cruising speed. On 65 percent power it travels at 192 mph, and it has a maximum range of 880 miles with 60-gallon tanks. The stall speed is 62 mph. Total take-off distance over a 50-foot obstacle is 990 feet, including a 550-foot ground run.

The old-fashioned location for the trim crank is still on the ceiling.

Bellanca 300 Viking
3,000 pounds gross weight

The four-seat, 1,900-pound EW Viking is the 300 hp version of the Bellanca 260-C. It has the fastest rate of climb of any single-engine unaspirated piston plane on the market, wheels sticking out of the belly or no: 1,940 feet per minute from sea level.

With the 300 hp fuel-injection Continental IO-520-D engine, it uses a 60-gallon fuel capacity to range up to 880 miles nonstop with its maximum useful load of 1,100 pounds. Service ceiling is 24,500 feet, and the Viking cruises on 65 *percent* power at 204 mph. Cruising speed on 75 percent power is 211 mph, and the top speed effort is 216 mph. Landing distances and stall speeds are the same as for the 260-C, and its shorter take-off distance over a 50-foot obstacle is only 850 feet, including a 490-foot ground run.

That's a lot more performance than delivered by its sister ship for only $2,000 more. Including the fully equipped panel and auto-pilot, price of the Viking 300 is still only $24,950.

Humphries is boosting even that kind of performance. The Super Viking 300 holds 76 gallons of fuel as standard, and it's all in the wing. The fuselage auxiliary tank has been eliminated to allow for more room in the back seats, which have been moved 3¼ inches aft. This makes ample leg room even for six-footers, even when the front seats are full back.

Wait yet! Bellanca also now has the Turbo Viking, which has one of the fastest top speeds of any single-engine plane short of a jet: over 255 mph. Except for its faster high-altitude speeds, specs are similar to those of the Viking 300, including weights. Not the price, though; the Turbo Viking sells for $31,500. The four-placer has a 290 hp Lycoming engine with fuel injection and Riley turbocharging.

Want more? The *Super* Turbo Viking, with the extra leg room and fuel capacity noted, is priced at $34,150. That's with a 310 hp Lycoming TSIO-540 engine and an increase in gross weight to 3,200 pounds, with an empty weight of 1,960 pounds for a 1,240-pound useful load. FAA-rated ceiling is 25,000 feet, but is actually closer to 40,000 feet.

A *derated* version, at 180 hp, is also due to appear soon with fixed gear to compete with the Cherokees, Cessna 182s, and Musketeers. Still on the drawing boards is a cylindrical all-metal fuselage, totally new for Bellanca, which is designed to take pressurization.

That kind of a program may call for Bellanca to scatter its corporate shot pretty thin. Before it's all gone, many pilots hope that the company's redesigners will do something about repositioning some of the existing ships' hard-to-get-at and poorly placed controls. Even the ashtrays are in lousy positions.

Aero Commander 200
3,000 pounds gross weight

This plane is out of production as of 1968. Maybe they couldn't think of a name of a bird, as for the rest of the Commanders. Or maybe the fact that only 24 of them were sold during 1967 had something to do with it. But the 200 is the company's only single-engine plane with retractable landing gear, and many people in the industry think that it is due for a comeback.

The 200 is not just the Aero Commander 100 (now Darter and Lark) with the fixed gear replaced, but an entirely different airplane. The four-seat 285 hp 200 weighs 1,940 pounds empty and has a useful load limit of 1,060 pounds. Price tag: a basic $29,500.

Unfortunately, it *looks* little. But the flush-riveted plane has a top speed of 215 mph, cruises at 210 mph on 75 percent power, and has a range of 1,040 miles on 65 percent power doing 201 mph TAS (true air speed). The 80-gallon fuel capacity is used at 14 gallons per hour.

The Continental I0-520-A six-cylinder engine behind the constant-speed prop climbs from sea level at 1,400 feet per minute, and the service ceiling is 18,500 feet. Stall speed: an

Aero Commander Model 200

appreciated 54 mph with gear and flaps down, or 67 mph clean. The stall break is heralded with plenty of advance warning by the buffeting as well as by the horn.

Total take-off and landing distances are both the same at about 1,175 feet over a 50-foot obstacle. Ground run is 900 feet. There's room for four radios on the professional-looking instrument panel, and the same post lighting is used on the 200 as on the company's big $335,000 Turbo II turboprop.

The 200 still has greatest speed range between stall speed and maximum cruise speed of any plane in its class. The hydraulically operated landing gear on the tough 200 has been extended for emergency deceleration at airspeeds up to 210 mph (not recommended). A couple of years ago the 200 finished 1, 2, and 3 in the Phoenix Air Races.

Bonanza, you should be ashamed of yourself for getting this one shelved.

Beech Bonanza E-33
3,050 pounds gross weight

The proud Bonanza should hang its head for letting the lesser Debonair model use its name. Admittedly, the name "Debonair" never was too good a name for an airplane, especially a Beech. The name not only was a little too cute but also had a feminine connotation in its nickname, "Debbie." In any case, it is now called the Bonanza E-33 in the 225 hp version, to cash in on Bonanza's worldwide reputation for excellence in the manner of the automobile industry, which allows its prestige names to filter down through the line of lesser models. The name may be Bonanza's but the conventional tail is still Debbie's.

In fact, except for that tail, the Debonair has always been essentially the same as the split-tail Bonanza. But like any younger sister, the E-33 has some good points of its own, too.

The E-33's six-cylinder Continental I0-470-K engine combines fuel-injection advantages with the ability to use low-cost, easily available 80-octane gas. It can thus deliver what Beech likes to call "compact-car economy" at its 180 mph cruising speed on 65 percent power.

Top speed is 195 mph, and there's only a 5 mph difference in cruising speed when power is decreased to 75 percent. It stalls

Beech Debonair

at a reluctant 60 mph with 1,196 pounds in useful load. Empty weight is 1,854 pounds. The strong four-seater is licensed not just in standard but in utility category by the FAA as well, to combine high-performance speeds with short, rough field capability.

Total take-off distance over a 50-foot obstacle is 1,290 feet, including a 980-foot ground run. With a 645-foot ground roll, total landing distance over a 50-foot obstacle is 1,290 feet. The two standard fuel tanks carry a 50-gallon total, but two optional tanks carry 40 gallons each, for a maximum range of 1,170 miles on 50 percent power at 7,000 feet altitude. Rate of climb at sea level is 930 feet per minute (it will do better than that), and service ceiling is pegged at 17,800 feet.

The $30,750 price covers full equipment, including a Narco Mark 12A 360-channel nav/com system. Just about everything but the reclining seats are electric, and the throw-over wheel for "your turn" piloting helps make the flight office just terrific. One of the options is a fifth seat that faces sideways.

Like all four Bonanza models, the E-33 has a slightly nose-high attitude when it's parked, a posture that makes it look like it's anxious to get going. The positive angle of attack is more than good-looking, though, as it causes the wings to lift weight off the gear early in the take-off run, which can be important on soft or rough fields. The rugged landing gear is the same that's used on the Beech Baron (which has a gross weight of 5,300 pounds). A Beech "Magic Hand" similar to the automatic gear system on the Piper Arrow remembers to put down the wheels if the pilot doesn't, and the option will prevent premature gear retraction on take-off, too.

Beech even makes the E-33 easy to buy with a finance/leasing plan.

Piper Comanche B
3,100 pounds gross weight

This 1,728-pound EW four-seater is the successor to Piper's hugely successful Comanche 260. With a 200-pound increase in gross weight certification, the B's useful load limit is 1,372 pounds.

The extended cabin has a new third window on each side and provisions for fifth and sixth seats in the back. Passengers for these "extra" seats can enter through the small left-side door to what used to be the baggage compartment.

Although the price is a relatively modest $24,990, the Comanche B holds the single-engine Class IV World Non-Stop Distance Record: a 7,668-mile flight by Max Conrad from North Africa to Los Angeles. The B is powered by a rugged 260 hp six-cylinder Lycoming 0-540-E dual-ignition engine, on which the normal operating period between overhauls is 1,200 hours— better than 200,000 miles. It's offered with either a standard carburetor or an optional fuel injection.

The Comanche B is also available with a Lycoming 10-540-D, inasmuch as the Comanche 400 (that's horsepower, son!) is no longer being built; the competitive turbocharged modifications have put it out of business.

Rate of climb for the new B is 1,370 feet per minute at sea level, service ceiling is 20,000 feet, and it cruises at 183 mph on 75 percent power or 175 mph on 65 percent. Top and stall speeds are 194 mph and 67 mph. Range with 90-gallon tanks, on 65 percent power at 10,800 feet, is 1,075 miles. Take-off run at gross is 760 feet, for total distance going over a 50-foot obstacle of 1,040 feet. Landing: a 655-foot ground roll out of a 1,015-foot total distance "over the 50."

With six people aboard, just remember: no baggage.

Bellanca 300TL Super Viking
3,200 pounds gross weight

See Bellanca 300 Viking.

North Star Riviera
3,270 pounds gross weight

Middle-class people in Europe are more likely to use bicycles for transportation than airplanes. The European who can afford to own a plane at all is usually so wealthy that he doesn't quibble about prices, and the North Star Riviera is priced accordingly at $35,000.

However, it's turning out that there may not be as many such prospects around as Siai-Marchetti thought. Sales have been less than record-breaking; bankroll-breaking would be more like it, and anybody who likes the looks of this four-seater had better get one while the getting is good.

The amphibian Riviera has not only retractable wheels but retractable balance floats as well. By thus forming low-drag wing tips, the Italian-built flying boat can achieve a top speed of 177 mph thanks to a small and highly loaded wing.

The take-off run on water is almost 1,500 feet. The 2,270-pound EW Riviera can carry a useful load of 1,000 pounds, and with its 1,250 hp Continental 10-470-P engine behind a three-blade reversible Hartzell propeller, the inordinately noisy amphib has a rate of climb booked at 1,220 feet per minute. Service ceiling is 18,500 feet, normal cruise speed on 65 percent power is 152 mph, and a 50 percent setting still gets 137 mph. The stall speed is 73 mph clean, or 67 mph with the big flaps down.

Take-off run on land is 1,000 feet for total take-off over a 50-foot obstacle of 1,400 feet. Total landing distance over a 50-foot obstacle is 1,100 feet, including a 660-foot ground roll. At 60 percent power, maximum fuel range is 865 miles and maximum payload range, 560 miles.

When landing on the hull, the Riviera sprays water every which way for 625 feet. Turns are inadvisable before getting rid of *all* airspeed lest the tip float disappear under water completely. The retractable water rudder might bend, too, at water speeds over 40 mph.

The Riviera is a lot of fun backing up, though.

Beech Bonanza E-33-A
3,300 pounds gross weight

In this version of the ex-Deb (see Beech Bonanza E-33), Beech uses the same 285 hp fuel-injection six-cylinder Continental I0-520-B engine as in the "real" Bonanza with the split tail. Otherwise, the conventionally tailed E-33-A is the same as the E-33 except for a little increase in empty weight to 1,900 pounds and a lot of increase in useful load certification to 1,400 pounds.

Price of the four- or five-seat E-33-A is $34,150, but the buyer gets considerably more in performance for his additional outlay over the cost of the E-33.

E-33-A has a top speed of 208 mph on full throttle at 2,700 rpm at sea level. Cruising on 75 percent power (2,500 rpm) at 6,500 ft, the speed is a flat 200 mph, and on 65 percent power at 10,000 feet, 195 mph. Cutting down to 45 percent power (2,100 rpm) at 10,000 feet produces a speed of 156 mph. These operating conditions result in a maximum range of 1,080 with the optional 80-gallon fuel capacity. The E-33-A can carry even more fuel with the installation of still more capacity in the wing tips, for a 120-gallon total.

The big constant-speed propeller is hydraulically controlled for continuously variable pitch, and the aluminum alloy blades are 84 inches in diameter. The rugged landing gear is exceptionally smooth for a system designed to withstand the shock of landing with vertical descent components to over 600 feet per minute. Beech's "Magic Hand" is available as an option for pilots who tend to be careless about lowering the gear themselves.

Lifting off at 80 mph at the end of an 880-foot ground run, total take-off distance to clear a 50-foot obstacle is 1,225 feet, with the best rate of climb speed only 115 mph. The book lists the E-33-A stall speed at 62 mph, but with three people aboard and gear and flaps down it kept flying recently all the way down to 50 mph indicated before a full stall developed—and grudgingly at that. Total landing distance over a 50-foot obstacle is 1,150 feet, including a 625-foot ground roll.

Full avionics and many other extras are included in the price. It's not exactly a bargain-basement special, but it's a lot of airplane, too. And all that visibility! The one-piece windshield is only the start of 27 square feet of glass, and the three windows on each side are 3 inches lower than on most low-wingers. The windows curve up into the roofline, too.

The E-33-A is an extremely sensitive airplane, and not for

a novice. Pitch trim, in particular, is devilishly sensitive, due in part to the wide range of speeds, and practically all first pilots have trouble with overtrimming at cruise speeds. Like the other models in line, the E-33-A yaws a bit in turbulence no matter how well piloted, even if not as badly as claimed by some of the competition. Beech sold 427 of them in 1967.

Sensitive means responsive, too.

Navion H
3,315 pounds gross weight

All through its checkered past of various configurations and gypsylike wanderings from home to home, the classic Navion design was something of a phenomenon. In many ways it still is. It now seats five, has a 285 hp engine (it once harbored 520 in a twin version), and weighs 1,965 pounds empty, but it still has the longest range—up to 1,800 miles on 65 percent power—of any single-engine plane on the market. There is a noticeable change in the "now" price: $29,500. That price, however, includes a full panel: 360-channel transceiver, a VOR/LOC receiver and indicator, and basic two-axis auto-pilot, among other goodies.

The pilot now sits so far forward that most of his visibility is through the windshield, and he can see the runway only 20 feet in front of the nose when taxiing. Sad to say, the sliding canopy that distinguished the Navion for so long is finally gone, and there's a new door on the left side in the H model.

The Continental IO-520-B engine can muscle a useful load weight of 1,350 pounds. This includes the weight of a loaded 108-gallon fuel capacity, which makes the long ranges possible. Rate of climb is a no-nonsense 1,375 foot per minute at sea level and full gross, and the service ceiling is 21,500 feet.

Top speed is 203 mph; cruise speed on 75 percent power is 191 mph and on 65 percent power settings is 183 mph. The Navion's rated stall speed of 58 mph has been bettered by almost every owner.

The Navion H has the shortest listed landing distance over a 50-foot obstacle of any single-engine plane with retractable gear:

750 feet. But this, too, has been bettered by countless pilots, who do all but drop 'er straight down over the treetops. The book's total take-off distance of 925 feet over a 50-foot obstacle is a modest claim, too. The Navion's long-famous capabilities for steep angles of approach are used for comparison when other manufacturers want to brag up *their* airplanes.

There are plenty of Navions around over voting age. The way these rugged planes are built, they might even make it to social security.

Cessna 210/Centurion
3,400 pounds gross weight

Take the fixed gear off a Super Skylane and presto! you've got a 210/Centurion. However, one improvement on a plane often begets a whole chain of others, and when Cessna engineers turbocharged the 1966 model they found that old bugaboo of high-wingers working against them: drag from the wing struts.

So they took 'em off. The result was not only higher performance, but also more headroom, more gross weight, and more fuel capacity. While they were at it, the engineers also revamped the model so that it is now bigger in all dimensions by as much as 3 inches, heavier by 100 pounds, faster by 2 to 4 mph, and now more expensive by $3,500. Cost of a 210/Centurion is now $29,475.

There's now a transverse beam across the top of the cabin, but it goes across the ceiling aft of the pilot's seat and does not interfere with the headroom of occupants in either front or back. Actually, a cantilever wing is nothing new to Cessna, which built strutless high-wing racing planes before World War II. The company even marketed a cantilevered high-wing plane for a time as the Cessna 195 until the middle 1950s. But a cantilever wing costs more to build than a conventional lift/strut design, and it was not until 1967 that Cessna felt they could afford to put the extra money into a plane where it would make all that difference.

The four- to six-seat 210/Centurion now has a fuel-injection

Cessna's wing-strutted 210/Centurion

Cessna 210's clean new look for turbocharging

285 hp Continental IO-520-A engine, weighs 1,960 pounds empty, and carries a useful load of 1,440 pounds. Rate of climb at sea level is 1,000 feet per minute, and service ceiling is 18,300 feet. Take-off distance to clear a 50-foot obstacle is 1,365 feet, including an 800-foot ground run. Including the 625-foot ground roll at gross weight, total landing distance is 1,355 feet.

Top speed is 200 mph, cruising speed on 75 percent power is 192 mph, and stall speed is 63 mph. The Centurion holds 90 gallons of fuel, uses it at 15.8 gallons per hour, and at 10,000 feet has a maximum range of 1,360 miles.

An optional de-icing system was introduced in 1968 to allow for a wider variety of weather conditions. The electrically de-iced propeller and pneumatically operated wing and stabilizer boots represent the only factory-installed de-icing system for single-engine planes of any major manufacturer. Electric elevator trim control, a boom mike, and a control-wheel map light are among the many other new Cessna options. Basic flight instruments are now in the standard T grouping on the new panel, an arrangement Cessna is using right down the line.

With a ceiling over 18,000 feet, a handy option for the 210/Centurion is the overhead oxygen console with a 76-cubic foot capacity. The system is standard in the turbocharged Centurion.

And that's what all these high-performance capabilities are all about. The turbosystem Centurion has a 30,200-foot service ceiling and a top speed of 234 mph to make the most of all the improvements.

The turbosystem is an integrated, three-part package including the 285 hp Continental TSIO-520-C engine, the exhaust-driven bootstrap turbocharger, and automatic controls. This lash-up enables the powerplant to maintain sea-level horsepower up to 19,000 feet.

Turbocharging is doing for planes today what retractable gear did when it was first introduced into production aircraft, and it is the most significant development in piston engines for general aviation to date. By cramming more fuel into the engine, the blower prevents an airplane engine from running out of steam above 10,000 feet, when the manifold pressure in unaspirated engines starts to drop.

Turbocharged Centurions not only can fly up over dirty weather but can get high enough to take advantage of tail winds an unblown plane only hears about. Operating from high-altitude airports is greatly improved, too. At 7,500 feet at gross weight and standard temperature, a turboed plane gets off and clears a 50-foot obstacle in nearly a third less distance than its normally aspirated brother.

Rate of climb improvement is even more impressive. At 10,000 feet the turbo is almost twice as good as the plain one;

at 15,000 feet it's three times as good. At 30,000 feet the turbo's feet per minute is double that of the unsupercharged airplane at 20,000 feet.

Basic price of the turbosystem Centurion is $33,675. For that it cruises at 24,000 feet on 75 percent power at 223 mph TAS or 197 mph at 10,000 feet, where its range is 765 miles with a "standard" 65-gallon fuel capacity compared to 860 miles at 24,000 feet. Optimum range with the optional big tanks is 1,450 miles. Rate of climb is 1,115 feet per minute; take-off and landing distances for both versions of this flying limousine are the same.

According to the book, total landing distance over a 50-foot obstacle is supposedly 1,355 feet, including a 625-foot ground roll. However, during a flight test last April at Williams Airport, where Flagstaff is 6,700 feet above sea level, a turbosystem Centurion lifted off in less than 300 feet of runway and could have cleared a 50-foot obstacle in 500. Okay, okay, so it was facing a little wind.

Almost all TS Centurions are being purchased with the optional three-blade propeller. This improves ground clearance, minimizes engine vibration, and provides a quieter ride—in a way, almost too quiet; first pilots may have a tendency to apply too much power for taxiing, which can shorten brake life. Other factors contributing to the remarkably low noise level are the dampening effect of the exhaust-using blower itself, exceptionally good soundproofing, and the single exhaust stack from the turbocharging system instead of the two on the ordinary Centurion.

The Centurion is *almost* big enough to be considered a regular six-seat plane, with two seats in the back really designed for children. However, a pretty-well-grown-up young lady who admits to weighing 115 pounds had plenty of head room as a fifth passenger on a recent test flight, if not as much as she would have liked for her long legs.

She didn't like wearing the oxygen mask at higher altitudes, either. A nose bag is far from flattering and dosn't do much for conversation, either. Maybe some day somebody will invent another pill.

Beech Bonanza V-35-A
3,400 pounds gross weight

Will the real Bonanza please stand up? (Not you, Debbie!) Ever since 1947, when the first revolutionary Bonanza showed its V tail to the competition, nobody has been able to catch up to it in admiring popularity. Still looking more like a fighter plane than a private airplane, the Bonanza of today is better than ever.

And why not? Current base price is $35,750, although this includes basic avionics, as any deluxe piece of travel machinery should.

With an empty weight of 1,950 pounds, the Bonanza V-35 carries a useful load of 1,450 pounds. The four-seater has a 285 hp fuel-injection Continental IO-520-B engine and climbs at 1,135 feet per minute with full gross, including 80 gallons of gas. Top speed is 210 mph, cruising speed on 75 percent power is 203 mph, and "economy cruise" on 65 percent power is at 198 mph, where it has a maximum range of 990 miles. Service ceiling is 17,500 feet; it stalls clean at 74 mph or at 63 mph with gear and flaps down.

Including a ground run of 965 feet, total take-off distance over a 50-foot obstacle is 1,320 feet. Total landing distance over a 50-foot obstacle is under 1,200 feet; ground roll, 645 feet. All these distances are figured with gross weight at sea level and zero wind conditions.

The split-tail Bonanza has a long string of firsts to its credit. One of the most important was when the old K-35 model was the first production plane to use the then-new continuous-flow fuel injection in place of the conventional carburetor. No Bonanza has ever iced up since.

The latest innovation is the optional "Magic Hand" that automatically drops the landing gear when airspeed is reduced to 120 mph and manifold pressure is below 18 inches. The "biggest" cabin can now hold up to six people, too.

The list of over 8,000 Bonanza owners is still growing. Which brings us to—you guessed it—the

Beech Bonanza, owned by Blommer Chocolate Company, Milwaukee, carries four passengers at a lower cost per seat mile than first-class airline fares.

Beech Bonanza V-35-TC

3,400 pounds gross weight

The turbocharged modification of the V-35-A costs over $5,000 more than its unblown brother (see preceding listing) and at a cost of $40,950 is the highest-price single-engine piston-powered airplane being made today.

One reason (and a good one) is Beech's automatic TC system. There is no separate turbocharger control, no extra set of turbines, pipes, or waste gate apparatus. As with an aspirated engine, the pilot adds power to compensate for falling manifold pressure to 5,000 or 6,000 feet. But then he never needs to touch the throttle again; the 285 hp Continental TS-IO-520-D engine and AiResearch turbocharger provide the right climb power until he levels off.

This automatic system eliminates the risk of overboosting the engine, which is all too easy to do on the manually controlled systems. A too-heavy overboost will result in engine failure, and a severe one could necessitate an engine overhaul.

The 2,000-pound EW Bonanza V-35-TC seats four (six if your flight log includes a couple of children or midgets). Useful load is 1,400 pounds, only 59 pounds less than in the standard

Bonanza. But its top speed is 250 mph (at 16,000 feet), it cruises on 75 percent power at 230 mph (21,000 feet), and up at 24,000 feet it cruises at 221 mph on just 65 percent power. Rate of climb is 1,225 feet per minute and service ceiling is 29,500 feet. Stall speeds are the same as for the regularly breathing Bonanza, as are take-off and landing distances. Range, too . . .

. . . but one helluva lot faster.

Mooney Mustang (M22)
3,680 pounds gross weight

As more and more single-engine planes were modified with turbocharging to get them into high-altitude operations, somebody was bound to try pressurizing the cabin. It was the ubiquitous outfit in Kerrville that gambled on it first, and the Mooney Mustang is the eye-popping result.

The company announced plans for it in 1963 with a $30,000 price goal, hedged a bit at $33,950 as the prototype flew in 1966, and settled on $46,320 as the deliveries started in 1967. However, this is about a fourth the cost of any other pressurized plane, and the competition starts with a $175,000 Cessna.

The Mustang's cabin is pressurized by bleed air off the engine supercharger, and the system is surprisingly easy to operate. The only special ground check necessary is to give the door a good hard slam and lock it from the inside. Except for pulling an "operable" control knob as he climbs for altitude, the pilot can ignore the pressurization system as long as he remembers to close the outside air vents before he goes through 8,000 feet, where the pressurization starts up automatically.

From there on up he has three more gauges than usual to monitor, but he wouldn't be heading for IFR territory in the first place if he wasn't already a pretty good pilot.

Inasmuch as cabin pressure depends on the operation of the engine, some pilots have been understandably concerned about the whole idea of flying a pressurized plane that has only one engine. In the event of an engine failure, sudden decompression followed by an inevitable descent can cause an emotional prob-

The five-place Mooney Mustang is the world's first commercial single-engine aircraft with cabin pressurization. At an altitude of 20,000 feet, passengers enjoy a cabin altitude of only 8,000 feet in shirt-sleeve comfort. The Mustang will cruise at speeds to 250 mph.

lem. A day spent at the FAA's physiological training center in Oklahoma City has been suggested as an integral part of every Mustang pilot's checkout.

However, the Mustang is so well built that the pressurization bleeds off slowly enough so that there is plenty of time to grab a mask. Furthermore, the Mustang can approach a TAS of 300 mph and can get out of high altitude pretty fast when it wants to. The builders might do well to consider a bigger emergency oxygen system than the one furnished as standard, though. It will last only about 12 minutes if there are five people in the plane, which might not be enough time to continue flying over the rough weather that the pilot climbed to 20,000 feet to get out of in the first place.

This top-of-the-line Mooney has the biggest powerplant of all single-engine planes, a 310 hp six-cylinder Lycoming TIO-541-A1A supercharged fuel-injection engine. Overall length of the Mustang is 27 feet, or about 4 feet longer than the Executive 21, which it resembles only in the fact that both have three windows on each side. These factors also make the Mustang the heaviest of all single-engine piston planes, with an empty weight of 2,380 pounds. Useful load is limited to 1,300 pounds.

Mooney's standard PC and full-length rudder may remind a Mustang pilot of the M20 series, but the upward folding door will remind him of a Mercedes 300SL, and the double-slotted flaps, of a jet plane. The lower profile of the Mustang results in its instrument panel being "higher" than most on light planes, which makes for something less than ideal visibility over the nose during taxiing or climb-out, where 15-degree S turns are highly recommended.

The landing-gear retraction system is automatic, and the rubber shock doughnuts used in lesser Mooneys have been replaced in the heavy Mustang with robust hydraulic absorbtion units on all three wheels. A three-blade Hartzell propeller furnishes the needed bite.

Engine supercharging and cabin pressure are provided by a Garrett AiResearch compressor. The supercharging is automatic, with no engaging or disengaging for the pilot to fret about. But the Mooney Mustang is not for beginners. Its 24,000-foot service ceiling not only means mandatory IFR operation, but the factory wants each new Mustang owner to go through an indoctrination and ground-school course of its own besides.

Maximum zap at 24,000 feet is 256 mph. Cruising speed under the same conditions but on 75 percent power is 230 mph, or 214 mph on 65 percent power. The 75 percent power cruise speed up there uses 18.5 gallons of fuel per hour, and cutting to 65 percent power reduces fuel consumption to 16 gallons per hour. The 92-gallon tanks can be milked for 926 miles on 65 percent power, or 838 miles on 75 percent. Rate of climb speed is 1,125 feet per minute, and the best rate of climb is 120 mph. Stall speed, gear and flaps down, is 67 mph.

Total take-off distance to clear a 50-foot obstacle is 2,080 feet—not exactly STOL with a ground run of 1,140 feet. Landing distance over a 50-foot obstacle is a 1,550-foot total, including the 960-foot ground roll.

Any high-performance plane performs best at high altitudes. But building a plane that will get up there really doesn't make a lot of sense when the result is clutter and discomfort for the occupants. Of all single-engine planes—and most of the twins —the pressurized Mustang is the only one that does something about it.

BEST OF CLASS

(Standards)

LEAST WEIGHT STANDARD—Piper Arrow: 1,380 lbs. empty

MOST SEATS—Cessna Super Skylane, Super Skywagon: 6

BIGGEST PAYLOAD—Beech Bonanza V-35: 1,459 lbs.

BEST LIFT RATIO: Piper Arrow: 1,120 lbs. useful load compared to 1,380 lbs. EW (certified to carry 81% of its own weight)

BIGGEST ENGINE—Mooney Mustang: 6-cylinder 310 hp Lycoming

SERVICE CEILING, UNASPIRATED—Navion H: 21,500 ft.

TAKE-OFF DISTANCE (RUN)—Lake LA-4: 450 ft.

TAKE-OFF DISTANCE (OVER 50-FT. OBSTACLE)—Lake LA-4: 650 ft.

LANDING DISTANCE (ROLL)—Bellanca 260C: 400 ft.

LANDING DISTANCE (OVER 50-FT. OBSTACLE)—Navion H: 750 ft.

RATE OF CLIMB—Bellanca 300 Viking: 1,940 fpm

AIRSPEEDS: TOP—Mooney Mustang: 256 mph; at 75% power—Waco TS-250-3 Meteor: 235 mph; at 65% power—Cessna TS Centurion 221 mph; at stall—Lake LA-4: 51 mph

RANGE, AT 65% POWER—Navion H: 1,800 miles with 45-minute reserve

FUEL CONSUMPTION—Palomino F-130: 5.9 gals. per hour

LOWEST PRICE STANDARD—Mooney Ranger: $16,600

CHAPTER 6

Light twins

Moving up in class from a single-engine plane to a twin will again roughly double the cost of the average such aircraft. Light twins (which the owner usually flies himself) range in price from under $40,000 for a four-seater to over $95,000, with well over a dozen good choices in between.

A twin-engine plane is a much different animal from a plane powered by just one engine. Cost of the second engine, as such, is only a good start. The control system is decidedly more complex compared to what's needed to fly a one-lunger. The airframe for a twin must incorporate stress factors that are far more demanding, too.

The pilot of a twin necessarily has to have a more advanced license than the pilot of a relatively simple single. Light twins all have retractable landing gear and make the most of variable-pitch constant-speed propeller capabilities—calling for skills the beginner would not be able to cope with, to say nothing of the quite more complicated job of operating two engines instead of just one.

The biggest single advantage of a twin-engine plane is the unadorned fact that in case of an engine failure up there, the pilot still has another engine to get home on. The added resultant weight generally calls for more wing, which in turn means that the bigger plane can carry more of a useful load—*if*, of course, the power is increased accordingly; light twins have a combined power package of never less than 300 hp, usually over 400, and all the way up to the turbo-Baron's thundering 760 hp.

One by-product of all the factors that have to be built into a light twin is waste. For example, there is no such thing as a standard one- or two-seat twin in the general aviation market. A man who does a lot of flying over big lakes or mountainous terrain might feel that he needs a twin-engine plane for its dependability; that second mill is mighty comforting when flying over the Everglades with all those alligators waiting down there. But how often does a businessman fully utilize a useful load capability of a ton or more? And if he's flying alone, what good are all those empty seats?

As for superior flight characteristics, turbocharged single-engine planes are getting mighty close to twin capabilities and are starting to cut into the market once enjoyed by twins exclusively. When the *twin* engines are turbocharged, of course, the performance approaches that of the seriously heavy-duty pure turboprop powerplants.

Anyone for speeds over 240 mph in a plane costing less than 50 grand?

Wing Derringer
2,900 *pounds gross weight*

In pistol parlance, a derringer is a murderous little two-barrel weapon that can fit in a vest pocket. That description pretty well fits the Wing Derringer, the lightest-weight (and once lowest-priced) twin on the market. Empty weight is only 1,920 pounds.

The prototype was designed as a two-seater, but when it was first flown in 1962 with 110 hp engines the engineers quickly decided to use a pair of 160 hp Lycoming 10-320s instead. They also put in a third seat for good measure (on the theory that potential buyers wouldn't like the idea of paying so much money per seat?). The market-ready version was introduced in late 1965 with a "hopeful delivery price" of $29,995, which then went up to a "realistic" price of $49,995 . . . and then dropped to $32,500 when deliveries started in 1968.

The Wing Derringer has a top speed of more than 240 mph, which is helped with exterior skin panels that are milled chemically and stretch-formed, like ski pants. Empty weight is only relatively small in a plane this little, though, and the Derringer carries a mere 980 pounds in maximum allowable useful load. With a full 88-gallon tank of gas aboard to make its 1,000-mile maximum range possible, there isn't much weight allowance left over. This is strictly a briefcase airplane.

Rate of climb is 1,900 feet per minute, and service ceiling is 21,500 feet or 8,500 feet with one engine out. The Derringer cruises on 65 percent hp at 218 mph and at 230 mph when goosed to 75 percent. Stall speed is a pretty fast 78 mph. Total take-off distance after a 750-foot ground run is 1,080 feet to clear a 50-foot obstacle. Landing distance from a 50-foot altitude is 1,700 feet, including only a 250-foot ground roll.

The Derringer from California is a regular zip gun.

Piper Twin Comanche B
3,600 pounds gross weight

The bigger, third-windowed, four- to six-seat B now supersedes the straightforward four-seat Twin Comanche, which has outsold all other twins except for Piper's Aztec. The Twin Comanche B, at $37,250, is still the lowest priced of all the standard twins.

The 160 hp Lycoming 10-320-B engines climb at 1,460 feet per minute. Service ceiling is 18,600 feet or 7,100 feet on one engine. Empty weight is 2,210 pounds, and useful load is 1,390 pounds. Top speed is 205 mph, cruising speed on 75 percent power is 194 mph, and she'll travel 885 miles on 90 gallons of fuel at 186 mph on 65 percent power. Maximum range on 65 percent power with optional fuel tanks is 1,360 miles.

Total take-off distance to a 50-foot altitude is 1,570 feet, including a 950-foot ground run. Total landing distance over a 50-foot obstacle, including a 700-foot ground roll, is 1,875 feet. Stall speed is 69 mph.

The fuselage has been beefed up over the single-engine Comanche considerably. There's a big 20-cubic foot baggage area that can handle 200 pounds of luggage with ease. But one reason why that little door is back there is because that baggage compartment is *also* the fifth and sixth seat area. One or the other; not both. Although the nose wheel has been moved forward nine inches, there's no baggage space up front on this model, that section of the plane being crowded with nose wheel, heater, and other esoteric equipment.

Do you like to risk overloads, with or without FAA sanction? Max Conrad once took off with a gross load three times the empty weight, with 720 gallons of fuel on board to set a Class V World Non-Stop Distance Record. Equivalent: 25 people!

Piper Turbo Twin Comanche B
3,725 pounds gross weight

This ship offers as good an example as any of what happens when the manufacturer starts hanging on extra engines and blowers. The single-engine Comanche B (already almost twice the price of the fixed-gear Cherokee 180, what with retractable gear) costs $24,990—or something like $12,250 less than the Twin Comanche B. Now comes the Turbo Twin Comanche B, where the price tag is an unabashed $45,680. These big price steps have gotten the price to well over the $10,000 per "real" seat that concerned Wing's engineers. And even with all that, the Turbo Twin Comanche B was *still* the least expensive turbocharged twin by some $24,000 until Cessna turbomodified its Skymaster.

In one way, some pilots consider the Turbo Twin Comanche B a rather dangerous piece of machinery. Price-wise, it is within reach of men who really don't have enough know-how to fly this

Piper Comanche B follows Twin Comanche B

hot an airplane. Even as in supercharged racing cars or boats, any open-throttle operation by the careless or inexperienced can result in big trouble in a big hurry. Wrecking the engine is only one (and lesser) risk.

Top speed for the Turbo Twin C/B is 240 mph, even with the smallest engines used on any twins (160 hp Lycoming 10-320-C1As with fuel injection). At 24,000 feet it cruises on 75 percent power at over 225 mph. On 65 percent power, it can range as far as 1,360 miles at over 200 mph.

Rate of climb is 1,460 feet per minute, and its service ceiling is 28,500 feet (19,000 feet on one engine). Empty weight is 2,408 pounds, and it carries a 1,317-pound useful load limit. Take-off and landing distances are the same on the turbocharged modification as on the unblown Twin Comanche B, and stall speed is only 1 mph faster.

To support this kind of performance, Piper builds in as standard equipment a complete oxygen system with the required 64-cubic foot bottle, as well as fuel tanks in the wings, which bring the total gas capacity to 120 gallons. On trips when the pilot encounters bad weather he wants to climb over, he can call on capabilities that include a rate of climb at 10,000 feet of 1,350 feet per minute.

This is the type of plane that depends heavily on full-service airports. The prop-to-ground clearance, which almost whimpers for paved airstrips exclusively, is only 10¼ inches.

The engines have manual cowl flaps, which are needed supposedly only for single-engine touch and go. But the tight cowlings are almost too efficient and can build up quite a bit of heat in taxi, run-up, and climb operations, and the pilot should keep full open cowl flaps up to cruising altitude. They should be open on the way down, too, to cool the flat "Tiger Shark" nacelles lest the fuel-injection lines develop vaporizing during any subsequent hot start.

There is so much instrumentation on the panel that some of it is hard to read in flight. Room for improvement: canting the right-hand side of the panel more toward the pilot's seat shouldn't be too much of a job. The pilot's seven-point prelanding check list is on his visor, because there just isn't room for it on the panel. Piper's familiar trim crank probably wouldn't be moved to a more "modern" location even if there was room for it down below, but in any case, it still lurks up there in its old slot on the ceiling.

When flying the Turbo Twin Comanche B, watch your head, bunkie. And not just to watch out for bumping that overhead trim crank, either.

United Consultants Twin Bee
3,800 pounds gross weight

This is an off-again on-again operation in which the manufacturer makes the customer furnish a Seabee airframe and finishes it off as an amphibian twin with a cruising speed of 131 mph on 75 percent power. The cost: $34,500.

The UC-1 seats five, carries a useful load of 1,300 pounds, and weighs 2,500 pounds empty. The 180 hp Lycoming IO-360-1D engines climb at 1,265 feet per minute at sea level, and the service ceiling is 18,000 feet. If one of the engines quits, the ceiling is a quick-drop 4,000 feet. Stall speed is, not surprisingly, the safest of all twins: 49 mph.

Top speed of this dragonfly is 147 mph, and it cruises at 124 mph on 65 percent power. With a 100-gallon fuel capacity, maximum range is 870 miles, which is about as much of a trip as anybody can reasonably endure in as noisy a contraption as this one.

On take-off from water, the splash rail gets a good work-out for 650 feet before lift-off, for a total take-off distance of 890 feet to clear a 50-foot obstacle. The aerodynamically designed hull is so good that when the plane lands it coasts for almost 600 feet to a full stop. Ground roll on land is considerably better for a landing: 350 feet. Take-off from land involves a 600-foot total distance to clear a 50-foot obstacle, including a 375-foot ground run.

United Consultants is primarily what the name implies, an engineering firm. Its marketing program is pretty spotty accordingly, and its service facilities could stand some improvement.

Beech Travel Air D-95-A
4,200 pounds gross weight

The lowest-priced twin in the Beech line also carries the oldest name in the company's history: the Travel Air at $53,500 (avionics included).

Thinking that a twin can be operated as economically as a high-performance single-engine plane is unrealistic, but the Travel Air D-95-A comes close. It will fly 11 miles on a gallon of gas, for example, and there are plenty of automobiles that don't do as well with only one engine. The D-95-A's two four-cylinder engines can be overhauled for little more than the cost of overhauling *one* six-cylinder engine of less total horsepower, even though its 2,650-pound EW airframe might not be as rugged as some.

The four-seater can carry a fifth seat well within its useful

Retractable landing gear increases air speed of 210 mph Travel Air
Twin operated by Barrett Motels, Inc., Augusta, Georgia

load limit of 1,550 pounds. The 180 hp fuel-injection Lycoming 10-360-B1B engines climb at 1,250 feet per minute, service ceiling is 18,100 feet, and single-engine operational ceiling is 8,400 feet.

Top speed is 210 mph, cruise speed on 75 percent power is 200 mph, and on 65 percent power it can cruise at 195 mph for a maximum range of 1,040 miles from its 112-gallon fuel capacity. Normal fuel consumption is 18 gallons per hour and the stall speed is 70 mph.

Total take-off distance to 50-foot altitude is 1,280 feet, including a 1,000-foot ground run. The D-95-A lands over a 50-foot obstacle in a total of 1,590 feet, out of which 980 feet is ground roll.

Competition is closing in on the Travel Air, and rumors have it that the D-95-A is being phased out of production as of the beginning of 1969. Too bad; along with the rest of its advantages, it has all the best of Beech's features, too, such as throw-over wheel, fast gear retraction, and free inspections. Nice airplane.

Morava L-200D
4,300 pounds gross weight

The National Aircraft Works in Yugoslavia has built over 1,000 of these unconventional twins since the L-200D was first flown in mid-1962, so it must be a pretty good plane. But it's a little hard to judge by the information dribbling out from behind The Curtain. The data below is based on secondhand information from England.

Price of the miniscule three-seater is worthy of the most dedicated capitalist, though: $46,200. The low-winger is powered by two 210 hp M337 supercharged engines pouring their air stream directly back onto two vertical tail sections, for a tail assembly that reminds some of the Twin Beech 18 transporter.

Apparently the L-200D really needs them to hold control, as the total length is only 28 feet 3 inches compared to a thin wing, which spans 40 feet 4½ inches. That big stretch accounts for only 186 square feet of wing area. That just *can't* supply enough lift for the 2,820-pound empty-weight and 1,480-pound useful-load registrations!

It does, though, with a total take-off distance over a 50-foot obstacle of 1,650 feet and a maximum rate of climb listed at 1,200 feet per minute. Maximum range in the oddly shaped critter is 1,055 miles at the economy cruising speed of 183 mph. Standard fuel capacity is 92 Imperial gallons. Total landing distance from a 50-foot altitude is 1,580 feet.

Service ceiling is listed at 16,240 feet, which doesn't seem a lot for a "supercharged" plane. Presumably neither of the engines would ever dare quit, because the figures covering single-engine operation are not offered.

Cessna Super Skymaster
4,400 pounds gross weight

One trouble with a standard twin is that when flying with one engine out, the resultant asymmetrical thrust forces present a real challenge for the pilot. The Skymaster's center-line thrust principle, with tandem-mounted engines, makes it the safest of all the "safer twins" to fly.

The pusher engine mounted at the back of the cabin eliminates the weight of the entire aft fuselage section, too, replaced with lightweight tail booms. The "price" for this advantage is the fact that useful storage space is eliminated, too; a good many Skymasters are being sold with the optional Cargo Pack, which carries up to 300 pounds of luggage under the fuselage. This attachable and removable belly pod is aerodynamically designed so that cruising speed is reduced by less than 4 mph.

Even with the wing struts on Cessna's beloved high wing, the top speed of the Skymaster has been 200 mph for several years now (it takes two 210 hp fuel-injection Continental 10-360-C engines to do the job, however). Cruising speed of 191 mph is admittedly the slowest speed on 75 percent power of all light twin-engine planes. The four-seater (with two more optional seats for shrimp-size passengers) has an empty weight of 2,650 pounds and carries a useful load of 1,750 pounds, a latter figure that has been increasing steadily over the years since the Skymaster was introduced in its 1965 model with retractable landing gear. Gross-weight certification is up in the 1968 model by another 125 pounds even over the 1967 figure. Another creeper: the price, now $44,500.

Rate of climb is 1,200 feet per minute for the Super Skymaster ("Super" is the *only* kind of Skymaster being built). On only the front engine, rate of climb is 335 feet per minute; the rear engine working alone pushes it up at 415 feet per minute. Service ceiling is 19,500 feet for twin-engine operation. On the front engine only, operational ceiling is 6,800 feet; it's 8,800 feet with just the rear engine working.

With its normally aspirated engines, the Skymaster's performance is best at 5,500 feet for both top and cruising speeds. With 93 gallons of fuel, she'll cruise for 5.6 hours at that pokey 191 mph for a range of 1,070 miles. Optimum range is 1,345 miles flying at 10,000 feet at 144 mph for a 9.5-hour nonstop trip with an optional fuel load of 128 gallons. Normal fuel consumption is 21 gallons per hour.

In fairness to the Skymaster, it should be pointed out that the above figures are all based on operations at the 4,400-pound maximum allowable gross weight. It really isn't that kind of an airplane; this is a luxury ship, not a workhorse, and a more normal flying weight would be, say, 3,900 pounds.

With that lighter load, the biggest differences are naturally in shorter take-off and landing distances. At 3,900 pounds, ground run is 680 feet to lift-off and a total take-off distance of 1,290 feet to clear a 50-foot obstacle. Landing distance from 50-feet up is 1,500 feet, including a 590-foot ground roll. Stall speed is 63 mph, power off.

The tail on this unique aircraft resembles nothing so much as a backless love seat. If not downright love, the tandem twin does engender a certain amount of affection; *Plane and Pilot* magazine named the 1967 model as Plane of the Year. The public likes it, too; 850 Skymasters were sold in its first five years of production.

Cessna Super Skymaster's "backless love seat"

Cessna Turbosystem Super Skymaster
4,500 pounds gross weight

The listed gross weight of the turbocharged version of the Super Skymaster (see preceding evaluation) may be a shade misleading. The FAA certification for the extra 100 pounds is allowable only for take-off. Allowable gross weight for landing is still the same as for the normally aspirated Skymaster.

In short, Cessna got through a certification for the benefit of long-distance flyers who need to take off with more gas. With optional fuel tanks, the TS Skymaster can use the 128 gallons on 65 percent power flying at 24,000 feet for a range up to 1,580 miles—a nonstop trip that would take almost 11 hours, and by which time the dry plane would have a gross weight of some 1,000 pounds less.

New automatic alternate-induction air systems starting with the 1968 model are much easier on the pilot than the former manually operated controls. And an extra new engine-driven hydraulic pump is available as an option for faster landing-gear retraction and to serve as an additional back-up system in addition to the standard auxiliary hand pump—all to make the TS Skymaster ever more safe to fly in. The new "T" arrangement of the standard instrument panel even makes it *look* safer to fly in.

Out of respect for high-altitude flight, there is also a new overhead console with oxygen outlets for the pilot and copilot, with stowage space for masks when they need the umbilicals.

The TS Skymaster uses fuel-injected 210 hp Continental TS10-360-D engines to accommodate the compressors, and the empty weight is thus up to 2,795 pounds. Useful allowable weight for landing is 1,605 pounds. Sea-level rate of climb is 1,155 feet per minute (375 fpm and 410 fpm operating on the front or rear engines alone, respectively). Service ceiling is 30,100 feet, or 18,600 feet with the front engine only (19,600 feet with just the rear engine).

The only differences in the landing and take-off distances between the two versions is an additional 40-foot ground run needed by the fully loaded TS modification. Stall speed is 1 mph faster. Fuel capacities and normal consumption for both are the same, at 21 gallons per hour.

The big differences come in when speed is considered. Top speed is 231 mph, cruising speed on 75 percent power is 224 mph, and 65 percent power delivers a TAS of 222 mph.

The versatile Skymaster can be equipped for many kinds of missions, including taxi and air cargo. The Air Force has even ordered a couple hundred of them.

Burns BA-42-P
4,500 pounds gross weight

Did you know that there's an airplane factory down in Starkville, Mississippi? They're building a pretty good airplane, too, even if not in volume. In fact, they haven't sold any yet. This report will thus be an inside look at what amounts to an aircraft birth in progress.

The prototype Burns BA-42 weighs 2,400 pounds empty and carries a useful load of 1,850 pounds. That, though, is without the turbocharging and pressurization the ruggedly built hull is designed to take. When so equipped, the six-seater will have an empty weight of 2,700 pounds and a useful load of 1,800 pounds. The optimistic price tag on the basic Burns BA-42, before being souped and pressurized, was $49,950 before the accountants started in where the engineers left off, and it is now $59,995.

The 210 hp Continental 10-360 engines climb at 1,500 feet per minute; the service ceiling is 20,000 feet or 7,000 feet with one engine out. Don't fool around, though, because stall speed is 80 mph. Top speed is 235 mph, cruising speed is very close at 233 mph on 75 percent power, and maximum range on 65 percent power at 225 mph is 870 miles whether at full 4,300-pound gross weight or with the whole 100 gallons of gas, which disappears at the rate of 21 gallons per hour.

The everything-and-pressurized version was first publicized as a $64,950 airplane, but on second thoughts another $25,000 has been added to make the price $89,950, flyaway Starkville.

Take-off and landing distances are the same for both models: 1,200-foot run to make a 1,750-foot total to 50-foot altitude, and a 1,000-foot ground roll to stop coming down in a total of 1,400 feet over a 50-foot obstacle. Rate of climb with the TS10-360-D engines is still 1,500 feet per minute, but service ceiling for the TS'd plane is at 30,000 feet on both or 15,000 feet running on one engine.

But speed ratings are something else. At 21,000 feet the BA-42-P can hit 265 mph. Cruise speed on 75 percent power at that altitude is *still* 265 mph. And it cruises at 24,000 feet on 65 percent power STILL at the same 265 mph with a 950-mile range.

There's nothing leisurely about *this* product of the ol' south!

Beech Baron 55—(B)
5,100 pounds gross weight

The biggest difference between the Barons (there are three of them) and the lesser-powered Travel Air is that the lighter plane is still considered as primarily a pleasure craft while the Baron aims squarely at the executive market.

The biggest recent change in the Baron 55-B, and one that amounted almost to heresy in the industry in 1968, was the fact that Beech cut the price by a full $4,000. Price of the 55-B is now $59,950, including a full package of avionics. This is one reason why there is so much scuttle-butt around about the probability of the Travel Air's days being numbered, now that *its* price has risen to within $6,500 of the cost of the much better 55-B.

This lowest-priced Baron has room for four to six seats and sports a pair of fuel-injection 260 hp Continental 10-470-L engines for a sea-level climb rate of 1,670 feet per minute and a service ceiling of 19,700 feet (16,600 feet on one engine). Empty weight is 3,075 pounds, for a useful load limit of 2,025 pounds.

Top speed is 236 mph, cruising speed on 75 percent power is 225 mph, and economy cruise on 65 percent power is 220 mph. Stall speed is 78 mph. Total take-off distance to 50-foot altitude is 1,255 feet, including a 910-foot ground run. Landing over a 50-foot obstacle at gross weight used a distance of 1,370 feet, including an 840-foot ground roll. The 55-B carries 142 gallons of gas, which it normally uses at 26.5 gallons per hour. Range with maximum fuel is 1,225 miles on optimum settings.

Although the empty weight of the Baron 55-C is the same as the 55-B, big brother is rated at 200 pounds more in gross weight and carries that much bigger a load accordingly. This is accounted for in the bigger 290 hp Continental 10-520-C engines. Rate of climb is the same, but the service ceiling is upped to 20,900 feet, while the single-engine ceiling is 13,500 feet.

Price of the avionics-equipped 55-C is up to $73,950, but this includes a lot of fancy stuff like a standard heated Pitot tube, optional anti-icer for the prop, and a de-icer for the wings. Speeds are increased to a top of 242 mph, 75 percent cruise to 230 mph, and to 225 mph on a 65 percent setting. Stall speed is 1 mph slower, too. Fuel capacity is the same, but the 55-C uses it faster: 28 gallons per hour in normal use. Maximum fuel range: 1,143 miles.

Some of the biggest differences are seen in the take-off and landing performance. The 55-C lifts off in less than a 600-foot run to clear a 50-foot obstacle in less than a total of 970 feet at gross weight. On the other hand, it uses almost 1,415 feet to land over a 50-foot obstacle, with nearly an 870-foot ground roll.

And (it had to figure) there's a new turbocharged Baron, too, the 56-TC. This modification is capable of exceeding 290 mph, and its service ceiling is 32,000 feet. Single-engine ceiling is 23,700 feet, where the 3,625-pound EW Beech can handle a useful load of 2,365 pounds.

The engines are massive 380 hp Lycoming TIO-541-E1B4 powerplants. High-altitude cruising speed on 75 percent power is 284 mph, and 266 mph can be expected on 65 percent power settings. Stall speed is 84 mph, and runway capabilities are relatively long: 1,420 feet to scale a 50-foot obstacle, including a 1,005-foot ground run, and a total landing distance of 2,080 feet coming in over a 50-foot obstacle when the 1,285-foot ground roll is included. Fuel capacity is the same as for the other Barons in the family, but the 56-TC uses it at 39 gallons per hour in normal operations. Range with maximum fuel load is 1,074 miles.

With automatic turbocharging, the gross weight is 5,990

pounds, which is hardly in the light-twin class any more. Neither is the price of $95,950.

The Turbo Baron joins the other Beech twins in using a one-piece windshield in the new models. Built-in oxygen outlets at each station are standard in the 56-TC, as is the businesslike avionics package.

All three Barons feature good luggage-loading capabilities, and the two big compartments fore and aft carry up to 670 pounds. Their weather-tight doors can be locked, and an optional cargo door is the biggest in any light twin: 22½ inches high by 38 inches wide. Another new luggage option is an additional compartment recessed behind the usual baggage area (or fifth and sixth seats) for 10½ cubic feet more of space.

The distinctive window-within-a-window next to the pilot's seat is indicative of the type of man the Baron is built for—a man whose time is valuable enough so that he doesn't like to waste any of it when he can conserve it with efficiency. Baron owners who fly just for the fun of it (and admit it) are very rare.

Piper Aztec C
5,200 pounds gross weight

"The Piper with the window curtains" has outsold any other twin and is the lowest-price twin primarily designed for business use. The 2,933-pound EW Aztec is big enough for six full-sized people and has big baggage compartments sandwiching the cabin. The interior has assist straps, arm rests, ash trays, magazine pockets, and individual fresh-air vents at each seat position as well as "airliner type" reading lights for each passenger. The $57,990 Aztec C carries well over a ton in useful load: 2,267 pounds.

Along with the bare airplane, Piper offers packages of instrumentation in a big option of operational groups. There are four "executive packages," from $5,565 to $17,040. Four "sportsman packages" go up to $17,420, "professional packages" to $19,765, and "corporate packages" to $26,155 (only $11,000 or so

Piper Aztec C

more than for what the company considers minimal instrumentation for "corporate" use). There is even a choice of instrument
packages termed "international," where the minimum costs $17,530
and from there on in "easy" stages goes up to $28,150. That sure
covers a whole gang of transistors.

The Aztec C is powered by a pair of fuel-injection Lycoming
1-540-D4-B5 engines, which produce 250 hp at 2,575 rpm. It takes
a darn good pilot to match the show-case performance of Piper's
ace professionals, but in tests run on a new Piper C equipped for
cross-country transportation under conditions considered by the
FAA as standard, top speed is 216 mph, optimum cruise speed
at 7,500 feet on 75 percent power is 206 mph, and on 65 percent
power at 10,000 feet the Aztec cruised at 202 mph for a range
of 1,030 miles. Cutting the power to 45 percent after going up
to 16,000 feet extends the range to 1,420 miles. Fuel capacity is
144 gallons (140 usable), and gas consumption is a normal 23.8
gallons per hour.

Rate of climb is 1,490 feet per minute and service ceiling is
21,100 feet. Absolute ceiling on one engine is 8,800 feet, but the
loner isn't really comfortable at gross weight until it gets down
to around 6,400 feet. The stall speed is 68 mph with flaps extended.

Take-off run to lift-off is 820 feet, and the Aztec can clear a 50-foot obstacle in a total take-off distance of 1,250 feet. It lands over a 50-foot obstruction in 1,680 feet, including an 860-foot ground roll.

As if all this wasn't enough, Piper has now turbocharged the Aztec, too. Not that the blower changes the take-off and landing distances or the stall speed, but for $72,400 the buyer gets an airplane that has a one-engine service ceiling of 18,500 feet— or a way-up 29,700 feet on two engines. They can head for the high country from sea level at 1,490 feet per minute. Not counting the IFR tools and the bag accouterments, the Turbo Aztec C weighs 3,127 pounds empty, which still leaves a useful load of 2,077 pounds.

The remarkably efficient AiResearch turbocharging system enables the 250 hp fuel-injected Lycoming 10-540-J4A5 engines to hit a top speed of 256 mph at 20,000 feet and cruise on 75 percent power 236 mph at 24,000 feet or at 224 mph on 65 percent power.

Normal fuel consumption from the 144-gallon capacity is 24.7 gallons per hour, but optimum range is 1,550 miles. For that $72,400 price the built-in oxygen system is included as standard. The instrumentation packages, of course, are still extra.

Cessna 310-N
5,200 pounds gross weight

Ever since the tip-tanked 310 was introduced so successfully in 1954, Cessna has had a hard time trying to find anything to improve for each successive year's model. After reversing an industry trend by cutting down on the number of windows on each side from three to two on the 1966 model K (for the 47-inch-long "Vista View" window), about the most evident change in the 1967 310-L was the one-piece windshield. The 1968 310-N introduced electroluminescent lighting for the newly squared-off T-formation instrument panel (also bigger by 16 square inches), where a sealed-in phosphorous coating emits light when the AC

Cessna 310-L

current is turned on. Advantage: more reliability compared to light bulbs, which do burn out or get broken once in a while.

The six-seat executive twin (presumably with minor executives in the two small back seats) actually doubled in sales one year to take first place in all twin sales for a while and may make it again. The 310 has a lot going for it.

It enjoys the advantage of being one of the best-looking planes around just about any airport. Those racy main tanks on the wing tips, optimizing roll stability, are not just canted for appearance but provide additional lift as well. The waist-high wing lockers in the aft sections of the engine nacelles, with almost 15 cubic feet of space for 240-pound capacity, are much-appreciated additions to the regular baggage compartments in the fuselage. Starting with the 310-N, there is also a large optional access door for loading bulky cargo. With full-feathering props and all the rest of Cessna's engineering successes, the 310 has room for improvement only in embellishment.

Empty weight of the $63,950 310-N is 3,125 pounds, and it carries 2,075 pounds in useful load limit. It is powered by 260 hp Continental I0-470-V0 fuel-injection engines with a rate of climb of 1,540 feet per minute. Rate of climb on one engine is 330 feet per minute. Full service ceiling is 19,900 feet and is 6,850 feet on one engine at full gross.

When showing off with only a 1,275-pound weight aboard (4,400-pound total lift-off weight), the 310 has a top speed of

242 mph. At 6,500 feet on 75 percent power, cruise speed is 228 mph. Maximum range on 140 gallons of gas (including 40 gallons in auxiliaries in addition to the standard 100 gallons) is 1,515 miles, traveling 173 mph at 10,000 feet. Even this can be boosted with the new optional wing-locker fuel tanks, which can increase total fuel capacity to 180 gallons. Total take-off distance for the lightened demonstrator to clear a 50-foot obstacle is 1,165 feet, including a 970-foot ground run. Total landing distance from 50 feet up is 1,275 feet, including a 695-foot ground roll.

All such figures are, of course, changed substantially with increases in weight of load. But then, the lively 310 is still a teen-ager.

One good example of its growing up, though, is the radome nose now available as an option for the installation of weather radar. There were a few gripes about hard touchdowns and rough taxiing on earlier models, but the complaints have been remedied now with a 28 percent increase in the shock-strut travel in the redesigned main landing gear. Another commonly heard beef has been lessened by the use of larger entrance steps for the passengers, and the new retractables are now nearly twice as large as on previous designs.

The 310's engineers have long believed in two of everything that counts most (starting with the engines). The 310 now has dual generators, dual regulators, dual dry vacuum pumps, and dual fuel pumps for each engine, all standard equipment.

To duel Piper's Aztec for first place again?

Beech Baron 55-C
5,300 pounds gross weight

See Beech Baron 55-B.

Beech Turbo Baron 56-TC
5,990 pounds gross weight

See Beech Baron 55-B.

BEST OF CLASS

(*Standards*)

LEAST WEIGHT—Wing Derringer: 1,920 lbs. empty

BEST SEATING CAPACITY—Piper Aztec C: 6

BIGGEST PAYLOAD—Beech Turbo Baron: 2,340 lbs.

BEST LIFT RATIO—Piper Aztec C: 2,267 lbs. useful load compared to 2,933 lbs. EW

BIGGEST ENGINES—Beech Turbo Baron: 380 hp Lycomings

SERVICE CEILING—Beech Turbo Baron: 32,000 ft.

TAKE-OFF DISTANCE (RUN)—United Consultants Twin Bee: 375 ft.

TAKE-OFF DISTANCE (OVER 50-FT. OBSTACLE)—UC-1 Twin Bee: 600 ft.

LANDING DISTANCE (ROLL)—Wing Derringer: 250 ft.

LANDING DISTANCE (OVER 50-FT. OBSTACLE)—Beech Baron 55-B: 1,400 ft.

RATE OF CLIMB FROM SEA LEVEL—Beech Turbo Baron: 2,200 fpm

AIRSPEEDS—Beech Turbo Baron fastest in all three settings: top, 290 mph; 75% power, 284 mph; 65% power, 266 mph

SLOWEST STALL SPEED—UC-1 Twin Bee: 49 mph

RANGE—Cessna Turbosystem Skymaster: 1,580 miles

NORMAL FUEL CONSUMPTION—Piper Twin Comanche: 15.2 gal. per hour

LOWEST PRICE—Piper Twin Comanche B: $37,250

CHAPTER 7

Heavy twins

The word "heavy" is strictly relative. Nobody has any trouble categorizing a four-place Piper Comanche as a light twin, and a $200,000 pressurized Grand Commander is universally recognized as a heavy twin. But the middle ground is something else again. Even the industry itself does not agree on any strict line of demarcation.

But as far as this book is concerned, the difference between light and heavy twins does not depend on weight. Or on price, either. Instead, the difference is arbitrarily decided according to use.

A light twin, then, is a plane that the owner most often flies himself, up to and including the "executive" twins. A heavy twin is considered any type of plane that is most often piloted by professionals or for "corporate" use. Sure, there are plenty of corporation presidents who are capable of taking over the controls of a 10-seat Queen Air; and any number of Cessna 310 company planes are operated by full-time professional pilots. But in general, if the passengers walk into a plane instead of climb into it, it's a heavy twin.

That's what it says here, anyhow.

Sud M-360-6 Jupiter
5,269 pounds gross weight

The 3,042-pound EW Jupiter is Europe's answer to the United States' Skymaster. But unlike its American counterpart, Sud's tandem twin has the aft engine all the way at the back of the plane, with the horizontal and vertical stabilizers on top of a standard fuselage well forward of the rear engine's air stream. The European tandem is also considerably bigger and heavier than the Skymaster's. It is built in either a six- or a seven-seat configuration, with plenty of legroom in each. It sells for $88,200 in United States currency. Basic.

The Jupiter is powered by 310 hp Lycoming TIO-541 engines. They are turbosupercharged for high-altitude performance, carrying a useful load of 2,227 pounds. Total take-off distance to clear a 50-foot obstacle is 1,380 feet, and the maximum rate of climb from sea level is 1,840 feet per minute.

Standard fuel capacity is 125 Imperial gallons, but this can be boosted to anything the customer wants through a series of optional auxiliaries up to a 220-gallon total. Service ceiling is 32,800 feet, the highest of any piston-engine plane on the market. When it gets down to earth, it lands from a 50-foot altitude in a total distance of 1,540 feet.

At this writing, Sud is also about ready to announce an 800 hp version powered by 400 hp turbocharged engines. The new plane will be called the M-360 Presidence. But not by Cessna.

Cessna Executive Skyknight
5,300 pounds gross weight

The 3,273-pound Skyknight is a stretched-out and turbocharged version of the model 310 design (in fact, the official designation for what Cessna salesmen call the Skyknight is the model 320). It carries a useful load of 2,027 pounds, is powered by 285 hp Continental TSIO-520-B six-cylinder fuel-injection engines, and costs $85,000.

Top speed for the six-seater is 275 mph at 6,000 feet. Cruising speed at 20,000 feet on 75 percent power is 260 mph, and it can go nonstop for 1,182 miles on a total fuel capacity of 140 gallons. Optimum range on a supplemented total of 140 gallons is 1,542 miles at 25,000 feet, fully loaded to the gross weight of 5,300 pounds and flying at 228 mph.

Twin-engine climb at sea level as 1,920 feet per minute, and on one engine the climb rate is 475 fpm. Service ceiling on both engines is 29,000 feet; 18,800 feet with one engine out. Ground run is 1,190 feet out of a total take-off distance of 1,514 feet to clear a 50-foot obstacle. The Skyknight lands over a 50-foot obstacle in 1,734 feet, including a 614-foot ground roll to full stop.

With one more window on each side than the 310, the Skyknight is even handsomer—in fact, downright pretty. The foul-weather window in the pilot's side window is now frameless, and the windshield is one piece, to make the Skyknight even sleeker than it already "finally" was in 1966. It also sports some of the classiest paint jobs to come out of any shop in the industry, in a dozen combinations.

Any way you look at it, the Skyknight is a capital B beauty.

Aerostar 600
5,500 pounds gross weight

If there's anything going on in the aviation industry that could be called revolutionary, this is it. The revolution comes in how the Aerostars are built. Guiding genius of the concept is Ted Smith, the self-same man who developed the Aero Commander line built by the then Rockwell Standard company. His Aerostar is a triple-threat innovation.

To begin with, the wing of the monocoque Aerostar has only 50 parts, compared to several hundred in a conventional wing. The resultant savings are possible through the utilization of a heavy skin, like the outer "skeleton" of an insect. Applying the same principle to all elements of the plane vastly reduces the number of parts used throughout the aircraft for minimal costs in tooling, parts manufacture, and assembly labor.

Second, individual parts designs serve multiple purposes. For example, there is only one fixed-tail surface design, which is used interchangeably as left or right horizontal stabilizer *or* left or right elevator and even as a rudder. Only one design for wing-control surfaces is used; attached outboard, the piece is an aileron, or inboard it is the flap. This further cuts tooling and parts manufacturing costs, and the airframe uses a total of only 25 percent of the parts used to start with in the typical light-skin, stringer frame design of practically all current general-aviation aircraft.

Furthermore, the *entire* airframe is used interchangeably as the Aerostar 320 (hp), 360, 500, 600, 601 (turbocharged), and 600P (pressurized). Nor will any basic changes be necessary for turboprop or jet power. It's almost like designing a shot glass that can handle anything from Rhine wine to 100-proof bourbon.

Ted Smith's "Rhine wine" version only got as far as mock-up, a single-engine, two-seat, fully aerobatic 160 hp trainer that supposedly would come out of the same jigs for a selling price of $5,000. The Aerostar 160 even had retractable landing gear at that target price, where a basic difference from other models was a nose gear that swiveled in to lie flat in the single-engine version.

The Aerostar line was originally opted by Rockwell Standard for $6.5 million to make that company's already "most comprehensive" line the most revolutionary as well. But the deal eventually fell through. Before it did, Smith announced the 4,000-pound GW model 400 as first in line, a 2,400-pound EW twin with a selling price of $42,000.

The "heavy" twin had entry through a split clamshell door for the passengers, just like on a $700,000 jet. The six-seater was designed for 200 hp Lycoming IO-360 fuel-injection engines, to carry a useful load of 1,600 pounds. Rate of climb: 1,750 feet per minute full on, or with one engine, 350 feet per minute. Maximum cruise speed at 10,000 feet: 220 mph, for an optimum range of 1,100 miles. Fuel capacity: 100 gallons; stall speed, 61 mph. Take-off run: 900 feet, for a total take-off distance of 1,150 feet over a 50-foot obstacle. That $42,000 price even included avionics —dual, yet.

Alas, production plans were shelved when the Rockwell deal

fizzled. So were the plans for the Aerostar 320, an even lighter twin powered by 160 hp Lycoming IO-320 engines. With gross weight at 200 pounds less, the 2,300-pound EW 320 was designed for a useful load of 1,500 pounds. The 320 was figured to climb at 1,600 feet per minute, or 340 feet per minute on one engine. Maximum cruise speed: 212 mph at 10,000 feet. Range: perhaps a 1,100-mile optimum. Total take-off distance over a 50-foot obstacle: 1,165 feet including a ground run of 945 feet. Stall speed: 58 mph. Price of the 320, fully equipped with dual electronics: $35,000.

The 1967 price of the 520 hp model was $45,000. The pressurized 620 hp Aerostar—with a cruising speed of 319 mph at 22,000 feet—was listed at $70,000. But then something happened. Namely, Smith had to go it on his own.

The first Aerostar off the production line was the model 600, when certification was announced in early 1968 after a FAA flight program that involved less than 20 hours of flying. The 600 was expected to be around $65,000, but it wound up with a somewhat disappointing $86,550 price tag.

This is a completely equipped IFR airplane, though. The price includes an avionics package with DME and transponder, dual rotating beacons, dual flight controls, electric gyros, a fuel capacity of 170 gallons, and a deluxe six-place leather interior. Narco equipment abounds.

Empty weight of the Aerostar 600 is 3,425 pounds with all standard equipment, for a useful load of 2,075 pounds. Loading for the 170-square foot wing is 32.3 pounds per square foot at the 5,500-pound gross weight. With 290 hp Lycoming IO-540 engines, rate of climb is 1,850 feet per minute or 450 fpm on one engine, both a little less than expected before the actual deliveries started.

So are the airspeeds. Top speed behind the fuel-injection engines is 260 mph at sea level. At 10,000 feet, 70 percent settings deliver 250 mph, 65 percent gets 240 mph, and the 600 travels at 225 mph on 55 percent power. Range on 65 percent power with a 30-minute reserve is 1,430 miles. Service ceiling is 22,000 feet, or 6,300 feet on one engine. Stall speed is 77 mph. Over a 50-foot obstacle, the 600 takes off in a total distance of 1,025 feet and lands in 1,100 feet.

A turbocharged version, the 601, is scheduled for deliveries in 1969. It is to be followed by the model 620 pressurized version with 310 hp Lycoming TIO-541 engines, an expected 30,000-foot ceiling, 310 mph top speed, and a climb rate of 2,300 feet per minute.

Plans for the production of the five-seat 360 and 400 models have not been finalized as of this writing, but both will have 21,000-foot ceilings, climb at 1,400 feet per minute, and have IO-360 Lycoming engines. The model 360 will have a top speed of 220 mph and will cruise on 65 percent power at 210 mph. The model 400 will be about 10 mph faster. This time, Smith isn't saying what the prices will be until he is ready to deliver.

In the meantime, his research and development team is deep in work on advanced designs for the 1970s. Smith already projects some 40 different models of radical (?) design.

BN-2A Islander
6,000 pounds gross weight

This plane looks like a cross between an Aero Commander Shrike 500 and something out of the 1930s . . . with fixed landing gear (the only nonretractable twin). The ten-seat high-winger is priced at a basic $62,000, which is much less than a lot of four-seat airplanes.

Most air-taxi and third-level air-transport routes involve flights of less than 40 minutes. When thus used commercially, the Islander's STOL capabilities make up for its slow speeds— slow indeed for a twin, with a 150 mph cruising speed at 59 percent power (13,000 feet). Top speed is the slowest in its class: 168 mph. Cruising speed on 75 percent power at 7,500 feet is 156 mph, but cruising on 67 percent power at 9,500 feet is only 1 mph slower.

Empty weight with basic equipment is 3,500 pounds, for a useful load limit of 2,500 pounds. The cabin floor is 41 square feet in area, and a good 10 feet stretches out behind the pilot's seat. With full radio, the Islander can carry nine 165-pound passengers plus the pilot, with 290 pounds available for fuel and baggage. This would mean flying for about two hours on 65 percent power. Putting in de-icing and cabin-heating equipment would add about 150 lbs., which would eliminate one of the passengers.

For use as a cargo plane, the Islander has three big doors, each 44 inches high. It's even roomy enough so that it can be rigged with sleeping accommodations for four, provided that two of the cheapskates are small children. The Islander is also a low-cost maintenance plane, with two six-cylinder Lycoming 540-E4-C5 engines, 260 hp each.

With a ground run of less than 700 feet, it can take off in a total distance of 900 feet to clear a 50-foot obstacle. It can land over a 50-foot obstacle in less than 1,000 feet, including a 500-foot ground roll. The two-blade Hartzell constant-speed feathering props are 80 inches in diameter, and the Islander carries 134 gallons of gas in its integral wing tanks. The main landing wheels, mounted under the engines, provide an exceptionally stable base (as well as considerable drag).

Built by Britten-Norman on England's Isle of Wight, the Islander is distributed in the United States by a New York organization with the somewhat sinister-sounding name of Jonas Aircraft & Arms Company. Cessna and Piper don't seem to be scared a bit.

Piper Navajo
6,200 pounds gross weight

With the air-taxi business mushrooming, Piper's entry into this field was almost inevitable. The result from Lock Haven is the 3,600-pound EW Navajo, Piper's first really new design since before the Apache gave way to the Aztec.

In the six-seat corporate configuration, the newest Indian is a flying executive suite with a separate crew compartment up front, pairs of facing seats "conference-style" if desired, and fold-away tables that can be used for anything from work to gin rummy. An aft refreshment console, an inflight luggage area big enough to hang up coats, and a camouflaged toilet all become

Piper Navajo

worthwhile replacements for additional seating capacity (one guy could ride in the john, though).

Without the frills, the commuter configuration can carry a pilot and seven passengers who can look out of windows bigger than they will see on any airliner. Piper built 200 Navajos in the first year for the taxi trade, which particularly appreciates the big spread between top speed and slow approach/landing speed, in the interests of minimizing take-off to touchdown time on the mostly short trips in such operations.

The Navajo is now powered by 300 hp fuel-injection 10-540 six-cylinder engines with direct drive and dual ignition (290 hp until 1968). Useful load is 2,600 pounds, including baggage capacity (aft plus fore) of 350 pounds. At sea level, top speed is 224 mph, and best rate of climb is 1,440 feet per minute.

On 75 percent power settings at 6,400 feet, the Navajo cruises at 210 mph, or at 205 mph on 65 percent power at 10,300 feet. Optimum range is 1,540 miles, flying at 19,400 feet on 45 percent power at 177 mph—still better than two and one-half times the stall speed of 70 mph. Fuel consumption runs from 21.6 gallons per hour at 45 percent to 31.4 gallons per hour at 75 percent power.

The ground run for short-field take-off is 930 feet, with total distance over a 50-foot obstacle of 1,950 feet. Landing on a short field over a 50-foot obstacle, total distance is 1,690 feet, including an 1,115-foot ground roll. Twin service ceiling is 20,500 feet; on one engine, 7,000 feet. Price, basic: $89,500.

And as expected, there's a turbocharged version. A new FAA rating ups the gross weight to 6,500 pounds, and useful weight is 2,741 pounds with the 3,759-pound empty weight. Top speed of the Turbo Navajo is up to 260 mph, cruising speed on 75 percent power (at 23,500 feet) is up to 247 mph, and airspeed at 65 percent power settings is 231 mph.

Optimum range is extended to 1,685 miles at 181 mph on the Turbo Navajo's 190-gallon fuel capacity (used at rates from 20.2 to 35.6 gallons per hour). Stall speed for the TS is a bit better at 1 mph slower: 71 mph. The automatically turbocharged powerplants are 310 hp fuel-injected Lycoming TIO-540-A engines; rate of climb, at best from sea level, 1,395 feet per minute; and the service ceilings are 26,300 and 16,400 feet for two and one engines respectively. Total short-field take-off capabilities are more than 200 feet better than for the nonbreather over a 50-foot obstacle, including a 40-foot improvement in ground run. Basic price of the Turbo Navajo is $97,290.

The Navajo is designed so that any good Aztec pilot can make a complete check-out in less than three hours. One change he will gladly get used to: that damn trip tab has finally been moved from the ceiling to the throttle area, where "big airplanes" have it.

Cessna 401/402
6,300 pounds gross weight

This hybrid combines the cabin of a 411 with the wings of a Skyknight. With its four round window ports on each side of the stateroom, the 401 looks like the more powerful, more expensive model 411, and it is a forerunner of the pressurized model 421. The turbosystem 401 has 300 hp Continental TSI0-520-E fuel-injected engines and a basic price of $99,800.

Empty weight is 3,641 pounds, and the 401 carries a useful load of 2,659 pounds. Passengers and crew board the 401 through an airline-type two-piece Air-Stair door. The upper half of the door provides a shelter and contains a courtesy light to illuminate the steps. With a span of 17 feet on the horizontal stabilizer, the 401's towering vertical fin makes the tail look for all the world like a smaller version of a commercial 727.

With the crew's quarters closed off, the passenger compartment still has 42 square feet of flat, carpeted floor area. Passengers in the 401 are surrounded by adjustable fresh-air outlets, reading lights, and oxygen ports . . . not to mention ash trays, recessed cigarette lighters, and tinted windows. The eight-seat 401 takes a back seat from very few flying machines in regality of appointments, and when two seats are taken out to make room for a snack bar, vanity, toilet, etc. . . . WOW.

The 401 and 402 are identical in basic specs and performance, but the 402 is designed for air-taxi and air-freight markets. *Aft* of the pilot's compartment the cabin is 14.5 feet long, and

Cessna Model 401

there are seven seats back there to get operating costs down to best potential on a seat-mile basis.

When converted to cargo use (which takes about 10 minutes), the 402 can carry up to 1,790 pounds of freight. An optional side-hinged cargo door aft of the Air-Stair door facilitates freight handling; with both doors open, the fuselage opening is 45 inches high and 40 inches wide. The cargo door can be locked in a closed position while the Air-Stair door is used independently.

Aimed squarely at the air-taxi market is the 402's capability of minimizing overall point-to-point trip time. It can maintain a 180 mph final-approach speed to within 1.5 miles of the runway, for fast deceleration with flaps that can extend to 15 degrees at 180 mph and landing gear that can be extended at speeds up to 160 mph. The heavy-duty gear allows for high-speed taxiing, too, with minimum braking action as well as positive steering.

The 401/402 has a maximum speed of 261 mph, at 16,000 feet. Maximum range is 1,131 miles, traveling at 25,000 feet on 75 percent power at 215 mph on 140 gallons of fuel (standard capacity: 102 gallons). Rate of climb on both engines: 1,610 feet per minute; on one engine, 255 fpm. Service ceiling is 26,180 feet, or on one engine an 11,700-foot altitude. The 401/402 breaks ground in 1,695 feet and clears a 50-foot obstacle in a total of 2,220 feet; it lands over the same obstacle in 1,765 feet, including a ground roll of 777 feet.

The air-taxi business, incidently, is the fastest-growing segment of all general aviation.

Cessna 411
6,500 pounds gross weight

When the 411 was introduced in 1965 as Cessna's top-of-the-line product, the new design was thought to be as good as a 3,865-pound airplane could get. But 300 improvements have since been made. The latest models involved only such minor fussing as the relocation of map pockets, and even the competition admits that the 411 now really does make fullest use of the industry's most advanced technology.

The eight-seat turbocharged 411 climbs at 1,900 feet per minute to a 26,000-foot service ceiling and can cruise on 75 percent power at 246 mph for 1,000 miles on its 175-gallon fuel capacity. Basic price is $113,950, and official designation is now 411-A.

About the only way to make an airplane like that appreciably better is to pressurize the cabin. Those little round windows on the 411 were the tip-off, and it now turns out that pressurization was what those cagey fellows in Wichita had in mind all along. The pressurized version of the 411, called the model 421, was introduced in mid-1967 as Cessna's "ultimate twin." It is the eighth plane in Cessna's line of twins, and the fourth developed in a single year to represent the company's heavy penetration of the corporate-twin market. Building in plans for the 421 made the basic 411 just that much better than it really had to be.

The 411 is indeed a pretty posh airplane. Up in captain country, the panel can utilize full dual instrumentation with everything up to and including latest weather radar equipment. Cessna's new white lighting is illuminating in more ways than one.

One of the problems on the early 411 was ice at high altitudes, which is nicely minimized on the 411-A with new props and spinners. Heated vents for the tip tanks and spring-loaded auxiliary vents facilitate high operations as well. A sliding curtain provides privacy for (or from) the crew.

The 411-A is powered by 340 hp Continental GTSIO-520-C engines, and the turbocharging system is automatic. All-weather ignition is a real revelation for pilots who have cursed balky-starting fuel-injection systems in the past. The propeller is a big-bite 90-inch three-blade McCauley, and the useful load limit is 2,635 pounds.

Normal fuel consumption is charted at 34 gallons per hour, but the standard 175-gallon tanks can be implemented for a 258-gallon total capacity, for an optimum range of 1,500 miles. The 411-A can cruise on 46 percent power at 20,000 feet at 176 mph. Top speed is a blistering 268 mph, and stall speed is 84 mph. Service ceiling on one engine is 13,000 feet.

The 411-A takes off over a 50-foot obstacle in a total distance of 2,010 feet, including a 1,560-foot ground run. From a 50-foot altitude it lands in a total of 1,815 feet, including a ground roll of 1,240 feet.

Cutting down to six seats provides room in the passenger area for such luxuries as a refreshment center and a head behind an aft cabin divider. People who travel in this kind of style often take a lot of luggage, and the 411-A is planned accordingly: 350-pound luggage capacity in the nose, 120 pounds in each wing locker, and 340 pounds in the aft cabin compartment.

When you've got almost half a ton of luggage, you should be set to go almost anywhere.

Piper Turbo Navajo
6,500 pounds gross weight

See Piper Navajo.

Beech Duke (model 60)
6,725 pounds gross weight

Two years' future deliveries were sold out on the Duke before the first one got on the market in 1968. It is pressurized, powered, and priced to compete with Cessna 421. The Duke goes for $166,500 with turbocharged six-cylinder Lycoming TIO-541-E1A-4 engines rated at 380 hp each, but the addition of optional equipment beyond the standard avionics package has upped the actual delivered price to an average of $204,785 on the first few months' deliveries.

Empty weight of the six-seat twin is 4,100 pounds, including flight instruments, cabin heating and ventilating system with windshield defrosting, night-flying equipment, soundproofing, and provisions for air conditioning. Useful load is thus 2,625 pounds. Cruise speed on 79 percent power at 15,000 feet is 252 mph, or 278 mph at 25,000 feet. Stall speed, clean, is 98 mph, or 87 mph with gear and flaps down. Service ceiling is 31,300 feet, or 15,700 feet on one engine. With weight cut to 5,200 pounds,

Beech Model 60 Duke

the ceilings are 35,800 feet and 23,800 feet when rate of climb is 2,373 feet per minute (739 fpm on one engine).

The new Duke is royalty all the way.

Shrike Commander
6,750 pounds gross weight

Before Aero Commander renamed all its regularly powered planes after various birds, the Shrike was the model 500-U. It evolved from Ted Smith's 1944 design and today is rivaled for longevity only by the Beech Bonanza (now that the venerable Twin Beech has been phased out). The Shrike looks for all the world like a flying boat or at least an amphibian. But it is a standard corporate twin for a' that.

The big high-winger (4,350 pounds EW) is also one of the toughest planes on the market; FAA utility-category certification allows operation of the aircraft under extreme conditions, with maneuverability and gust loads up to 4.4 Gs and landings at a

Shrike Commander

descent rate of 15 feet per second. Even so, for a four-seat plane it costs a lot of pretty pennies: $99,950. This 1968 price is $5,000 more than the 1967 price and is about 10 percent over the price of the competition.

At that price and weight, the Shrike is more of a corporate than an executive plane in terms of definition. To substantiate this premise, the plane can be opted with various configurations all the way up to eight seats. This is a lot of people to cram into a cabin less than 11 feet long, but the useful weight *is* a big 2,400 pounds.

Passengers walk into a Shrike and sit down as if in a miniature airliner, and the pilot has a standard door all to himself. Because the rear windows are under the wing, where high-pressure eddies create a lot of drumming, the noise level can be pretty bad, but this is due to the original conception of the plane as a utility aircraft rather than primarily as a passenger ship.

The 290 hp six-cylinder IO-540-E1A5 fuel-injection engines climb at 1,450 feet per minute (340 fpm is the limit on one engine). Cruising speed on 70 percent power at 10,000 feet is a relatively slow 215 mph behind the three-blade Hartzell props.

The strutless wing stalls at 68 mph, with gear and flaps down. Service ceiling on one engine is 6,000 feet, or 17,500 feet on full power.

Optimum range with a 30-minute reserve is 1,230 miles, with a 156-gallon fuel capacity. Take-off and landing distances are 1,375 feet and 1,235 feet respectively over a 50-foot obstacle. Top speed is an eye-opening 288 mph.

That's a pretty fast foot for a workhorse.

Cessna 421
6,800 pounds gross weight

The $159,950 model 421 is the result of ten years of study and evaluation of pressurization systems and more than five years of pioneering in turbocharged engine power systems. The power system was guinea-pigged by the 411, but the pressurizing is all the 421's own. Marketing of the 421 started in late 1967, and the plane now has users on five continents.

The pressurization system operates off bleed air from the engines' exhaust-driven turbosystem units. Either engine operating on as low as 60 percent power can supply enough air for pressurization and ventilation, for "dual reliability." Cabin altitude pressures can be preselected by the pilot for maximal passenger comfort.

With an empty weight of 4,237 pounds, the 421 has useful load limit of 2,563 pounds. Maximum speed is 276 mph and cruise speed at 20,000 feet and 75 percent power is 255 mph. The model 421 takes off over a 50-foot barrier in 2,516 feet at sea level and climbs at 1,700 feet per minute. Landing distance over a 50-foot obstacle is 2,110 feet, with a landing weight of 6,500 pounds.

The pressure capsule is exceptionally quiet. Sound is muted with floor panels and fore and aft bulkheads of crushed aluminum honeycomb. Even the thick carpeting helps, as do the three-blade, low-rpm props.

The exhaust-driven turbines in the engines' turbosystem units enable the GTSIO-520-D to develop a full 375 hp each from sea

Cessna's pressurized Model 421

level to 16,000 feet. Service ceiling of the six-seater is 26,000 feet, or 13,340 feet on one engine. The standard fuel system consists of 50-gallon tanks in each of the canted wing tips, plus two 35-gallon wing auxiliary tanks for a total 170-gallon capacity. Maximum range is 1,174 miles. However, optional tanks in wing lockers can increase fuel capacity to 248 gallons, which ups maximum range to 1,710 miles.

The airline-type two-section Air-Stair is the same as the one that impresses the passenger so much on the model 401. The cabin interior is, of course, almost sybaritic in its appointments, starting with walnut partitions to close off the flight deck. Options include a cabin intercom and an eight-track stereo tape system, not to mention air conditioning.

All-weather systems include anti-icing options for wings, props, tail surfaces, and windshield. The 421 is designed to go anywhere, anytime.

Beagle B-206
7,500 pounds gross weight

This six- to eight- (!) seat plane weighs 4,567 pounds empty, with a long nose and a longer, skinny aft section of fuselage that makes it look smaller than it really is. The British aircraft industry apparently does not subscribe to the reputed policy of understatement, and ads as late as 1968 proclaim the B-206 as having the longest range, the largest aft-wing door, the biggest windows, and so on, of any six- to eight-seat plane going (check the specs and capabilities of a few planes like the Skyknight, 411, and Baron, chaps). The Beagle 206 is also declared to be "the best buy" in the six-to-eight–seat class, with a price of $106,000.

A-l-l-l rightie, let's see. A quick check shows that only planes in the Queen Air class and up cost more (except for the fabulous and turbocharged Cessna 411). Piper's Turbo Navajo and the Shrike Commander even cost less. The Beagle's engines are 310 hp (ha!), and it carries a useful load of 2,933 pounds . . . well, what do you know, it *does* carry more weight than anything smaller than a Courser Commander. Total take-off and landing distances over a 50-foot obstacle are 2,340 feet and 2,290 feet respectively—nothing to get excited about. Neither is the rate of climb at 1,100 feet per minute, the cruising speed of 195 mph, the service ceiling of 17,500 feet, or the maximum range of 1,475 miles on 195 *Imperial* gallons of gas (with *half* a payload).

Fuel capacity can be augmented to 235 gallons, and the Beagle can use it . . . normal consumption is 28 gallons per hour. Top speed is 225 mph, cruise on 75 percent power is 212 mph, and stall speed is 78 mph. The panoramic windshield is big all right, but in being so big that it would look more at home on a helicopter, it contributes to the Beagle's curious effect of looking smaller than it is. The panel really *is* big—54 inches wide—but some of its rather old-fashioned features seem more military than the Buck Rogers stuff seen on some of the Wichita products. A supercharged version, the Beagle B-206-S, is also on the market at $115,000. And that's not considered darts money.

The turboed Beagle has a 200-pound heavier empty weight,

340 hp GTSI0-520-C engines, three-blade feathering McCauley props, twin- and single-engine ceilings of 24,000 feet and 14,000 feet respectively, and a sea-level rate of climb of 1,340 feet per minute. Take-off to clear a 50-foot obstacle is 2,380 feet, including a 1,560-foot ground run; landing distance over a 50-foot obstacle is a 2,485-foot total, including a ground roll of 1,242 feet. Top speed is pretty good: 310 mph; and 65 percent cruise speed isn't bad either, at 290 mph. Normal fuel consumption is 34 gallons per hour, but maximum range with a full payload is only 500 miles.

But what's this? The Beagle 206 meets full airline standards of nav/com equipment and coupled auto-pilot. Okay, we're impressed. And the engines are made by Rolls-Royce! Well, we've *still* got the biggest door.

Beech Queen Air A-65
7,700 pounds gross weight

The model 65 was introduced in 1958 as the smallest of the big twins—the lightest-weight as well as the least expensive. It still is. Empty weight is 4,890 pounds, and the basic price is $133,500.

In the six-seat configuration most often used (the factory also installs seating arrangements to accommodate up to nine people), there are three compartments. The front office has a sliding door for privacy, the passengers can loll in anything from "conference type" facing lounge chairs to a full-length stretch-out couch in the salon, and the aft compartment is closed off for a lavatory and baggage section. Air conditioning is optional. The swept-back tail, new in 1968, makes the A-65 look more like the bigger and sleeker Queen Air B-80.

Supercharged 340 hp Lycoming IGS0-480-A1E6 engines provide the muscle for the shortest take-off distance over a 50-foot obstacle of any heavy twin in the corporate class: 1,560 feet, including a 1,180-foot ground run. Initial rate of climb from sea level is 1,300 feet per minute and the service ceiling is a gee-whiz

Beech Queen Air A-65

31,300 feet (or 15,500 feet operating on one engine). Useful load limit is 2,810 pounds.

Top speed is 239 mph, cruising speeds are 214 mph and 210 mph respectively for 75 percent and 65 percent power, and stall speed is 80 mph. The A-65 can carry 264 gallons of fuel for maximum range of 1,660 miles. Total landing distance over a 50-foot obstacle is 1,750 feet, including a 1,330-foot roll.

There's even a little window in the washroom.

Piaggio P-166C
7,708 pounds gross weight

When is a flying machine a production plane? As of 1968, only one Piaggio P-166C had been delivered. But the factory is ready and waiting for anybody else who wants to go to Italy with the money to buy the $168,000 plane.

Piaggio has a long and honorable history in the manufacture of military aircraft, as well as a working partnership with Douglas for the production of civilian jets for the corporate market (see

Piaggio-Douglas PD-808). The P-166C is a far and relatively weak cry from either.

It has two 380 hp Lycoming IGS0-540-A1C engines on a shoulder gull wing, and the 39-foot "full utilization" fuselage holds 13 seats. Empty weight is only 5,020 pounds, and useful load is 2,688 pounds. Best rate of climb from sea level is 1,415 feet per minute, and the service ceiling is 27,000 feet.

The fuel capacity is only 112 gallons, which limits the maximum range to 631 nautical miles even when carrying a gross weight trimmed to 6,950 pounds (1,000 pounds over the weight of gas and oil). That range is at a cruising speed of 168 knots per hour.

Although its general appearance resembles that of a stepped-on Shrike Commander, there's a considerable difference in performance. The Piaggio P-166C uses a total distance of 1,950 feet to take off over a 50-foot obstacle and 1,860 feet to land over the same obstruction. It's sure got one thing going for it, though: a man who is not too tall can stand up in it.

Courser Commander

8,500 pounds gross weight

The $159,950 Courser Commander uses the same high wing as the lower-priced Shrike Commander, but the fuselage is more than six feet longer. The Courser weighs 5,450 pounds empty and carries a useful load of 3,050 pounds, figuring on a crew of two with the standard three seats in the passenger compartment. This is with fabric upholstery; leather seats weigh 20 pounds more and cost another $550. A lavatory costs $1,100 and weighs 35 pounds.

Seating capacity aft of the crew's quarters can be increased all the way up to nine, for people who like to ride three abreast. Aviation seating does not come cheap. For example, the buyer who wants six leather seats in the passenger area instead of the standard three will have to come up with another $3,175 over the base price. Such a customer wouldn't have the expense of a lavatory, though, because it wouldn't fit.

The Courser Commander is powered by 380 hp Lycoming IGSO-540-B1A engines turning three-blade constant-speed Hartzell props. Initial rate of climb from sea level is 1,285 feet per minute (240 fpm on one engine). Twin service ceiling is 27,500 feet, or 11,500 feet with one engine out. Top speed is 288 mph, and maximum cruising speed on 70 percent power is 240 mph at 10,000 feet. Up at 16,000 feet, the cruising speed is 230 mph on 65 percent power or 210 mph on 55 percent. Optimum cruise range is 1,310 miles with a 30-minute reserve.

Stall speed with gear and flaps extended is 82 mph, and the minimum speed for single-engine control is 90 mph. Take-off and landing distances over a 50-foot obstacle are 1,560 feet and 1,360 feet respectively.

For $50,000 more, the Courser comes pressurized (same gross weight, but with an empty weight of 500 pounds more, for a maximum useful load limit of 2,800 pounds). The base price of $199,950 still does not cover any more than the three standard seats in the stateroom, but a pressurized Courser Commander is seldom seen with three-abreast seating except for the aftmost divan. Pressurization does not change any of the performance figures—just makes the passengers more comfortable at high altitudes by eliminating the cumbersome nose bags for oxygen. The plane is air conditioned not just in flight but on the ground as well.

Some guy from Madison Avenue must have gotten to Aero Commander's marketing division, because they sure picked some of the damnedest names for the planes. All the Commanders were renamed for birds, and a "courser" is a running bird of the ostrich family. A "shrike" is even worse: sometimes known as the butcher bird, he is a nasty specimen who preys on small birds and impales them on thorns to eat them conveniently. A "darter" is a bird that flits around erratically, and a "lark" spends most of his time singing and has limited flying ability. It sounds like something from *Mad* magazine.

Beech Queen Air B-80
8,800 pounds gross weight

A revamped edition of the Queen Air A-65, the model B-80 is a heavier, faster, and costlier six-seater in the corporate configuration or an eleven-place commuter for the air-taxi trade. Empty weight is 5,120 pounds, top speed is 248 mph, and it costs $193,000.

But as a profit maker it can be well worth it. It carries a 27.5 percent bigger useful payload: 3,680 pounds.

The supercharged 380 hp Lycoming IGSO-540-A1D engines have a service ceiling of 26,800 feet (14,500 feet on one engine). Full-feathering three-blade Hartzell props are standard. Best initial rate of climb at sea level is 1,275 feet per minute. The Queen Air B-80 cruises at 229 mph on 70 percent power, or at 222 mph on 65 percent power, for a range of 1,300 miles on 264 gallons of fuel.

Beech Queen Air Model B-80

Endurance at 5,000 feet has been achieved on 32 percent power for 14.3 hours. Total take-off distance over a 50-foot obstacle is 1,800 feet, including a 1,370-foot ground run. Landing over the same obstacle, total distance is 2,310 feet, 1,340-foot ground roll included.

In order to give the B-80 a sleeker look to go along with its improved performance, the swept-back vertical tail section distinguished the B-80 until 1968, when "the new look" was also passed on down to the smaller A-65. Even the little rear peek-a-boo window is a look-alike on the latest models.

When an airplane gets up around the $200,000 mark, the manufacturers can afford to use the best of everything in what are relatively minor cost items such as appointments. The model B-80 skimps on nothing; even the dividers for the fancy little aft lavatory are glossy hardwood finishes. A B-80 is as good as a piston plane can be made without pressurizing.

Beech Queen Air 88
8,800 pounds gross weight

Pressurization and a complete panel of avionics get the price of the Queen Air 88 up to $259,500—the highest list price of any piston-engine aircraft being built for the general aviation market today. Its gross weight is the same as that of the Queen Air B 80, but with the empty weight up to 6,000 pounds, useful load of the model 88 is cut to 2,800 pounds. Seating options are for seven to nine people.

The maskless Queen Air 88 isn't quite as fast as its sister ship, either, and corresponding performance characteristics are cut accordingly. Top speed of the 88 is 246 mph, cruising speed on 75 percent power is 221 mph, and a 65 percent setting delivers a speed of 217 mph. Stall speed is the same 82 mph. Best climb rates are also the same, as are the service ceilings and the distances for take-off and landing. Maximum range, though, is cut to 1,270 miles.

However, that range is enough to fly nonstop—between meals—from Charleston to Cheyenne or from St. Louis to Spokane. Loafing along on a 65 percent power setting at 217 mph at a 17,000-foot altitude, the Queen Air 88 can beat many airline times between smaller cities when ground travel is considered— and between many metropolitan areas as well, considering the kinds of airports the 88 can use.

Anti-icing equipment and air conditioning are standard. For a quarter of a million dollars, Beech can afford to put in everything *including* a "kitchen" sink. There's even a safety belt in the john.

Piper PA-35

9,000 pounds gross weight

Third-level airlines are mushrooming so fast that even Piper couldn't resist getting into this lush market. PA-35 is the biggest plane Piper has ever attempted, an 18-passenger commuter airliner powered by two 470 hp Lycoming T10-720 turbocharged engines. The fat little plane (39 feet long with a 16-foot height) is also the first totally new airframe specifically designed for third-level operators.

Government regulations limit such aircraft to 20 seats and 4,000 to 5,000 pounds of useful load within the gross-weight category of 12,500 pounds or less. The PA-35 is getting pretty close, with a useful load of 4,100 pounds and a 4,900-pound empty weight.

Top speed is 242 mph at 10,000 feet. Cruise speed on 75 percent power at 10,000 feet is 216 mph, or 230 mph at 17,000 feet. Rate of climb is 1,630 feet per minute, stall speed is 74 mph, and single-engine ceiling is 14,000 feet. Range on 75 percent power is 650 miles, and 810 miles on 55 percent power. Standard fuel capacity is 200 gallons. General performance is similar to that of the Aztec C, including short-field capabilities and handling.

The cabin area totals 530 cubic feet, and there's another 100 cubic feet in luggage compartments. Are you *sure* that this is the great grandson of the Piper Cub?

Beech Super 18, Ol' Twin Beech

Beech Super 18

9,900 pounds gross weight

Here's one that's really going to be missed.

There are a lot of Beech airplanes with two engines, but there is only one "Twin Beech" as far as most airport personnel are concerned: the model 18. The dual-tail twin, with a separate vertical tail surface behind each engine, has been in continuous production since 1937 and is probably the most-flown airframe in the world. The refined version, the Super 18, was introduced in 1954 and has been in a class by itself as a corporate workhorse ever since.

Some horse! The latest Super 18 is powered by 450 hp Pratt & Whitney R-985-AN-14B engines, for a power package unsurpassed in the piston-engine field. Empty weight is 5,680 pounds, and the Super 18 carries a useful load of 4,220 pounds—more than any other piston plane regardless of size or turbocharging.

It can carry up to 11 people (rarely) and has one-stop coast-to-coast range with a 318-gallon fuel capacity.

Base price on the last Super 18 is $179,500. But it also has a top speed of 236 mph and cruises at 220 mph on 65 percent power. Total take-off distance over a 50-foot obstacle is 2,070 feet, and the service ceiling is 20,300 feet (11,500 feet on one engine). Stall speed is 87 mph and total landing distance over a 50-foot obstacle is 1,850 feet.

Unfortunately, the venerable Twin Beech is being phased out as of 1968. It is simply too old-fashioned to compete with more sophisticated rivals in today's aviation market. But this is the airplane that established Beech Aircraft firmly in the general aviation market, more than any other design.

Walter Beech couldn't have asked for a better monument.

BEST OF CLASS

(Standards)

LEAST EMPTY WEIGHT—Sud 360-6 Jupiter: 3,042 lbs.

MOST SEATS (PRODUCTION)—Beech Queen Air B-80: 11

BIGGEST USEFUL LOAD—Beech Super 18: 4,220 lbs.

BEST LIFT RATIO—Beech Super 18: 4,220 lbs., compared to 5,680 lbs. EW

BIGGEST ENGINES (STANDARD)—Beech Super 18: 450 hp Pratt & Whitney R-985s

SERVICE CEILING—Beech Queen Air A-65: 31,300 ft.; on one engine—Cessna Skyknight 320: 18,800 ft.

SHORT-FIELD CAPABILITIES—BN-2A Islander, best in all categories: take-off run, 680 ft.; total take-off distance to clear 50-ft. obstacle, 900 ft.; total landing distance over 50-ft. obstacle, 1,000 ft.; landing roll, 500 ft.

BEST SEA-LEVEL RATE OF CLIMB—Aerostar 600: 1,950 fpm

AIRSPEED: TOP—Shrike Commander: 288 mph; at 75 percent power —Aerostar 600: 270 mph; at 65 percent power—Cessna Skyknight 320: 260 mph; at stall—BN-2A Islander: 49 mph

RANGE (AUGMENTED)—Cessna 421: 1,710 miles

LOWEST PRICE—BN-2A Islander: $62,000

CHAPTER 8

Turboprops

The aviation industry has been "revolution-ized" many times. One of the very few real revolutions, though, was the development of the turbine engine. In exactly the same way that the diesel engine virtually replaced steam engines for the railroads almost overnight, turbine engines have replaced piston engines in heavy-duty, prop-driven aircraft.

The standard reciprocal piston engine is one of the most inefficient contraptions ever conceived. Each of the cylinders has to do four separate jobs at a time: compress the gas mixture, sleeve back at explosion for the actual power stroke, pump in to exhaust the dregs, and then draw in more fuel. A single-cylinder engine would shake itself to pieces in no time, and the multiplicity of cylinders is simply an effort to cut down vibration by spreading it out on a reciprocal basis.

This entire Rube Goldberg process necessarily has to be controlled by critically adjusted distributors for firing sequence, an involved crankshaft that even looks incredible, and a whole system of checks and balances that can be ignored by the turbine powerplant.

A turbine engine utilizes one of mankind's earliest forms of power: wind. Except that it is a windmill that creates its own wind, it is only a little more complicated than the grist mills that dot the Netherlands. In effect, the turbine engine could almost be compared to a tornado in a metal box.

It contains only one-fifth the number of parts in a conventional piston engine. Horsepower for horsepower, it consequently weighs only about half as much as a piston engine—a tremendously important factor in an airplane. There are no pistons, no carburetor or distributor, no crankshaft.

There is only one spark plug, which fires only once: when the engine is started up; the turbine engine keeps burning like a plumber's blowtorch once it's lit. "Standard" tune-ups, stock service, and the constant fiddling-type maintenance the piston engine requires are not needed for the turbine. Basically, the only moving part in a turbine engine is a simple straight shaft spinning on plain sleeve bearings.

A piston engine requires one whale of a lot of designing, machining, milling, fitting, assembling, and just plain work that are totally unnecessary in building turbine engines. The same applies to service, where the piston mechanic often has to be pretty much of an engineer in his own right. The mighty lighter-weight, simpler-to-build, and easier-to-maintain turbine engine has still one more plus factor: it's vibrationless.

Ah, then why don't *all* airplanes use turbine engines? The answer, in a word: cost. A turbine engine is little more than a jet engine with a "windmill" in the jet stream—and jet engines can each cost half a million dollars and more, primarily because the heat that is generated demands such sophisticated metallurgy.

With the turbine wheel spinning at supersonic speeds, the resulting temperatures would melt ordinary steel in minutes. Until the industry finds a way to mass-produce them, without the use of precious metals, turbine engines are priced off the market for light aircraft.

Note to Casual Readers: A turbine engine is a far cry from the "turbocharged engines" discussed in the previous chapters. Turbocharging (also known as supercharging) is simply used on ordinary piston engines to maintain manifold pressures at high altitudes to the same air pressures as at sea level, where a piston engine works best. A turbocharged engine can thus take advantage of high-altitude flight, where the blower enables the air-breathing aircraft to fly above foul weather. Turbocharging is merely an *addition* to piston engines, whereas the turbine engine itself is a completely different breed of animal.

Burns BA-42-T

4,800 pounds gross weight

Only the addition of a "T" to the stock number of Burns' pressurized twin designates this little shrimp of a turboprop for what it is. The BA-42-T costs a flat $60,000 more than the piston-engine version, although with a price tag of $149,950 it is still less than half the price of any other turboprop on the market.

But with an empty weight of only 2,400 pounds, it is also by far and away the lightest-weight turboprop going. This helps give it the best rate of climb in its class: 3,000 feet per minute from sea level. Not surprisingly, the fuel consumption is only 50 gallons per hour, not to mention a short take-off distance over a 50-foot obstacle: 1,400 feet, including a 1,000-foot ground run.

With an empty weight of 300 pounds less than its piston sister's, the six-seat "Model T" increases its useful load to 2,400 pounds, and the service ceiling is 30,000 feet (15,000 feet on one engine). Stall speed is a relatively comfortable 82 mph.

Top speed is 310 mph at 18,000 feet, where its maximum cruising speed is still close to 300 mph. Optimum cruising speed is 280 mph at 20,000 feet, where range is 1,200 miles with the 170-gallon fuel capacity, figuring on a 45-minute reserve. Coming down over a 50-foot obstacle, the Burns lands in 1,500 feet, including a 1,000-foot ground roll. This powerful little runt handles almost like a fighter plane; only good pilots need apply.

Mooney MU-2
8,930 pounds gross weight

This is the airplane that caused all the confusion about the name "Mooney" being synonymous with "Made in Japan." Mooney does, of course, build most of its own aircraft in Texas, although the MU-2 is Japanese designed and built. However, not by any newcomer to aviation; Mitsubishi Heavy Industries, Ltd., has been building airplanes since 1920, including the Zero fighter and Betty bomber of World War II. The company has since been licensed to build the North American F-86 Sabrejets, the Sikorsky S-61, S-62, and SH-3A helicopters, and the Lockheed F-104 Starfighters.

Mooney Aircraft, Inc., which is marketing the MU-2 in the United States along with its own growing line of private planes, assembles and equips the MU-2 at its new San Angelo facilities. When the deal was announced in 1965, the price of the MU-2 was heralded as $260,000, but within a year the turboprop was "improved" to the point where the price went up $100,000 more . . . which has since been cut in half for a 1968 price of $311,850. Did somebody's original pencil slip?

The six-seat MU-2 now has two 605 shaft-horsepower (s-hp) Garrett-AiResearch TPE331 turbine engines. Unlike many monkeyed-with turboprops, the MU-2 airframe was designed *for* turbine power. Empty weight is 5,430 pounds, as against a 3,500-pound useful load limit. Rate of climb at sea level is 1,860 feet per minute and the service ceiling is 26,500 feet, or 12,500 feet on one engine.

Over 50-foot obstacles, the MU-2 takes off and lands in 1,500 feet and 1,100 feet respectively. This beats any other turboprop in its class for short-field capability. The MU-2 also has the slowest stall speed of any of the turboprops: 74 mph. Top speed is rated at 325 mph. Best cruising speed, 310 mph, is at 10,000-foot altitudes. At 20,000 feet, the range is 1,200 miles, using 57 gallons per hour from the 295-gallon usable fuel capacity.

MU-2 salesmen like to say that the blatter can fly seven

Mooney's Turbo-Prop MU-2

people, but even six are crowded. The cabin is actually the smallest in its class, with the entire cabin behind the pilot's partition only six feet long.

Norman Hoffman, Mooney's vice-president in charge of marketing, expects to sell 1,000 MU-2s in the next 10 years. Rots of ruck, Normansan!

Beech King Air A-90
9,300 pounds gross weight

At $442,000, the King Air costs $182,500 more than the look-alike Queen Air 88. But that resemblance is strictly superficial. With an empty weight that is well under the weight of the piston version, the King Air (EW 5,600 pounds) can carry a useful load of 3,700 pounds, compared to 2,800 pounds for the Queen Air 88. The King Air carries 384 gallons of fuel for a maximum range of well over 1,450 miles, with six to ten passengers in the various optional configurations.

The A-90 is powered by a couple of 550 s-hp Pratt & Whitney turbine engines, which give it a service ceiling of 27,200 feet (17,700 feet on one engine). It also requires the shortest take-off run to lift-off of any of the big turboprops: 1,010 feet. Total take-off distance over a 50-foot obstacle is only 1,200 feet. The landing distance over a 50-foot obstacle is an unassisted 2,050 feet, but this can be improved to 1,680 feet with reverse props, including a 775-foot ground roll.

Speeds to 280 mph are possible in the fully pressurized King Air, but maximum cruising speed is 256 mph. Optimum cruising speed is 231 mph. With flaps down, stalling speed is 88 mph.

As in all Beech products, the appointments in the King Air are excellent—and at prices like these, Beech can afford not to skimp. The interiors are custom-designed for each individual buyer, with all the leather, paneling, and hide from that elusive Nauga that anybody could reasonably desire. Large and/or re-clining chairs, work tables that fold out of the way, refreshment centers, and enough closets to challenge Mother Hubbard can be included in the various seating plans. All-weather electronics, oxygen, and air conditioning are part of the King Air pressuriza-tion package covered by the price.

The crew is supposed to stay where it belongs, and privacy for executive conferences is assured by folding doors between the passenger cabin and the pilot compartment. When a company plane gets up into this bracket, it is no longer a fly-it-your-self aircraft . . . you get hired help to fly it. The King Air is Beech's royal top of the line as far as hard-working executives are concerned.

Turbo II Commander
9,450 pounds gross weight

The Aero Commander divisions keep improving their prod-ucts steadily, and the Turbo Commander is an outstanding example of the policy that proclaims "specs subject to change without notice." The most recent changes have been an increase in empty weight to 5,783 pounds at the sacrifice of some of the short-field characteristics but with a compensating gain in speed and comfort.

The Turbo Commander is now the only plane in the family that's not named after some bird. It is also now the only pres-surized twin in its class providing dual pressurizing reliability, with a system that functions on either or both of the 575 s-hp Garrett-AiResearch TPE331 engines. Current price is $335,000.

The Turbo Commander is built with various passenger configurations accommodating from five to ten people, including the pilot. Built for a newly classified 9,450-pound gross weight, it handles a useful load of 3,667 pounds with ease. Service ceiling is now 25,000 feet, or 11,000 feet on one turbine.

When it is fully loaded, the take-off distance to a 50-foot altitude is 1,975 feet, and it climbs at 2,025 feet per minute with 10-degree flaps at sea level. Top speed is 280 mph at 10,000 feet, and maximum cruising speed is still the same at 15,000 feet. Optimum cruising speed, at 20,000 feet, is a zippy 270 mph.

From a 20,000-foot altitude, the T2-C requires about 90 statute miles for the let-down, and it lands over a 50-foot obstacle in 2,460 feet. Stall speed, with full weight in a standard landing configuration, is 94 mph with power at zero thrust. Fuel

Turbo II Commander

load with maximum payload is 1,360 pounds. Range with the whole 287 gallons of fuel capacity (figuring a 45-minute reserve) is 1,050 miles, at optimum cruising speed using 60 gallons of fuel per hour of flight.

Aero engineers of today are bugged on passenger comfort to a degree that Ted Smith never was. The high-wing T2-C design provides not only exceptional stability along with the panoramic scenery, but ease of entry and exit, too; a single step at low level makes boarding as easy as entering an automobile. Without ladders to climb on or wings to crawl over, the only complaints come from the hanger-side miniskirt watchers. The 50-cubic foot baggage compartment is also at a handy knee-high level, where the 19 by 30–inch door minimizes rat-holing.

The cabin in this model is so well soundproofed that the already-quiet engines are barely audible in flight. A doored flight deck helps make a veritable salon of the cabin, where the floor is completely flat, wall to wall, for easy mobility.

From the first-flight celebration on New Year's Day 1966 to the time of writing, well over 400 T2-Cs have been ordered by an elite of corporate buyers.

Swearingen Merlin II-A
9,800 pounds gross weight

A few years ago, some of the backers of this San Antonio company had been disappointed in the public's acceptance of Swearingen's product. For one thing, the manufacturer's image had been clouded by a lot of activity with conversions, with research and development work for other manufacturers, and so on. But the Merlin II represents a roll of the dice at the big table, with a $380,000 entry in the turboprop field. The first Merlin was delivered in late 1966, and, happily, 18 were sold during 1967. The Texas plant is now building four a month.

The eight-seat Merlin II is powered by 550 s-hp Pratt & Whitney PT6A-20 engines, and the dual-bleed air-pressurization system operates from either or both. The empty operating weight is 6,525 pounds, and useful weight is now 3,275 pounds, a ratio

Merlin II-A from Swearingen

that became newly possible with a 1967 increase in certified gross weight of an additional 500 pounds. Passenger compartment in the roomy Merlin is the biggest of any plane designed primarily for corporate use (almost twice as long, for example, as the cabin in the Mooney MU-2).

Service ceiling is 28,750 feet, or 12,600 feet with one engine out. Take-off and landing distances are both 2,400 feet over a 50-foot obstacle, with a stall speed of 86 mph. Rate of climb at sea level is 1,950 feet per minute on full power, or 420 fpm on one engine.

With 385-gallon fuel capacity, optimum range is 1,700 miles. Range at gross weight: 975 miles. Cruise speed at 17,000 feet, using 67 gallons per hour, is 270 mph, and at 17,500 feet the cruise speed is 250 mph using only 48 gallons per hour.

Merlin was a magician, wasn't he?

NOTE: Up to this point, prime consideration has been given to "small" aircraft designed mostly for recreational and/or (especially in the case of turboprops) business use. The planes covered in the balance of this chapter, however, are "big" airplanes that can and have been used in commercial transport, from air-taxi and third-level feeder airlines to regularly scheduled service by the majors.

Plenty of the smaller planes previously discussed *are* used steadily in commercial service. And any number of the "big" planes are operated strictly for private use, up to and including corporate configurations of Convairs and FH-227s. But the arbitrary dividing line is the 12,500-pound gross weight point, where the FAA says a plane has to meet the same type of operational and safety standards required of the giants used by the scheduled airlines.

Here again, exceptions prove the rule that sensible classification has to go according to actual use of the intended design. The Beech King Air's gross weight until 1967, for example, was better than 3,000 pounds over the FAA's 12,500-pound line of demarcation, although it is designed to handle at best six passengers.

So to start with (not that it will make the rules any more clear), let's begin the rest of this chapter with a plane with a gross weight well *under* the FAA's magic number.

Beech 99 Airliner
10,200 pounds gross weight

Not even bothering to develop a corporate configuration, the model 99 is Beech's bid for the commuter and local-service airlines market. Designed as a 17-passenger money maker, it has an empty operating weight (with all-weather IFR equipment) of only 5,875 pounds, even allowing 200 pounds for the pilot and his lunch bucket. At lift-off, this gives model 99 a useful load of 4,325 pounds for passengers and/or cargo as well as gas and oil.

Carrying capability is excellent on a ton-miles per hour basis, where it even outperforms the famous DC-3 by 24 percent. Based on a revenue of 12 cents per seat-mile, a model 99 flying 1,500 hours a year will make money every time it carries more than *two* passengers.

Reversible three-blade Hartzell aluminum alloy props enable the model 99 to land over a 50-foot obstacle in 1,800 feet, so it

17-place Beech 99

can use short airstrips at small (high-profit) airports. The low-maintenance 550 s-hp Pratt & Whitney engines can run on anything from kerosene to greasy kid stuff.

With 374 gallons of fuel, the model 99 can carry 16 passengers, the pilot, and 480 pounds of baggage 375 miles at a block speed of 250 mph at 10,000 feet, with a 45-minute reserve. At sea level it climbs at 1,910 feet per minute on full power, and the service ceiling is 25,000 feet. On one engine, climb rate is 450 fpm and the service ceiling is 10,000 feet. Normal take-off distance with 30-degree flaps is 2,025 feet.

Sounds good? THERE AIN'T NO PRESSURIZATION!

Handley Page Jetstream
12,250 pounds gross weight

Modesty is not one of the failings of Handley Page, Ltd., of Hertfordshire, England. They claim, quote, "the Jetstream is the biggest, fastest, most versatile aircraft in the under 12,500-lb. category, operating with ease from the shortest airstrips anywhere in the world. Add to all this its amazingly low cost and you have the world's most eligible business aircraft."

The "amazingly low cost" is $480,000 . . . less avionics, interior, and even final painting. The United States market has apparently not yet grasped the significance of these claims, and the Jetstream is still being outsold by practically all its serious competitors.

Not to mention being outperformed.

Empty weight of the Handley Page turboprop is 7,800 pounds, and adding a useful load of 4,700 pounds brings the rated gross weight to within a scant 250 pounds of the FAA limitation where an airplane can get away with not conforming to the same standards that have to be met by the airlines. This can save a lot of money, even if it doesn't do much for the passengers' peace of mind.

There's no doubt about its being big, though. The pressurized turboprop can seat up to 18 people in a cabin almost 24 feet long behind the flight deck. More realistically, however, it seats 8 in an air-conditioned corporate configuration. The Jetstream sports two whopping big 850 equivalent-shaft horsepower (es-hp)

Handley Page Jetstream

Turbomeca Astazou XIV engines and has reverse props with 99-inch three-bladers. Company spokesmen do not like the term "turboprop" and would rather have one refer to the Jetstream as a "prop-jet aircraft."

Service ceiling is 30,000 feet, or 14,200 feet on one engine. Rate of climb from sea level is 2,100 feet per minute. On take-off and landing, total distances over a 50-foot obstacle are admitted to be 2,660 feet and 2,480 feet respectively. Ground run is 1,925 feet, and roll coming down is 1,555 feet. Stall speed is 85 mph.

Maximum cruising speed is 305 mph, and optimum cruise speed is 240 mph. With maximum fuel capacity of 456 gallons, range is an impressive 2,100 miles. But with maximum payload, range is 350 miles.

That won't get you far in Texas, Jeeves!

Potez 841-B
19,620 pounds gross weight

This baby's got *four* turbine engines on it and weighs in at 11,950 pounds empty. It has a useful load limit of 7,670 pounds and can carry up to 24 passengers plus a crew of two.

The 841-B uses 495 s-hp Pratt & Whitney PT6-A-20 engines, and the same basic model is also built as the 842-B with four 630 s-hp Turbomeca Astazou XII engines. The planes are in production at Toulouse and at—of all places—Baldonnel, Ireland.

The 841-B has a maximum sea-level rate of climb at 1,810 feet per minute. Take-off distance to a 50-foot altitude is 1,970 feet, and the service ceiling is 25,000 feet. "Economical" cruise speed is 280 mph with a range of 1,990 miles using 5,270 pounds of fuel. Total landing distance over a 50-foot obstacle is 1,640 feet.

Inasmuch as the total number of deliveries of this plane can be counted on one hand (with fingers left over), prices are still by negotiation.

Nord 262
22,930 pounds gross weight

This is another "in-between" plane, aimed at a slot in the aircraft market above commuter-type planes and below the really heavy ships used by scheduled airlines. In short, it is a transport designed for small airline operations. However, just so they make sure that they're not missing out on anything, the French manufacturers also offer the Nord in a corporate configuration.

The 262 seats up to 29 people in a 35-foot-long pressurized cabin. Empty weight is 13,500 pounds, and useful weight is 9,430 pounds at take-off. The engines are 1,065 es-hp Turbomeca Bastan 6-C turbines driving Ratier-Figeac three-blade feathering props.

The United States selling price sounds as if it were figured by an accountant strictly by mathematical mark-up over costs, with little regard for the niceties of rounding off the figures: its tag reads $456,715. But that's how the translation from francs comes out.

The Nord takes off over a 35-foot French obstacle (fewer high-rise apartment buildings over there) in 2,640 feet and climbs from sea level at 1,500 feet per minute. Service ceiling is 19,800 feet, or 12,000 feet with one of the engines inoperative.

With 2,130 hp going for it, the model 262 has only one operational airspeed: 247 mph, which is the same for top speed, maximum cruising speed, and optimum cruising speed at specific altitudes. Stall speed is 81 mph, which is pretty good for a plane this big, and it lands over a 35-foot obstacle in a total of 1,275 feet. The thirsty plane uses 120 gallons of fuel per hour from the 685-gallon capacity, and its range is 1,260 miles figured with either maximum fuel or maximum payload behind those big turbo engines.

Intermediate cargo carriers, who have long had to make do with stretched-out corporate airplanes or scaled-down versions of some larger existing transport, will appreciate the offerings of the Nord 262 in particular.

Grumman Gulfstream I
36,000 pounds gross weight

This is the Rolls-Royce of American turboprops with a price to match: $1,119,000 per copy. Almost 200 were delivered in the 10 years following the Gulfstream I's first flight, in 1958.

The powerplant consists of twin Rolls-Royce Dart Mark 529-8X engines, which each provide a take-off rating of 2,210 es-hp. The passenger configurations range from the mouth-watering luxury of 8 to a maximum of 26 people, including a crew of 2. An enclosed lavatory with hot and cold water, as well as a fully equipped galley, are usually included in the interior planning. The 32-foot cabin has walk-around headroom for a six-footer.

The empty weight of 21,775 pounds includes almost 3,000 pounds of customizing and avionics. In typical figuring, another 840 pounds is allowed for the weight of the crew, their luggage, wash water and lavatory supplies, galley and bar provisions, and so on. This brings the basic operating weight to 22,615 pounds.

Allowing about 1.5 tons for payload (passengers, plus luggage or cargo), this leaves enough of the allowable useful weight for almost 2,000 gallons of fuel, for a big maximum range of over 3,000 miles.

Service ceiling is over 30,000 feet on full power, or 14,000 feet on one of the engines. Maximum rate of climb is 1,900 feet per minute. Taking off fully loaded over a 35-foot obstacle, total distance is 4,725 feet. Total trip-end landing distance over the same obstacle is 2,740 feet, including a ground roll of 2,140 feet. Stall: 99 mph.

Top recommended speed is 357 mph—although she'll do considerably better. Maximum cruise and optimum cruise are the same 357 mph. Fuel consumption is at the rate of 195 gallons per hour.

Grumman makes a lot of its safety features, and rightly so. The Gulfstream was designed in strict accordance with fail-safe philosophy, which means extra safety precautions in all possible

Grumman Gulfstream I

areas. For example, the auxiliary gas-turbine power unit in the tail has a fire-detection device and its own fire-extinguishing system. There's an overhead escape hatch in the passenger compartment, in addition to seven other exits. In the event of an unmentionable, a gear-up landing can be made on the retracted wheels without the fuselage touching the ground.

These and many other cross-checks reflect Grumman's long experience in building airplanes—more than 25,000 of them. And none of them cheap.

Fairchild Hiller F-27J
42,000 pounds gross weight

The F-27 is somewhat like a truck driver masquerading in a tuxedo. It's a good airplane, but it was primarily designed for airline operations rather than for its advertised corporate use. In a transport configuration, it seats up to 48 people. FH is pushing it as a private plane for the pure and simple reason that there are a lot more corporations than there are airlines.

Fairchild Hiller F-27J

Even so, there are fewer than four dozen companies who have found a need for the private airliner, whereas almost 300 F-27s are used by airlines around the world.

Since the F-27 was certified by the FAA in 1958, the gross weight has been increased steadily to its present 42,000 pounds. Of this, 15,500 pounds is useful load, with an empty weight of 26,500 pounds. The ship is powered by two 2,250 es-hp Rolls-Royce Dart Mark 532-7 engines, either of which can function efficiently at 11,400 feet on its own. With both on, service ceiling is 25,000 feet.

Take-off distance to clear a 35-foot obstacle is over a mile, and the F-27 also likes a good half-mile of hard-surface runway for a landing. Maximum rate of climb is 2,380 feet per minute. Top speed is 324 mph; stall speed, 89 mph. Using 194 gallons of gas per hour from its 1,365-gallon fuel capacity, the F-27 has a range of 1,720 miles at optimum cruising speed of 294 mph.

The price is $1,145,000, less electronics and interior. But with a cabin more than 47 feet long, it's like having a private railroad car of your own on wings.

Fairchild Hiller 227-B
45,500 pounds gross weight

This new (since 1966) version of the F-27 concept is the biggest and most expensive corporate turboprop on the market (except for revamping an out-and-out airliner). It costs $1,295,-000 and in a pinch it can accommodate 52 seats, although about a dozen is more usual.

The same Rolls-Royce engines are used on the 227-B as on the F-27 (see above), and fuel capacity, speeds, and service ceilings are identical, too. But with a 95-foot wing span and 83 feet in length, it needs 5,650 feet to take off over a 35-foot obstacle. Gulping close to 200 gallons of fuel an hour, it has a range cut to about 1,480 miles.

The 227-B has a 45,550-pound gross weight, or 29,000 pounds empty (2,500 pounds more than its sister ship), but it carries a useful load of a "mere" 16,500 pounds (only 1,000 pounds more than the F-27).

Manufactured under Fokker license at the Hagerstown, Maryland, plant, over 100 have already been ordered. Naturally, mostly by small airlines.

Convair 600
46,800 pounds gross weight

Anybody who is willing to supply the airframe of a regular Convair can have General Dynamics build a corporate conversion for a half-million-dollar fee.

For a start, they replace the piston engines with a pair of 3,025 es-hp Rolls-Royce Dart 10 engines, which drive 13-foot, four-blade hydraulically operated and electrically controlled variable-pitch propellers. The air-conditioned and pressurized flying office also gets an auxiliary gas-turbine unit to provide engine-starting power, to allow the 600 to operate from airfields any-

Convair 600

where. The self-sufficient, radar-equipped model 600 also has hydraulic stairways, including the one that goes up under the tail. The sofas scattered around can be made up into beds.

Empty weight is 30,500 pounds, and useful load limit is 16,300 pounds. Sea-level rate of climb is 1,400 feet per minute, and full-power service ceiling is 20,000 feet (10,500 feet on one engine). Take-off and landing distances over a 35-foot obstacle are 4,520 feet and 4,020 feet respectively.

With its power, the Convair 600's top, maximum cruise, and optimum cruise speeds are all the same: 318 mph at appropriate altitudes. Stall speed is 94 mph. The plane gets a range of 1,530 miles on its maximum fuel capacity of 1,000 gallons, or 350 miles with maximum payload. It burns 305 gallons of fuel per hour.

It's about as high class as executive riding can get for anybody who can't afford a jet of his own.

Convair 640
55,000 pounds gross weight

This is General Dynamics' version of the "light commercial" conversion of the Convair, on the same principle as the Convair 600. Price for the revamp job, with the customer supplying the airframe, is also the same half-million dollars.

Although GD does build an all-cargo version of the 640 that can carry more than 18,500 pounds of payload for short-haul operations, the most popular configuration is one called the Super Metropolitan, with 56 seats. The operator who is willing to give the passengers another 5 inches of leg room can still pack in 44 customers.

Although the empty weight of model 640 is 3,150 pounds less than model 600, the gross weight is 8,200 pounds more, which gives the 640 a total useful load of 27,650 pounds. Only the stall speed is the same for both.

Rate of climb from sea level is 1,150 feet per minute and full-power service ceiling is 23,000 feet (8,500 feet on one engine). Take-off and landing distances over a 35-foot obstacle are 5,130 feet and 4,380 feet respectively. The 640 has a 1,730-gallon fuel capacity, operational airspeeds are 6 mph slower than on the 600, and using the same rate of fuel the 640 has a 1,230-mile range on maximum fuel or 850 miles with a maximum payload.

Even some 640s are used privately. When used by companies for their own operations, though, the owners treat them like airliners, complete with well-planned schedules, reservations, and flight manifests that duplicate airline operations.

And All the Other "Brand" Names . . .

Almost any list of turboprop aircraft will have a lot of names on it that are relatively unknown to the general public. This is because the turboprop market, more than any other branch of the industry, is particularly attractive to small companies that specialize in conversions (see Chapter 10). Few such lists are ever the same twice.

The performance of just about any plane can be improved by modifying it for special purposes—for example, putting in a better power system than the airframe manufacturer originally used . . . and a turbine engine is more efficient than a piston engine in most relatively big planes. Stretching out the fuselage of a good airframe is not all that big a challenge, either, for the corporate and air-taxi market.

Planes like the Volpar Turbo 18, PAC Tradewind, AIC Jobmaster, and Dumod are all good aircraft. But what the passenger seldom knows is that he's riding in a rebuilt airplane. The model 18 of the durable Twin Beech is one of the most rugged and adaptable airframes ever built, and these converters find it almost ideal as a turboprop vehicle.

The Riley Turbo Executive and the Carstedt Jetliner 19-seat commuter are conversions of the De Havilland Dove. McKinnon revamps Grumman amphibians. Performance on most of these (and many others) can surpass the original models, too—and they cost a fraction of the "factory" competition.

The Volpar Turboliner, for example, seats 17, has a useful load over 4,600 pounds, cruises at 266 mph, and can be shipped from Van Nuys for $225,000—and is comparable in performance to a new $480,000 Handley Page Jetstream.

TIP: one of the best ways to disguise a standard airframe is to put more windows in it for the commuters.

BEST OF CLASS

(*Standards*)

LEAST EMPTY WEIGHT—Mooney MU-2: 5,540 lbs.

MOST SEATS—Nord 262: to 29

BIGGEST PAYLOAD—Fairchild Hiller 227B: 16,500 lbs.

BEST LIFT RATIO—Nord 262: 9,430 lbs. in useful load compared to 13,500 lbs. EW

BIGGEST ENGINES—Fairchild Hillers: twin 2,250 es-hp Rolls-Royce Dart Mark 532-7s

SERVICE CEILING—Grumman Gulfstream I: 30,400 ft.

TAKE-OFF DISTANCES (BOTH)—Beech King Air A-90: 1,010 ft. run; 1,280 ft. over 50-ft. obstacle

LANDING DISTANCES (BOTH)—Mooney MU-2: 1,100 ft. over 50-ft. obstacle; 760-ft. ground roll

RATE OF CLIMB, SEA LEVEL—Fairchild Hiller F27-J: 2,380 fpm

AIRSPEEDS—Grumman Gulfstream I: 357 mph at top, maximum cruise, and optimum cruise speeds per altitude

STALL SPEED—Mooney MU-2: 74 mph

RANGE WITH MAXIMUM PAYLOAD—Grumman Gulfstream I: 2,060 miles; also best on maximum fuel: 3,025 miles

LOWEST PRICE—Mooney MU-2: $311,850

CHAPTER 9

Jets

"I got to move, man," says James Brown. "I live out on Long Island, and I make maybe 300 trips a year *all* over the country. Lotsa cats got airplanes of their own, but when I want to save time I wanta save lots of it. That's why I got a jet."

If this speech hardly sounds like that of a corporation executive, it's because that assumption is correct. James Brown sings rock 'n' roll music to teeny-boppers ("groupies" he would say) at schools, clubs, auditoriums, dance halls, and ball parks. He represents the growing jet market that was not even considered just a couple of years ago, when only the biggest corporations in America plus a few superstars like Frank Sinatra owned private jets.

The jet market didn't exist at all until September 1961 when Superior Oil Company of Houston took delivery on its Lockheed Jetstar. By mid-1968 there were over 700 private jets in operation —with several hundred more already on order. The FAA predicts that there will be 3,500 by 1971. The jet engine is starting to do to the turboprop engine what the turbine is doing to the piston engine, and the winner of the fight will be the public.

Lear Jet 24

Combining most of the advantages of conventionally powered aircraft with the speed of the commercial jets, the private jet is the ultimate as a "manpower multiplier." For example, James Brown and the rest of his group, known as the Famous Flames, could make little more than 200 dates a year before they got their own jet.

Flying from New York to Los Angeles in a few hours is no trick at all for the citizen who uses the airlines. But getting from Snodgrass, Arkansas, to Wheatfield, Montana, may take him a day and a half. The way most of the major airlines are cutting service, even travel between the relatively big cities can be handled more efficiently by private jet. A trip from Pittsburgh to Oklahoma City, for example, takes about two hours by private jet . . . and takes almost seven hours by commercial airliners, which stop at Indianapolis, St. Louis, and Tulsa on the way to destination.

Regardless of price, most of the jets built for the private market have one thing in common: location of the engines aft of the fuselage. The thus cleaner wing provides better lift, and the chance of objects being sucked into the engines from the runway is reduced, too. Almost as important as far as sales appeal is concerned, the cabin noise is reduced to a minimum.

Inside the pressurized cabin, the appointments are often downright opulent. Most often, they are designed and built to the customer's individual requirements and may include not just conference tables and desks, but movie-projection equipment and air-to-ground telephones as well. Such "standard" facilities as complete galleys, foldaway bars, and restrooms are almost taken for granted.

Ever try to justify your big salary by leafing through a few papers in the seat of a commercial airliner while trying to avoid the questions of the passenger in the next seat? Best possible answer: buy your own jet.

Lear Jet 24
13,000 pounds gross weight

Dynamic Bill Lear was one of the first to break the million-dollar price barrier, and he cracked the jet market reasonably wide open with the $489,000 model 23 in October 1963. One of the ways he did it was to keep the weight under 12,500 pounds, at which point the FAA says that a plane has to conform to the same standards as planes built for airline use.

Although the price went up to $595,000 by the time deliveries got under way, Lear could stay under the weight limitation (so that what Bill Lear considered "frills" could be eliminated) only by sacrificing some of the component elements that were subsequently found to be desirable after all. Putting it bluntly, there were just too many pilots of model 23 who were having too many accidents. Even Frank Sinatra traded in his Lear Jet for a Hawker Siddeley De Havilland 125.

The 6,880-pound EW Lear 24 now costs $649,000, with a custom interior and full avionics. The compact eight-seater carries a useful load of 6,120 pounds behind (or in front of) its two 2,850-pound-thrust GE CJ610-4 engines. Service ceiling has been upped to 45,000 feet (26,000 on one engine) and the model 24 has a rate of climb upped to 6,350 feet per minute from sea-level altitude.

It cruises at maximum speed of 540 mph (553 top), and the most efficient cruise speed is 508 mph. Stall speed is 104 mph.

Required take-off distance over a 35-foot obstacle has been cut to 3,000 feet, including a 2,500-foot ground run. Landing distance, however, is now up to 3,300 feet over the 35-footer, with an 1,850-foot ground roll. Even though model 24 uses less fuel (191 gallons per hour at optimum cruise speed), it gets a lesser 1,565-mile range from its 834-gallon capacity. In short, the new model sacrifices nothing to expediency any more. Best range with maximum payload is now just over 1,000 miles.

The bigger model 25 costs $795,000 fully equipped and carries a 27 percent bigger payload in certified useful weight than the $649,000 model. Empty weight is 7,295 pounds, and useful load is 7,705 pounds, making the Lear 25 the only jet that can carry more in payload than the empty weight of the plane itself.

The 10-seater is powered by 2,950-pound-thrust GE-CJG10-6 engines, and service ceiling is 45,000 feet (27,500 feet on one engine). Rate of climb is 5,600 feet per minute, but the rest of the speeds are the same as for model 24 (except for stall speed: 118 mph for the 25).

After a 3,150-foot run, model 25 needs a total of 3,700 feet to take off over a 35-foot obstacle. Landing over it requires 3,650 feet, including a 2,450-foot ground roll. Model 25 uses 225 gallons per hour from a 915-gallon fuel capacity at optimum cruise, for a range of 1,670 miles (or 1,280 miles with a maximum payload).

But neither of these planes realized Bill Lear's original dream of marketing a successful jet that would not have to conform to airline regulations. When he turned over United States distribution to the Gates Rubber Company in 1967, he also had a feeder-line jet in the works, the model 40, with a capacity up to 43 seats. When (and if) it hits the market, here are the specs:

Power: two 8,740-pound-thrust Rolls-Royce Spey RB163-25 engines. Weights: empty, 29,500 pounds; useful, 22,300 pounds; gross, 51,800 pounds. Service ceiling: 45,000 feet, or on single engine, 26,500 feet. SL R/C (sea level rate of climb), 5,000 feet per minute. Take-off and landing distances over a 35-foot obstacle: 3,550 feet and 3,430 feet respectively. Speeds: 580 mph top; 555 mph maximum cruise; 510 mph optimum cruise; 118 mph stall. Using 435 gallons per hour from a 915-gallon fuel capacity at optimum cruise speed, range: 3,430 miles (or 2,000 miles with a maximum payload). Price: an un-Lear-like $1,750,000. The only competition close to that model 40 in seating capacity, though, costs more than twice as much.

Lear Jet 25
15,000 pounds gross weight

See Lear Jet.

Jet Commander
16,395 pounds gross weight

Rockwell Standard first flew *its* version of a bargain jet eight months before Bill Lear got his model 23 in the air, but with a big difference: the Commander did meet the same standards the FAA requires of commercial jet airliners. Even though the Jet Commander has since changed management, it is now the lowest-*base*-price jet in production, at "Lear's" old price of $595,000. The IFR avionics, all-weather capabilities, and so on can easily get the ready-to-operate cost over $700,000. More than 100 Jet Commanders have been delivered (compared to more than 150 built by Lear).

With six to eight seats, the Jet Commander weighs in at 9,155 pounds EW, with a useful load of 7,240 pounds. Service ceiling is 45,000 feet, or 20,000 feet on one of its two 2,850-pound-thrust GE-CJ610 engines. It will climb at 5,000 feet per minute from sea level and has a top speed of 525 mph. Maximum cruise speed is a flat 500 mph, and optimum cruise is at 470 mph, where the Commander has a range of 1,585 miles using 225 gallons per hour from the 926-gallon fuel capacity.

Jet Commander

Take-off and landing distances over a 35-foot obstacle are 3,200 feet and 3,900 feet respectively. The stall speed is 112 mph.

There must be something discouraging about building $595,-000 jets; the Jet Commander, too, was "sold out" in late 1967. The new owners of the entire Commander jet project: Israel Aircraft Industries, Ltd., of Tel Aviv, Israel.

Piaggio-Douglas 808
18,000 pounds gross weight

This Italian/American product is really bigger than it looks. Although the wing span is only 43 feet, the 808 can carry up to 11 people at a stop speed of 550 mph at an eye-popping service ceiling of 48,500 feet. Even the single-engine ceiling is 32,000 feet.

The powerplant is a pair of 3,360-pound-thrust BS-Viper-526 engines. Empty weight (fully factory-equipped) is 10,310 pounds, and useful weight is rated at 7,690 pounds. Rate of climb is 6,300 feet per minute at sea level, with the take-off and landing distances over a 35-foot obstacle 3,200 feet and 2,750 feet respectively.

This rich relative of the P-166-C piston twin has a top speed of 550 mph. Optimum cruise speed is 500 mph, where the 808 uses 289 gallons of fuel per hour from the 995-gallon capacity. With maximum fuel, range is 1,250 miles, and with a maximum payload, 1,100 miles. Stall speed is 102 mph.

Too bad you didn't buy one last year, pal, because the current $1 million price is $175,000 more than the 1967 price.

North American Sabreliner
18,650 pounds gross weight

This 9- to 11-seat jet is a direct descendant of the Los Angeles company's World War II Mustang and its postwar F-86. As the T-39, almost 200 were built before the present deluxe design was finalized, and another 100 or more have been built since. Now that the company has merged with what were the Aircraft Divisions of Rockwell Standard Corporation, the aircraft industry expects the resultant Aero Commander Division of the new North American Rockwell Corporation to strengthen its market position even more.

The Sabreliner weighs 9,895 pounds empty with two 3,300-pound-thrust Pratt & Whitney JT1aA-8 engines, for a useful load

North American Sabreliner

of 8,755 pounds. From sea level it can climb at 4,620 feet per minute, and its service ceiling is 45,000 feet. Stall speed is 114 mph. Ground run to lift-off is 2,520 feet, and in landing it has a ground roll of 2,050 feet.

Maximum cruise speed is 515 mph. The Sabreliner carries 1,063 gallons of fuel, which gives it a range of over 2,000 miles when using it at 184 gallons per hour at the optimum cruise speed of 460 mph.

With full avionics and a custom interior, the Sabreliner 40 is also now a flat $1 million. But there was good news for 1968; there is now a new model 60 Sabreliner available big enough for *12* seats . . . for $1,240,000.

HFB 320/Hansa
19,400 pounds gross weight

Purely from the standpoint of aerodynamic design, a wing in the middle of the fuselage is better than either a high-wing or a low-wing plane. The first objection to *that* idea is that the result would be a waist-high spar going straight through the middle of the executive suite.

HFB has solved this problem by using *forward* swept wing designs, which means that the main spar can be brought *behind* the cabin. The forward-reaching Hansa can thus seat its 9 to 13 people in an unusually commodious cabin without making the plane any bigger. Cost for the midfuselage-winged Hansa: just $700,000.

The two GE CJ610-1 engines each have 2,850 pounds of thrust, and the 19,400-pound GW Hansa climbs at 3,500 feet per minute, with a service ceiling of 37,500 feet. It can operate handsomely on one engine at 16,500 feet. Empty weight of "The Hamburger Deluxe" is 12,125 pounds, for a useful load certification of 7,275 pounds.

HFB Hansa 320

After a ground run of 3,870 feet, it lifts off over a 35-foot obstacle in a total of 4,535 feet. It lands from a 35-foot altitude in a total of 3,080 feet, including a 2,060-foot ground roll. Maximum cruising speed is the same as its top speed: 495 mph. Optimum cruise speed is 425 mph, and stall speed is 108 mph. The plane carries 1,075 gallons of fuel, which it uses at an optimum rate of 225 gallons per hour for a 1,660-mile range.

With a maximum payload, though, the range is cut to 970 miles. Even so, if American bizjet manufacturers ever see an airplane coming after them "backwards," it just might be HFB's 320/Hansa.

Hawker Siddeley DH-125 3-AR
23,100 pounds gross weight

HS sold 27 of its British-built DH-125s during 1967, which is a pretty good indication of public acceptance in a field where foreign-built products do not move too well—particularly when they cost around $800,000 a copy. But as of the spring of 1968, 80 had been sold in North America out of a world total of 133.

Mainly, the DH-125 is a lot of airplane for the money, and it keeps improving year by year. Example: the latest model's ice detector not only activates the warning lights, but also starts the de-icing system automatically—and even that has a back-up system. The changes are seldom drastic, but they have been constant ever since the plane was first flown in late August 1962.

Even the price changes are conservative; almost all aircraft prices have been shooting up in the last few years, but the DH-125 went up less than 5 percent to the 1966 price of $822,400. Devaluation of the pound surely wasn't overlooked, though, and the price has since gone up another 7 percent to the present price of $882,400.

The DH-125 seats six to nine and has a 19-foot passenger compartment aft of the flight deck. The plane is powered by two 3,360-pound-thrust BS-Viper-522 engines, which give it a service ceiling of 41,000 feet (26,000 feet on a single engine).

Empty weight is 12,000 pounds, for a useful weight limit of 11,100 pounds with the new fuel allowance.

With maximum fuel capacity of 1,365 gallons, range is 1,840 miles with a 1,000-pound payload. Maximum cruise speed is 510 mph, and on optimum cruise speed of 445 mph the DH-125 uses 254 gallons of fuel per hour.

Hawker Siddeley DH-125

After a ground run of 2,000 feet, it will clear a 35-foot obstacle in a total of 3,800 feet. Rate of climb is 4,500 feet per minute at sea level. Landing requires 2,450 feet to come down over a 35-foot obstacle, including less than 1,000 feet for the ground roll. Stall speed: 100 mph.

Hawker Siddeley has absorbed De Havilland of England, although DH of Canada still runs independently. Hawker Siddeley is the only manufacturer with previous experience of both jet airliners and executive aircraft.

Dassault Falcon

26,455 pounds gross weight

During 1967, France's Dassault sold 54 of its fan jet Falcons, for which Pan Am's Business Jets Division is United States distributor. Except for the fact that so many Americans became disenchanted with M. de Gaulle, even better sales were anticipated for 1968. But after the general strikes in May hurt Dassault so badly, deliveries not only did not improve but fell off rather drastically. Nobody can blame the airplane, though.

With a top speed of 587 mph, the Falcon is right up there with the commercial airliners. Even maximum cruise speed is 570 mph, with optimum cruising rated at 450 mph. Stall speed is 100 mph. Empty weight of the Falcon is 15,500 pounds, and it is certified for 10,955 pounds in useful load.

From sea level, it climbs out at 3,500 feet per minute, with a service ceiling of 42,000 feet. The fan jet flies at 21,000 feet on one of the two 4,125-pounds-thrust GE CE700-2C engines. One disadvantage, though, is the fact that it needs more than a mile of runway to take off over a 35-foot obstacle—a total of 5,650 feet after a 3,750-foot ground run. It lands back again in 3,800 feet, including a 2,400-foot ground roll.

Using 225 gallons of fuel an hour at optimum cruise speed and altitude, the Falcon has a range of 1,875 miles with the maximum 1,257 gallons of fuel. Range with maximum payload is almost as good: 1,600 miles.

The above factors all relate primarily to the pilot. From the standpoint of the purchaser, the fan jet Falcon has a big strike against it: Dassault's price tag of $1,240,000 . . . bare. What do those guys think we are—tourists?

Lockheed Dash-8 Jetstar

42,500 pounds gross weight

This is the airplane that started the whole bizjet business, and it was first flown with two BS Orpheus engines in 1957. Re-engined two years later, it now mounts four 3,300-pound-thrust Pratt & Whitney JT12A-8 engines in lateral pairs at the sides of the rear fuselage. The only four-engine jet built in the United States for the corporate market (even the DC-20 and 737-E "conversions" get along with only two apiece), the Jetstar seats 12 to 15, including a crew of two.

For a price of $1,590,000, buyers are entitled to expect every new improvement that comes along and they are seldom disappointed. The 1968 model has a new useful weight certification and a new top speed of 575 mph to go with it. Empty weight is now 22,074 pounds, with 20,426 pounds rated as useful load.

The new service ceiling is 43,000 feet, and even the 36,000-foot single-engine ceiling is almost as good as the *top* ceiling was just a year before. Rate of climb is still 4,600 feet per minute, but maximum cruise speed has been increased to 570 mph. Optimum cruise is 507 mph, and stall speed is 123 mph.

Total take-off distance to clear a 35-foot obstacle is 4,880 feet, including a run of 3,740 feet. Coming down from 35 feet requires a total distance of 3,770 feet, including 2,450 feet of runway. At optimum cruise the engines use 465 gallons of fuel per hour, and the Jetstar has a 2,660-gallon capacity accordingly. With a 45-minute reserve, range on maximum fuel is 2,460 miles, or 2,190 miles with a maximum payload.

The Marietta, Georgia, plant delivered only 32 Jetstars during 1967. However, that's better than $50 million worth of airplanes, which is a nice sideline in anybody's business.

Grumman Gulfstream II
58,000 pounds gross weight

The executive shopping for a bargain in jet aircraft will do well to look elsewhere than in Bethpage, Long Island. Grumman has a money's-no-object policy . . . and it's justified. Anything Grumman makes is very, very expensive—and is absolutely the best that money can buy.

Grumman Gulfstream II

Grumman's enviable reputation is based on its record of production of military aircraft, notably for the Navy. In the corporate market, LeRoi Grumman's magnificent Gulfstream I has always been recognized as the Rolls-Royce of private planes up to the turboprop class, too, and over 200 of them will have been built by the time production is phased out in 1968.

A prime example of Grumman's corporate image is the fact that the company had orders for 53 Gulfstream IIs before it even flew—46 of them from operators of the Gulfstream I. And every one of these sight-unseen buyers plunked down a minimum deposit of $200,000 of their company's money on a plane they were only told would cost $2–$2.5 million.

Well, it's a little over that now, and today's price is $2,525,-000, but nobody counts any small change in the bizjet market when it gets to this level. But the Gulfstream II is not only the most expensive aircraft that has ever been designed specifically for the corporate market, but also is the most luxurious and highest-performance plane by quite a margin.

With up to 19 seats, the Gulfstream II is superbly overpowered with two 11,400-pound-thrust Rolls-Royce Spey Mk 511 engines (which alone cost $865,000 a pair . . . wholesale). Empty weight is 29,100 pounds, against a useful load of 28,900 pounds. Service ceiling is 46,500 feet, or 37,000 feet on one engine.

After a 4,225-foot take-off over a 35-foot obstacle, the Gulfstream II climbs at 5,000 feet per minute from sea level. With a stall speed of 116 mph, it lands from a 35-foot altitude in a total distance of 2,540 feet, including a ground roll of 1,750 feet.

Maximum cruise is at top speed: 590 mph. Long-range cruise speed is 500 mph, where fuel is used at 388 gallons per hour from the 3,460-gallon capacity. Cruising at 40,000 feet, fuel range is 3,650 miles, or 2,950 miles with maximum payload.

Short of the modified jets actually designed for airline use, there just ain't nothin' better.

BAC 1-11 400S Executive
87,000 pounds gross weight

Basically, this British plane uses the same engines as the Grumman Gulfstream II but in an airframe more than half again as big. In fact, the 400S Executive was designed primarily for commercial airline service, and the offering herewith is simply a corporate configuration.

Empty weight is 50,400 pounds, and seating capacity can be anything up to 30 people for a useful load of 36,600 pounds. With the two Rolls-Royce Spey Mk 511 engines (11,400 pounds of thrust for each), service ceiling is 40,000 feet, or, if one engine is out, 20,000 feet.

Over a 50-foot obstacle, the ground run is 2,500 feet and the total distance is 3,200 feet. At sea-level altitude it climbs at 3,900 feet per minute. Top, maximum cruise, and optimum cruise speeds are all rated the same: 550 mph at the right altitudes. With a 4,996-gallon fuel capacity, it uses 610 gallons per hour, for a 3,580-mile range.

In short, performance for the bigger plane in almost all respects falls short of what the Gulfstream II can do (except carry more passengers, and few company planes ever use anything even close to "pack 'em in" configurations). However, the British competitor still costs almost $1 million more than the Gulfstream II. The price tag for the BAC 1-11 is $3.5 million, up $500,000 from the 1967 price.

Douglas DC-9-20 Business Jet
98,000 pounds gross weight

When used by commercial airlines, this jet seats up to 80 people. As a bizjet, when modified for as few as 10 passengers, it can be roomy indeed. Its market includes major corporations whose use of jet transportation is so heavy that, in effect, they run private airlines of their own. This one is a $3.6 million airplane.

The two Pratt & Whitney JT8D-9 engines have a combined power of 29,000 pounds of static thrust, and they operate at a service ceiling of 35,000 feet. Empty weight is 55,600 pounds, and useful weight is certified at 42,400 pounds.

Over a 35-foot obstacle, total take-off and landing distances are 4,650 feet and 3,300 feet respectively. At sea level, the rate of climb is 4,850 feet per minute. The stall speed, which is remarkable in an aircraft this big, is only 80.5 mph.

Douglas DC-9 tail, big enough to fly alone

Top speed is 585 mph, and maximum cruise speed is 550 mph. Optimum cruising speed is at 495 mph, when the DC-20 uses 640 gallons of fuel per hour for a maximum fuel range of 3,725 miles (fuel capacity is 5,459 gallons). Even with a maximum payload, its range is almost 3,500 miles.

Although basically the same as the bizjet configuration called the DC-9-10 until 1966, the new DC-9-20 is different in almost all performance characteristics and specifications. And except for the price (which has been raised by another half-million dollars), most of them to the better.

Boeing 737E Business Jet
108,000 pounds gross weight

The 737 is, of course, one of the most famous designs for a commercial airliner ever to come off the drawing boards. As the model E Business Jet, the seats for paying passengers have been taken out and replaced with some lounges and so on for the executive trade.

Seating up to 30 people, the 737E weighs 55,000 pounds empty, for a useful load limit of 53,000 pounds. Service ceiling is 40,000 feet, or 18,000 feet on just one of the two 14,500-pound-thrust Pratt & Whitney JT8D-9 powerplants.

On take-off, this baby needs 7,300 feet to reach an altitude of 35 feet, and from there it climbs at 3,500 feet per minute. Coming down from 35 feet requires a total of 2,500 feet in landing distance. Stall speed is 98 mph.

Top speed is the fastest of any plane available on the market for corporate use: 600 mph. Maximum cruise speed is 580 mph, but optimum cruise speed for long-range operation is 485 mph, when the 737E uses 660 gallons of fuel out of a 4,670-gallon capacity. There is also an optional fuel capacity of 6,420 gallons total, primarily meant for overseas operation, where the range is 4,500 miles.

Basic price: $3,600,000. And that's pretty basic.

BEST OF CLASS

(*Standards*)

LEAST WEIGHT—Lear 24: 6,880 lbs. EW

MOST SEATS—DC-9-20: 80 possible

BIGGEST PAYLOAD—737E: 53,000 lbs.

BEST LIFT RATIO—Lear 25: 7,705 lbs. in useful load compared to 7,295 lbs. EW

BIGGEST ENGINES—737E or DC-9-20: 14,500-lb.-thrust Pratt & Whitney JT8D-9s

SERVICE CEILING—Piaggio PD-808: 48,500 ft.; on one engine— Gulfstream II: 37,000 ft.

TAKE-OFF DISTANCE (RUN)—DH-125: 2,000 ft.

TAKE-OFF DISTANCE (OVER 35-FT. OBSTACLE)—Lear 24: 3,000 ft.

LANDING DISTANCE (ROLL)—DH-125: 990 ft.

LANDING DISTANCE (TOTAL, FROM 35-FT. ALTITUDE)—BAC 1-11: 2,200 ft.

SEA-LEVEL RATE OF CLIMB—Lear 24: 6,350 fpm

AIRSPEEDS: TOP—Boeing 737E 600 mph; maximum cruise—Gulfstream II: 590 mph; optimum cruise—BAC 1-11 400S: 550 mph; at stall—DC-9-20: 80.5 mph

RANGE AT OPTIMUM CRUISE SPEED—737E: 4,500 miles

FUEL USE—North American Sabreliner: 184 gals. per hour

LOWEST PRICE (BASE COST ONLY)—Jet Commander: $595,000

CHAPTER 10

Conversions

Five minutes after the Wright brothers' first plane landed at Kitty Hawk, they started tinkering with it to make it better—this, despite the fact that it was at the time, without any doubt, "the finest aircraft the world has ever seen."

Aeronautical tinkerers are still at it. Even today, regardless of how well a manufacturer builds an airplane, there's always a guy somewhere who thinks he can figure out how to make it better—"better" for more speed, improved lift ratio, bigger payload, faster lift-off, or capabilities for special utilization—all at the sacrifice of some other factor, admittedly. Every plane ever built is the result of compromise, but every model ever designed has had a specific purpose for making it different, with a definite reason for the modification.

Many independent modifications have been so good that they have subsequently been adapted by the industry in general. The automobile industry uses the Memorial Day 500 at the Indianapolis speedway to publicly explore ideas and try out new equipment and systems, and hundreds of components in current production models were first tried out in those races. This is the real reason, incidentally, for all the grousing about the turbine cars having taken over domination of the Indianapolis 500 since the 1968 race; a turbine engine is remarkably efficient for sustained operations, as in a long race (or an airplane), but with the turbine wheel spinning at 35,000 rpm at operational speeds, the system is not well adapted for start-stop, stop-start family cars.

The aviation industry had a comparable guinea pig in the big air races of the 1930s, and many an improvement is the result of tryouts under strain conditions at the Cleveland wring-outs. But the big air races never revived after World War II knocked them out; the novelty of airplanes had worn off for the public, sponsors were hard to come by, and speed capabilities had developed to the point in the interim that pylon-type races were no longer practical.

Whether the major manufacturers will admit it or not, today they depend heavily on the independent modifiers who have figuratively inherited the silk scarves of the racing pilots of the 1930s. Many a tinkerer who started in a corner of a drafty hanger is now a respectable manufacturer in his own right, too. Others have sizable factories still devoted to nothing but the modification of existing models.

Quite a few have been bought out by the majors. But almost all of them, if they have a basic idea that looks any good at all, are closely watched by the rest of the industry.

Some develop an idea that does not have a big enough market to warrant serious attention from the major manufacturers. Others capitalize on aeronautical advances that the major firms have not yet caught up with (some of their basic airframes were "perfected" in the early 1950s). For an independent to solve a problem that has stumped the big-time engineers isn't too unusual, either.

In any case, the converters all have a good reason of their own for being in business. The planes rebuilt by some of them are so thoroughly revamped that the conversions are unrecognizable as the original airframes, especially when they use imaginative new brand names.

Not just anybody can modify an existing plane and put it out on the market under his own name. Even the experimental planes, which are never used by the public, are kept under the eagle eye of the FAA in the interests of protecting the citizenry. Anybody who monkeys with the powerplant, airfoil, weight ratios, or anything else basic can do so only with the sanction of a government team of examiners.

An airplane manufacturer sometimes has to spend years building and rebuilding a new model before getting it certified. Thus, the FAA is sometimes inclined to look with a jaundiced eye upon the converter's plans to improve on such supposed perfection (as far as compromise will allow). However, the government policy really is to help promote the growth and advancement of the aviation industry in all its phases, and if the applicant has anything on the ball at all, in due course he can expect to get his STC (Supplemental Type Certificate), which allows for installation and/or manufacture for the general market's use. After the converter has convinced the FAA that he has something worthwhile, of course, he then has to convince the buying public.

One of the easiest conversions, of course, is to reconfigure a heavy-duty aircraft for lesser service. Douglas hasn't built any DC-3s since 1951, but it is the workhorse of many corporations who have simply had it changed from a flying bus to a flying office. Companies like AiResearch do a lot more than replace the no-longer-needed seats with davenports, but there are still plenty of DC-3s in service where the only basic changes have been in the cabin appointments.

Many military planes have also been converted to corporate use with minimal trouble, especially paratroop carriers, cargo planes, glider towers, hospital planes, and troop transports. One of the best is the Lockheed PV-1 Lodestar, which entered service in 1939 *as* an executive aircraft and converted to military use. After the war, it was simply reconverted back to its original purpose. The typical Howard 500 conversion has a pressurized range of 2,100 miles and carries 10 passengers.

The Super Ventura PV-1 owned by the Chicago *Tribune* is a 32,000-pound plane with bigger engines, more fuel capacity, and a "lie down" lounge with food facilities for hot lunches; it cost less than $335,000. This is cheap, considering the fact

Converted Lockheed Bomber

that the three or four executives it usually carries have salaries that average around $1,000 a day.

Heavy demand keeps the prices up on these durable old-timers, and they are hard to find. Iver O. Tandy, chief pilot for the Natural Gas Company of Illinois, is lucky enough to have not just one but *two* Howard conversions under his command.

Conversion companies go in and out of business so fast, and so many duplicate each other's efforts, that only a coverage of representative well-established firms is possible in this chapter. The following listings concentrate on conversions that offer the most meaningful modifications.

Grumman Amphibians

MCKINNON ENTERPRISES, INC., has been overhauling, modernizing, and converting Grumman multiengine amphibians since 1952. A. G. McKinnon, then in the construction business, was using a Grumman Widgeon as a company plane in which he replaced the Ranger engines with Lycoming GO-435 powerplants. Performance was so much improved that he got into the aviation business with both feet, and the firm has since converted 73 Widgeons to turboprops.

McKinnon also did such a good job in converting the Grumman Goose to turbine power that he now holds an FAA-type certificate for the McKinnon Goose, complete with his own model numbers.

The base cost of the McKinnon G21C Goose is $312,500. With 550 es-hp Pratt & Whitney engines driving three-blade 96-inch Hartzell constant-speed feathering props, the twin operates at 211 mph, has a 1,200-mile range, has a useful load of 4,700 pounds, and can seat 17 people.

Adding 15 inches to the nose to accommodate sophisticated electronic gear adds $25,000 to the price and changes the model number to G21D. Or if the buyer is willing to settle for Grumman's original seven- to nine-place configuration, where the only change in the Goose is the engine change, the price for the G21A is $287,500. McKinnon will also convert the Grumman product

McKinnon Goose

to a four-engine version "to order." Where he gets the Gooses, McKinnon isn't saying, as Grumman only built 350 of them. If a customer brings in his own Goose for modification, the basic engine change costs $162,500.

Next in the expansion program: conversion of the Mallard to turboprop. McKinnon also has an eye on the Navy's Albatross, where turbine power and other McKinnon modifications will make so much of a change in performance that the landing speed, for example, will be reduced from 97 mph to 55 mph. Maybe Mc-Kinnon will *never* run out of Grummans!

De Havilland Dove

CARSTEDT AVIATION   doesn't advertise the fact that its many-windowed 18-passenger turboprop commuter is a conversion of a DH Dove, but it doesn't fool anybody except perhaps the passengers. Like many conversions for the third-level airlines market, gross weight of the Carstedt CJ660-A Jetliner is kept under the FAA's "naughty finger" 12,500-pound gross-weight limitation, and a lot of "frills" can be eliminated accordingly.

Carstedt charges $250,000 for the comprehensive conversion job, and the customer supplies the airframe to start with. However, he winds up with a twin that will cruise at 10,000 at 250 mph with full useful load of 5,185 pounds, which is more than the empty weight of the plane itself—including the weight of those 18 knee-bumping seats, not overlooking the one where a copilot usually sits.

RILEY AERONAUTICS CORPORATION   has figured out how to get even more people into a De Havilland Dove conversion than Carstedt if the publicity is to be believed, but Riley includes the pilot when they say "19." The Riley Turbo Skyliner is not, as a matter of fact, a turboprop like the Carstedt but uses 290 hp Lycoming engines with turbo*charging* on the powerplants.

Empty weight of the Riley Skyliner is 6,483 pounds and the useful load is 6,016 pounds, which makes the certified gross weight 12,499 pounds—just 16 ounces below the FAA's line of demarcation where the tougher regulations go into effect. If a user/airline ever gets up to gross weight and the pilot climbs aboard with a couple of apples in his lunch bucket, BOOM goes the license.

Riley also gets $250,000 for the Dove conversion, but that includes the airframe and all. The model from Florida is also about 10 mph faster than Carstedt's and has a service ceiling of better than 30,000 feet with the blowers. There are four of them, with two engines on each wing for a total of 1,160 hp.

Riley sweeps back the tail for a twin-engine conversion of the Dove into the Riley Turbo Executive 400, which seats six to eight in executive splendor. With fuel-injected and turbocharged 400 hp Lycoming engines, the E-400 has a cruising speed on 75 percent power of 285 mph, a service ceiling of 32,400 feet, and a useful load limit of 3,000 pounds out of an 8,800-pound gross. The stall speed is only 61 mph, which is better than any factory-built retractable twin on the market, regardless of size.

The E-400 conversion carries 201 gallons of fuel, which it uses sparingly for a 1,120-mile range. The base price is $174,500 . . . complete.

Twin Beech

This durable and adaptable airframe is used in more heavy-duty conversions than any other. Many a fancily renamed commuter "started" life as a 20-year-old Beech 18 when the converter started work on it. The model also has the longest record of continuous production of any plane ever built, and there are plenty of them around to work on.

AIRCRAFT INDUSTRIES OF CANADA, LTD., has done one of the best jobs in converting the Twin Beech to turboprop power. The AIC Jobmaster, a nine-seat twin with 575 es-hp Pratt & Whitney engines can carry more in useful load (5,435 pounds) than its own empty weight (5,265 pounds). AIC has not only decreased the empty weight but increased the gross-weight certification as well; the result between represents one of the best weight/lift ratios in the industry.

The AIC Jobmaster cruises at 260 mph. Fuel capacity is a generous 500 gallons, which provides the workhorse capabilities this kind of airplane is redesigned for as a no-nonsense corporate aircraft, with a maximum range of 1,560 miles. Service ceiling is limited to 16,500 feet, or 10,500 feet on one engine.

Base prices for the custom-built configurations start at a relatively modest $150,000.

VOLPAR, INC., began building modifications of the Twin Beech in 1959 with the conversion of "conventional" landing gear to tricycle equipment. Complicated engineering was so successful that the Beech factory itself subsequently replaced its long-standard gear with the similar landing gear as original equipment. In short, Volpar had been so successful that the California company had practically put itself out of business on "new" conversions.

But before the phones quit ringing, Volpar had still another refinement of the Beech 18: replacing the piston engines with turboprops. Since Volpar began marketing the "Volpar Super 18" in 1965, Beech has announced the imminent phasing out of the model 18 altogether, but with more than 1,500 of the Twin Beeches around the world still operating, Volpar has a pretty good market to work on. Turboprop modification with reversible props costs a Twin Beech owner $147,438.80 (plus another $25,500 for the tricycle landing-gear conversion), even though his as-is plane may have a book value of only $40,000 or $50,000.

Volpar sells its 11-seat Turbo 18 outright for $230,000 (closest thing to it in a new turboprop is the seven-seat Mooney at $311,850). Volpar's conversion has the same powerplants, too: a pair of 605 es-hp Garrett AiResearch engines. Cruising speed is 266 mph, the maximum range is 2,180 miles, and the useful load is 4,065 pounds out of a 10,285-pounds gross-weight limit. However, this kind of performance is only possible with the 1967 change to bigger turbines from the 575 es-hp engines formerly offered.

Volpar Turboliner

One reason for the engine change is because Volpar has also added the Turboliner to its catalog, a stretched-out conversion of the Twin Beech for the commuter trade. The 15-passenger Volpar Turboliner twin utilizes the same AiResearch engines as in the regular Volpar Turbo 18. Volpar's engineering is such that the 7-foot-longer Turboliner still retains the same empty weight as the unstretched version. Most performance characteristics remain the same, too, except for a drop in range to a 1,380-mile maximum.

The basic Turboliner goes for $250,000. For another $20,000 or so, the buyer gets wing and prop de-icing, plus extra 165-gallon fuel tanks and 350-pound baggage lockers on each wing. A third-level airline would also spend another $15,000 to $20,000 for an electronics package for this kind of airplane, to get a total operational cost of about $290,000. The closest thing to that in a new turboprop would be the Handley Page Jetstream, which is about 35 mph faster, has 700 miles more range, and costs twice as much without avionics.

In effect, Volpar offers two commuters for the price of one.

PACIFIC AIRMOTIVE CORPORATION   is one of the busiest outfits in all aviation. With its "something for everybody" concept, it offers the PAC Tradewind as a turboprop model with a top speed of 308 mph and a 1,580-mile range. The nine-seat configuration uses 500 es-hp Pratt & Whitney engines and is a top-quality airplane in all respects.

It should be; it's a converted Beech 18, with one of the best airframes in the world. The Tradewind is also one of the best-disguised conversions ever built, and the "conventional" dual-tailed Twin Beech has been modified for a single-tail version. The *con*version costs $250,000, and Pacific Airmotive can provide everything to go with it right down to the flying lessons if required.

PAC also builds a piston-engine model of the crop-tailed Tradewind called the Presidential for $150,000. Range is 2,000 miles on maximum 402-gallon fuel capacity, but the top speed is a "mere" 254 mph. Both Tradewinds are tricycled for improved ground operations, and both have the same 10,200 pounds gross weight. The Tradewind Presidential weighs 200 pounds more empty and thus carries a bit less useful load than the 6,300-pound EW turboprop Tradewind.

At 6,500 pounds EW, the Presidential twin is the heaviest piston-engine plane in the world. Its 450 hp engines also make it the most powerful conversion, with its 900 horses being matched only by the latest model of the Super 18 made at the Beech factory. Another version of the piston-powered Tradewind, with 11 seats for the commuter trade and logically called the Tradewind Commuter, is the same price with the same basic performance as the Presidential (more usually equipped with seven seats for the corporate configuration).

PAC usually changes the name of the Tradewind with each different interior in the corporate models, too. Chaired for six passengers, it is the Clubman; for five, the Executive. A private lavatory compartment is standard in all three corporate stylings, which is more than the buyer could expect from the original at the Beech factory, that's for sure.

DUMOD CORPORATION, of Opa-Locka, Florida, may well represent the conversion companies that never get to fly very high because their offerings are too close to the competition's. The Dumod Liner was aimed at the profitable air-taxi business, and although it made a lot of news when it was brought out on the market in 1966, there were few takers.

Its biggest distinction was the fact that it had the most windows of any piston-engine plane that had ever been built: 16 in all. But the price for the conversion was $169,000, and there were just too many other Twin Beech conversions in that price range (or a little below) with comparable performance. The cost-conscious third-level airline operators were not impressed with the 15-seat "Beechie" made by the new company, inasmuch as it had a rather mediocre cruise speed on 65 percent power of 220 mph.

Most of the news made by Dumod was channeled through newspaper people who did not know a lot about airplanes. The company's ads never made any mention of the fact that the Dumod Liner was in fact a rebuilt Beech 18. A new 15-seat, heavily powered plane *would* be big news, but nobody who was actually a prospective customer could possibly be naïve enough not to know what the Dumod Liner really was, and there didn't seem to be much point in trying to scratch sand over that particular track. That policy didn't help Dumod a bit.

The conversion was also offered as the Dumod Executive for the corporate trade with seating for eight at the same price. However, it carried only 200 gallons of gas, and with a full load at 220 mph the range was limited to 454 miles. That might be okay for an air taxi, but the average company plane needs a little more reach than that.

Life is not always a bed of roses for the converters.

DEE HOWARD COMPANY is so big in the conversion business that the San Antonio firm serves as a supplier to other converters. The name "Howard" is so widely known and so highly respected that many pilots have a higher regard for a Howard product than for the manufacturer who made the original equipment.

There are many Howard conversions of many types of planes, fuselages, powerplants, and operational systems of all sizes, purposes, and designs. Serving as a distributor, Howard supplies more center-section spar modifications for Twin Beech conversions, for example, than anybody else in the country.

Beech Queen Air

SWEARINGEN AIRCRAFT has pulled a switch on the industry by converting the supercharged Queen Air to an unblown power system, despite the fact that many manufacturers are riding the trend by doing just the opposite. Or maybe because of it.

The only way anybody can buy a new Queen Air today is with the turbocharged piston engines, which operate so much more efficiently at high altitudes. Like other aircraft manufacturers, Beech uses the blower because an ordinarily aspirated engine's power falls off starting from sea level on up; at 9,000 feet it actually produces less than 75 percent of its rated power, and at 18,000 feet, less than half. After turbocharging, the engine produces more power per size and holds it to a higher altitude.

However, a turbocharged engine costs more to buy, to maintain, and to operate. Swearingen is capitalizing on the fact that in much of the eastern two-thirds of the United States the high-altitude performance of turbocharged planes is seldom used to its potential. In a plush but unpressurized cabin like the Queen 65's, many executives instruct the pilot that they would rather not bother with oxygen masks and to forget about going up to the altitudes for which the turbocharging was actually designed. This can add up to a lot of wasted investment.

For aircraft owners who are concerned with saving money, Swearingen replaces the geared and mechanically supercharged six-cylinder 340 hp engines in the Queen 65 with the new eight-cylinder Lycoming 400 hp engines, which cost less to fly because they are unblown and ungeared. The eight-cylinder engines not only cost less to operate than the stock engines but cost less to overhaul and have longer TBOs (time between overhauls) besides.

A sideline advantage in the "reverting" conversion is better visibility over humpless nacelles and lessened air drag. The increase in number of cylinders from six to eight minimizes vibration to boot. The modification also increases the Queen 65's gross-weight allowance to 7,900 pounds.

Ed Swearingen charges $48,195 for the conversion job, but allows up to $8,445 in exchange for the engines he replaces (depending on engine time of the used IGSO-480 powerplants). Is this expenditure justified as a money-saving measure? Not for everybody. Here's how the two planes stack up against each other:

	Beech's Queen Air 65	Swearingen's Queen Air 800
Direct operating costs based on 65% power at 10,000 ft., flying 10,000 mi./mo.	200 mph 50 hrs./mo.	225 mph 44–48 hrs./mo.
Gasoline @ 40¢ per gal. QA 65—39 gal./hr. QA 800—37 gal./hr.	$780.00	$663.20
Oil—same, $1.04/hr.	52.00	46.59
Inspections—same, $6.30/hr.	315.00	282.25
Engine allowance IGSO-480-AlA6 factory-remanufactured exchange, $6,384 ea. @ 900 hrs., $14.18/hr. 10-720-Ala, factory-remanufactured exchange, $5,360 ea. @ 1,000 hrs., $10.72/hr.	709.00	480.28
For one month, total	$1,856.00	$1,472.32
Direct operating cost per mile	18½ ¢/mile	14¼ ¢/mile

Thus, the man who flies the Queen 800 only 120,000 miles a year will save $4,484.16 in direct operating costs. If he paid Swearingen, say, $40,000 with the stock engine exchange, it will take him almost nine years to save what he laid out. He will still have some equity in the 400 hp engines at the end of the nine years, but even figuring the deal straight down the line, the investment realizes about an 11 percent return—which makes good sense only if the owner uses money that's costing maybe 6 percent or 7 percent a year. And he still won't have all that high-altitude performance that Beech went to all the trouble for in the first place.

Twin Bonanza, Beech

SWEARINGEN AVIATION began building conversions of the Twin Bonanza within a year after Beech quit making the model in 1963. Swearingen's result: the Excalibur. It depends for its future on the fact that the Twin Bonanza was phased out of production only after Beech had built over 500 of them. More than 400 that can be made into Excaliburs are still around, and Ed Swearingen has a list of every one of them.

The Excalibur is more of a straightforward modernization job than a real conversion. The original engines are replaced with 340 hp Lycoming IGSO-540 engines, and distinctive pointed spinners front the three-blade, full-feathering, constant-speed Hartzell propellers. Drag is cut with svelte nacelles and fully enclosed gear doors, and several dozen improvements are made on each old-timer being doctored to bring it up to date. The resulting Excalibur is a faster, smoother, more dependable plane with a cruising speed on 75 percent power of 260 mph (Vne [velocity never to be exceeded] 270 mph). Useful load: 2,179 pounds, with six seats.

The conversion costs a Twin Bonanza owner $52,100. If a nonowner wants to buy one outright, it will cost him around $80,000 (depending on what Swearingen has to pay for the Twin Bonanza he builds from), and fitted out with the proper electronics, total cost will run from $100,000 to $110,000. The Excalibur is almost as big as a Queen Air, compared to the current single-engine Bonanzas coming out of Wichita.

Swearingen also builds the Excalibur 800, which has a gross weight within 100 pounds of the 7,700-pound GW Queen 65-A, and in fact surpasses it in empty weight. With a 5,200-pound EW and a pair of 400 hp Lycoming 10-720-A1A engines, this brute can just barely still be called a light twin. The direct-drive, eight-cylinder engines are noted for low operating, overhaul, and replacement costs; the Excalibur 800 conversion of the Twin Bonanza airframe costs less, too: $42,100. Biggest advantages in the six-seat monster are in better take-off and landing distances and in rate of climb, which is 1,860 feet per minute at sea level.

Only a wing as well-built as the Twin Bonanza's can take that kind of treatment. That wing, incidentally, today supports Beech's line of bigger twins and, in fact, is used on Swearingen's own pressurized Merlin II.

Piper Apache

GERONIMO CONVERSION CORPORATION confidently expects to convert 25 percent of all 2,000 or so Apache twins to the better-performing Geronimo modernization. By the time Piper quit making the Apache, there *was* plenty of room for improvement, and Geronimo has taken over where Piper left off.

The basic change is the replacement of the 150 hp and 160 hp engines in the discontinued Apaches with 180 hp Lycomings. Along with aerodynamic and other operational refinements, the additional moxie gives the conversion 24 to 37 mph more cruising speed, lowers stall speed by 6 mph, provides over three times as much single-engine rate of climb, gives an additional 4,200 feet of single-engine ceiling, and cuts take-off distance by at least 300 feet. The Geronimo also has air inlets like nostrils.

Geronimo conversions can be done at home by do-it-yourself Apache owners by buying kits ranging in price from $7,450 for the engine kit with exchange to a dorsal fin for $225. Everything the company has to offer, from the extended nose to aerodynamically improved wing tips, costs $13,638.50. For another $2,340 the whole works can be installed at the San Antonio shop, or the kits can be installed progressively as the owner's budget allows.

The company will also sell a complete Geronimo outright, with everything on it. The complete price, avionics included, is

$39,800. The Geronimo will not only better the stock Apache's performance, as expected, but also surpass all the performance specs of Piper's newest Twin Comanche B—the Indian that supposedly killed off the Apache.

FRANKLIN AIRCRAFT ENGINES is having a tough time finding customers among the major airplane manufacturers. One of the ways the company seeks a market is with an airplane of its own to put the engine into. The light twin Franklin Star is one of the results.

The Franklin Star is actually another conversion of the Piper Apache. As a matter of fact, the actual converting job is not done by Franklin at all, but is built by the James Miller Company of San Antonio. But as far as the market is concerned, the Star is sold as an outright airplane by the Franklin division of Allied Aero Industries from Pottstown, Pennsylvania, with a price tag of $38,850.

Modification of the stock Apache includes installation of 220 hp Franklin engines, an extended nose for more speed, wheel well doors to cut drag, a square-tip rudder that reduces yaw, high-speed wing tips, and rear windows so that the fifth passenger can see out. Feathering props help make the Franklin Star outperform the old Apache in almost every respect, and plenty of new competitors in its class as well.

For example, the six-cylinder Franklins can lift the Star off the runway in as little as 475 feet. At 7,500 feet the Star can hit 205 mph TAS (true air speed) using 68 percent of power, where it uses fuel at the rate of 70 pints per hour compared to 48 pph using 41 percent power at 5,000 feet for a TAS of 171 mph. Good plane.

Cessna 310

RILEY AERONAUTICS CORPORATION is not the only converter to revamp Cessna's good-looking 310, but it has done the best job. Renamed the Riley Turborocket and sold outright for $73,950, the conversion is the fastest twin-engine piston plane on the market.

Top cruising speed is over 300 mph—on 75 percent power. Rate of climb at sea level is 2,200 feet per minute, the service ceiling is over 35,000 feet, and it will operate on one engine at 28,000 feet at 220 mph TAS.

The answer for that kind of performance, of course, has got to be Riley's turbocharging of the 290 hp Lycoming TSIO-540 engines, which replace the 260 hp Continentals in the original 310. Although the Turborocket carries only 1,530 pounds in useful load, compared to 2,075 pounds for the 310, gross weight has been cut from 5,200 pounds to 4,830 pounds in the Riley version.

Despite all the speed, stall speed is only 68 mph (compared to 75 mph for the 310), and the Turborocket can take off over a 50-foot obstacle in 985 feet fully loaded. Fuel consumption is not bad, either: 20 gallons per hour at economy cruise. Capacity in the rebuilt is 170 gallons.

The high noise level in flight, incidentally, is one of the most uncomfortable ever. What did you expect?

Cessna Cardinal

DOYN AIRCRAFT, INC., was not even satisfied with the brand-new Cardinal, which many people in the industry hail as the biggest improvement in "family aircraft" in years. If there was anything wrong with the Cardinal, it could be faulted only for underpowered performance, notably in take-off and climb characteristics.

Wichita insiders aver that the 150 hp Cessna Cardinal was originally designed *for* the engine Doyn uses in the conversion. They like to point to the panel on the factory Cardinal, where there is a blank instrument hole where a manifold pressure gauge seems to belong. Doyn's conversion fills in this vacant spot with a perfectly fitting manifold gauge, adds a vernier pitch-control knob for the Hartzell variable-pitch, constant-speed prop that replaces the Cessna fixed-pitch prop and uses a 180 hp Lycoming 0-360 engine for the kind of power the Cardinal seems to appreciate most.

The Doyn Cardinal takes off in 460 feet (compared to 845 feet for the factory version). Climb rate is increased from 670 feet per minute to over 1,000 fpm. One slight disadvantage: Doyn's conversion adds about 37 pounds to the empty weight, which cuts down the useful load limit to well under 900 pounds. By the time a practical package of radio gear is installed, you no longer have legal room for four adults and their baggage. Doyn is still working on getting the conversion certified for a higher gross-weight allowance, which seems reasonable enough but which the stiff-necked FAA is never very anxious to hand out to all applicants.

With a new engine exchange, Doyn charges $2,450 for the conversion. The shop is right in Wichita, so that Cardinal buyers can have Doyn pick up the plane directly from the Cessna plant and get right to work on it.

Cessna 172

ATLAS AVIATION has converted over 400 Cessna 172s from 145 hp to 180 hp powerplants and is only one of several converters who have concentrated on this job. Cessna itself has made several attempts to upgrade the performance of the 172 while still retaining its economy and easy handling, but the 175 hp Continental engine they used in the ill-fated model 175 and 172-P turned out to be something of a dog. Discontinuance of the models left the field wide open for converters like Atlas; result: the Atlas Skyrocket, which uses the same four-cylinder engine used in the small but fast Mooney Mark 21.

The Skyrocket increases rate of climb from 645 feet per minute to better than 1,100. On 75 percent power at 7,500 feet, cruising speed is upped from 130 mph to 155 mph; top speed, from 138 to 160 mph; take-off run, from 865 feet to 400 feet. Service ceiling behind that Hartzell controllable-pitch prop in the Rocket is 19,500 feet, compared to the factory version's 13,100 feet.

Atlas sells the complete conversion kit for $4,175 and will install it for an average of another $250 (depending on what shape the presently flying 172 or 175 is in). Or, in an increasing number of cases, Atlas will buy a new 172 from Cessna and deliver a zero-time Skyrocket for $15,950. The closest Cessna itself can come to that in a comparably powered plane is $17,995 for the 182.

FRANKLIN AIRCRAFT ENGINES convert the Cessna 172s into veritable STOL aircraft. At a recent test flight in the Franklin Scorpio, at sea level with the temperature at 85°F. and facing a 5K headwind, the plane broke ground in 225 feet with two-thirds the maximum gross weight . . . and cleared a 50-foot obstacle in less than 500 feet.

Cruise at 7,500 feet on less than 75 percent power was at 160 mph. Initial rate of climb was 2,000 feet per minute, and the steady rate of climb, from sea level to 5,000 feet, was 1,400 feet per minute. And this was in the "cheap" Scorpio, with nothing changed but the switch to Franklin's 215 hp engine and a controllable-pitch prop. With engine exchange, the conversion kit is $4,298 on a do-it-yourself basis or $4,775 installed. If Franklin buys a new 172 for the customer, the zero-time Scorpio costs $14,450.

That's only a start, excellent though it may be. The Scorpio Mark II has a new leading edge on the wing and a lash-up that couples the flaps with a droop-aileron system to increase the lift-to-drag ratio. This lowers the stall speed about 10 mph in almost every configuration, increases the climb performance, and further increases the cruise speed. Franklin sells the Scorpio MK II for $18,950.

The man who wants the ultimate in 172 STOL performance can even get a Beta prop for reverse thrust on the ground. Floats, skis, and so on are also available. The Scorpio only *looks* like Cessna's original 172.

Robertson/Cessna Aircraft

Robertson Aircraft Corporation specializes in converting single-engine Cessnas to STOL utility aircraft and is modifying 15 planes a month for outright sale. The latest modification to get FAA approval is the model 206, and aside from the Skywagon revamp the factory also converts the Cessna 180 and 182, Skylane, 185, 205, and 210, with a similar certification being prepared for the Skymaster. Jim Robertson designed the remarkable Sky Shark for the Navy back in 1961, a remarkable 420 hp airplane capable of flying under full control at less than 25 mph—which the military should have bought but didn't. He did not break away and start on his own in full production until 1967, but he is already doing so well that he tripled the new plant's size in less than a year.

The Robertson miracles are achieved without replacing the engines (which is about all that many conversion shops ever do). Robertson is a wing man. The stall-resistant leading edge on the recontoured wing provides mild stalls even under the most extreme conditions as well as easy stall recoveries. The flap/aileron system accounts for more than a fourth of the entire wing area. A stall fence between the flaps and ailerons generates amazingly responsive control at low airspeeds, and an elevator boost system increases power-off flare capability by 30 percent.

The result is a plane that can be flown at control speeds down to 38 mph instead of 61 mph and—what is perhaps even more startling—at top speeds to 208 mph instead of 200 mph for the factory version of the turbocharged Super Skylane/Skywagon airframe. At 3,600 pounds GW, Robertson's STOL 206 can clear a 50-foot obstacle in 865 feet, including a 435-foot ground run (compared to 1,810 feet with a 910-foot run). Robertson's price is $28,000.

Robertson's $19,245 STOL 180 cuts the regular take-off distances in half, increases cruising speeds by 3 mph, and cuts stall speed from 58 mph to 34 mph.

Modifications on already-flying customer aircraft run from

$3,500 to $3,950, and all Cessna models and years (except the 1967 210) may be modified to STOL, floatplane, or amphibian. The Navy might be coming around yet.

Wren/Cessna 182

Wren Aircraft Corporation builds a plane that could just barely be called a conversion (and the Wren people get sore when you call it that). However, the Wren 460 does start with a Cessna 182 airframe (just as Cessna itself buys engines, tires, brakes, radios, electrical fixtures, fittings, and so on from *its* suppliers). But the Ft. Worth plant tears down the Cessna product almost completely and builds in features not found on any other plane to effect its STOL capabilities.

Wren engineers don't bother with modifying the engine. They don't need to. By the time they finish putting in 1,064 Wren parts, 2,114 pieces of standard hardware (and only *one* new Cessna 182 airframe, as they like to point out), the result is a 2,800-pound-GW airplane that can take off with 1,120 pounds in useful weight from 270 feet of runway to clear a 50-foot obstacle in 560 feet. It climbs at 1,080 feet per minute, and although the top speed is a nonspectacular 160 mph, the stall speed is 26 mph—less than half of what the 182 was designed for.

The wing is mostly Wren's own, and it holds the plane in a level attitude at all operational speeds. Its most distinctive features are the "Wren's teeth" on the top of each wing section ahead of and linked with the ailerons. At normal cruise the teeth trail in the air stream, but these drag plates turn as much as 60 degrees broadside to the air stream ahead of an aileron in slow flight to produce a balancing drag to offset the otherwise adverse yaw created by the drag of the "down" aileron of the opposite wing. They can also provide a directional or rudder effect. Each wing has double-slotted flaps . . . full span.

The leading edge of the wing also has a cuff that serves the same purpose as a leading edge slot, but without any moving parts. It results in a "trailing edge" stall from which recovery is immediate with only a very slight reduction in angle of attack, with no loss of control or altitude.

The Wren shows her teeth

The Wren also has a set of silly-looking horizontal stabilizers and elevators mounted on the nose directly in back of the propeller disc, which look like something from an amusement-park ride. However, by utilizing the high energy of the propeller slipstream blast, these nose fins give the Wren an additional 100 feet per minute rate of climb as well as increased overall lift—enough so that the nose wheel of the tricycle gear can be lifted clear of the ground in less than the plane's length at the start of a take-off when operating from muddy or sandy surfaces, slush, and so on. An extrastrength nosewheel, incidentally, with oversized tires for nose and main wheels alike, is an option taken by almost all Wren buyers. This is strictly a bush plane for people who don't use regular airports.

In fact, that's why Wren says that they use a Cessna 182 airframe instead of building their own—and they say it with a straight face. The advantage, of course, is that Wren owners can use the worldwide organization for service and parts that Cessna maintains for routine items.

A Wren is not cheap. In fact, it is the most expensive single-engine fixed-gear plane on the market, with a price tag of $32,720 (or almost $15,000 more than the standard Cessna 182 it started as). And that's the base price; all optional equipment is extra.

However, the Wren *can* land almost like a helicopter. Especially with the optional Wren Beta prop ($1,995), which was developed in conjunction with Hartzell. The pilot who knows how to use the reversible Beta prop can make such steep precision approaches that the Wren looks like it has been shot out of the sky. And after touchdown, the Beta prop's reverse thrust can stop the Wren like throwing out an anchor.

It can even back into a parking place.

CHAPTER 11

Heterogeneous
aircraft

The aviation industry is similar to the automobile industry in many ways. Both have histories of sporadic
brilliant successes and dismal flops, of harebrained schemes and
painstaking engineering, and of splintered companies resulting
from personality clashes as well as consolidations in the face of
mounting competition.

Both industries started with daring imagination and both
have tended to stiffen up with conservatism with growth. One
of the most striking similarities between the two industries is the
way they have fragmented their markets with specialization.

The automobile industry was the first to evolve production
for specific markets, with specialized products for sharply defined
purposes. What started as the automobile has also become the
station wagon, sports car, pick-up truck, highway transport, military tank, industrial lift truck, tractor, bulldozer, and even golf
cart. The aviation industry now does much the same thing only
more so because every airplane model is so much more a matter
of compromise, with almost every advantage being weighed
against the sacrifice of another.

STOL Aircraft

The NATO international STOL standard for single-engine aircraft is defined as the capability to operate in and out of a single strip with 200 meters (660 feet) between 50-foot obstacles and maintain good maneuverability with full stall-proof safety in the event of heavy turbulence and sharp-edged gusts.

However, any number of manufacturers who advertise "Short Take-Off and Landing" aircraft simply ignore those arbitrary limitations, which do call for quite a sacrifice in speed and/or useful load-carrying capacities. Not counting the excellent Robertson and Wren conversions (sorry about that word again, Wren), there are only four makes of genuine STOL aircraft available in the United States. And only one of them is made in this country specifically for use from short, rough, unimproved, and sometimes even rocky air strips.

HELIO AIRCRAFT CORPORATION, of Bedford, Massachusetts, makes STOL planes exclusively—five of them. The progenitor was the Helioplane, developed in the 1940s by Dr. Otto Koppen of MIT and Dr. Lynn Bollinger, of Harvard Business School. It has evolved into one of the homeliest-looking high-wing taildraggers ever to head for a cow pasture, but at full gross weight of 3,400 pounds the basic model can land over a 50-foot silo in 535 feet, including a 210-foot ground roll.

It can take off again after a 420-foot ground run to clear a 50-foot obstacle in a total of 890 feet with the 1,510-pound useful load limit. This, says Helio, is still an official "NATO-defined STOL" because with the useful load cut down to 1,110 pounds it *can* clear a 50-foot obstacle in 660 feet. With the lesser load, the Helio Courier Mark II is fully maneuverable at 28 mph while still able to hit a top speed of 163 mph. The 250 hp STOL costs $33,900.

With a 295 hp Lycoming engine the Super Courier improves take-off distance by 150 feet to clear a 50-footer and increases speeds by 7 mph at top speed to 20 mph better at 65 percent power for 155 mph cruising. The Super costs $38,980.

The Helio Couriers get almost twice as much lift in the wing as conventional airfoils, with large slotted flaps on the trailing edge working with the automatic lead-edge slats. These distinctive slats extend or retract in response to changes in air pressure to prevent stall-spin, and aileron-linked airflow interceptors act as spoilers like the dive brakes on sailplanes.

Helio also makes two versions of its turbine-powered Stallion, a 2,600-pound EW 10-seater with a useful load of 2,500 pounds and a $110,000 price tag. With a 550-s-hp United Aircraft of Canada (UACL) PT6A-20 engine, the Stallion can climb at 1,640 feet per minute, has a maximum speed of 227 mph, and has a service ceiling over 25,000 feet. With a Beta prop approach and reverse thrust on the ground roll, the Stallion can land over a 50-foot obstacle in a total of 504 feet, including a 197-foot roll. The Stallion is also available either with a PT6A-6 engine or in a Garrett TPE 331-2-1 version.

Two Helio twin-engine STOLs are in the process of certification. Model 503 is powered by 250 hp Lycoming 10-540 engines, and turbosupercharged it has a service ceiling of 30,000 feet (12,500 feet on one engine). The 4,500-pound GW model 503 has six seats and cruises at 177 mph on 75 percent power, carrying a useful load of 1,374 pounds.

The Twin Stallion is a big 9,350-pound GW plane with up to 18 seats and a useful load limit of 4,940 pounds. It is powered by 600 hp UACL PT6A-23 engines and has a top speed of 290 mph, climbs at 2,500 feet per minute, has two-engine ceiling of 32,400 feet, or 15,000 feet on one engine, and a stall speed slower than most small "sport" planes: 45 mph.

DE HAVILLAND OF CANADA has had more experience building STOL aircraft than any other manufacturer in the world. The first Beaver was built in 1947, and bush pilots around the globe have since put 1,600 of them into service before the piston-powered old-timer was overshadowed by the 1965 introduction of the Turbo Beaver. Operators in remote areas far from "ordinary" service facilities particularly like the way the Beaver achieves its STOL performance without the use of any complex mechanisms.

The Turbo Beaver DHC Mark II can accommodate 9 people and has a 500-pound additional payload advantage over the standard version (useful load of the Mk II: 2,610 pounds out of a 5,370-pound allowable gross weight). The 578 es-hp UACL PT6A-6 engine has a service ceiling of 23,500 feet and operates at 163 mph on all operational settings (with a 60 mph stall speed). Price: $131,400. The standard Beaver is still available at $49,250 with a 450 hp Pratt & Whitney engine, but its performance is considerably less right down the line, except for that same "magic" 60 mph stall speed.

Although there are over 500 DHC Otters around the world, this larger single-engine plane never did meet with the acceptance received by the Beaver. But the new Twin Otter, which received its certification of airworthiness in mid-1966, is something else again. For one thing, the 19-passenger turboprop is aimed at the third-level commuter airlines—*the* twin market of today.

The DHC-6 trigear has a useful load of 5,629 pounds compared to its empty weight of 5,950 pounds and is powered by 579 es-hp UACL PT6A-20 engines. Lift-off is in 750 feet, top speed is 190 mph, stall speed is 67 mph, and ground roll is 495 feet at gross weight. Price: $350,000.

De Havilland of Canada also makes even bigger planes like the Caribou and the Buffalo (which is primarily a tactical transport for the military). In a deluxe passenger configuration, the Caribou has 24 comfortable chairs, buffet, toilet, and so on and can still land *or* take off over a 50-foot obstacle in 1,020 feet provided only that it has 540 feet of dry concrete to work on; it weighs 26,000 pounds on the ramp. As a cargo plane it can carry 8,620 pounds, and the big "drive-in" cargo door opening in the back belly can be left open in flight (as for carrying very long items such as pipe) without affecting the Caribou's flight and handling performance.

FAIRCHILD HILLER has tried hard to market the Swiss-built Heli-Porter, but even changing the name from Turbo-Porter doesn't seem to have helped much. Selling European designs in the United States is a tough proposition, even though FH actually

De Havilland Turbo Beaver

DHC-6 Twin Otter built by de Havilland of Canada accommodates up to 19 passengers in the high-density seating configuration, operates from grass and gravel airstrips only 1,000 feet long. Here the Twin Otter is seen approaching a small downtown airport opposite the Toronto waterfront.

does make the plane at its Hagerstown, Maryland, plant under license from the Pilatus Aircraft Works, Ltd.

The Heli-Porter does get reasonably close to the performance of a helicopter, too, and can take off at full gross of 4,850 pounds over a 50-foot obstacle in 550 feet including a ground run (hop?) of only 305 feet. Rather than gimmicks, it owes its lift to the big wing area (310 square feet). The high-wing tail-dragger has a useful load limit of 2,390 pounds when powered by a 575 s-hp Garrett TPE-331 engine and costs $95,000. Using a 550 s-hp UACL PT6A-6 engine, the eight-seat turboprop has an increase in useful load to 2,510 pounds due to the lesser empty weight and costs $104,000.

Using flat pitch on the Hartzell three-blader enables the Heli-Porter to approach a landing strip almost straight down. Once on the turf, reverse thrust can cut the landing roll to as little as 128 feet.

The Heli-Porter is a comparatively recent graduate from piston to turbine power, but this does not seem to be quite enough for the Swiss to yodel about. How about a little price cutting?

DORNIER GMBH, of West Germany, did not do too well trying to market its eight-seat high-wing STOL tail-dragger in the United States on its own and called in Butler Aviation to improve the situation. One of Butler's ideas is to concentrate on the 12-seat Skyservant model equipped complete with avionics in an air-taxi/commuter configuration.

The 8,050-pound GW Dornier Skyservant carries a useful load of 3,435 pounds and is powered by 380 hp Lycoming IGSO-540 engines. It lands and takes off over a 50-foot obstacle in 1,020 feet, including 600 feet for either the ground run or roll. Top speed is 200 mph, cruise on 65 percent power is 165 mph, and the Dornier Skyservant has a range of 1,225 miles. The base price in the United States was cut in 1968 from $190,000 to $170,000.

Dornier has built and sold over 900 of its STOL twins. *Prosit!*

Ag Planes

The typical agricultural plane is a cross between a STOL plane and a bronco. Ag planes put in some of the most rugged hours-per-week flying schedules in all aviation and have to be built to take the kind of punishment few other planes have the stress resistance to endure. Most ag planes have stick controls for fastest possible response, are built with external wing bracing, and have wire cutters and antisnag cables to protect the pilot.

AERO COMMANDER.   North American Rockwell builds the biggest line of ag planes on the market, and after a series of mergers and consolidations can now offer crop sprayers anything from a 230 hp plane with a 170-gallon chemical capacity to a 600 hp beast that can carry 400 gallons.

Aero Commander Thrush

The new (1968) Sparrow sells for $15,750 with its six-cylinder Lycoming 0-540 engine, weighs 1,600 pounds empty, and has a useful load limit of 1,400 pounds. It carries 40 gallons of gas, on which it can operate about three hours at around 100 mph. At sea level, it climbs at 650 feet per minute.

The $17,900 Quail has a fuel-injected 290 hp Lycoming I0-540 engine, and 1,600 pounds of its 3,600-pound GW is useful allowable load, figuring a 210-gallon chemical tank. Sea-level climb rate is 850 feet per minute, and the Quail goes 115 mph on 75 percent power.

Another new model is the Snipe, powered by a 450 hp Pratt & Whitney R-985 engine, at $25,150. Useful load limit is 2,400 pounds out of the 4,500-pound GW, with a 300-gallon sprayer tank. The nine-cylinder engine uses 20 gallons of fuel per hour, and the rate of climb is 650 feet per minute. "Cruise" speed: 115 mph.

Top of the ag line is the $39,500 Thrush, powered by a nine-cylinder 600 hp Pratt & Whitney R-1340-AN-1 engine. The 6,000-pound GW Thrush can carry 3,280 pounds in useful load, including 400 gallons of chemicals. It climbs at 1,000 feet per minute, has a top speed of 140 mph, and carries 110 gallons of fuel, which is enough for four hours of work.

PIPER.   Safety is stressed in Piper's two new models, from the burst-resistant polyurethane fuel tank and progressive-collapse fuselage design to roll bars, cushioned head rest, recessed instruments and controls, and a cockpit floor 10 inches above the bottom of the fuselage.

The 2,900-pound GW Pawnee costs $16,490 with a six-cylinder 235 hp Lycoming 0-540 engine (and a useful load of 1,480 pounds) or $16,990 with a 260 hp Lycoming—1,360 pounds in useful load. Climb rate is under 700 feet per minute for both, and both have top speeds of 126 mph, 75 percent power speed of 115 mph, and 65 percent power speed of 107 mph. Stall speed is 61 mph in both versions, and both carry 38 gallons of fuel for a good morning's work.

CESSNA. The main difference in Cessna's two Agwagons is in the powerplants for the 3,300-pound GW workhorse. With a 230 hp Continental 0-470-R engine and 1,520 pounds in useful load, the Agwagon is priced at $16,695. It takes off over a 50-foot obstacle in 1,320 feet, climbs at 755 feet per minute, has a top speed of 138 mph, goes 128 mph on 75 percent power, and stalls at 56 mph.

But what a difference a couple of thousand dollars can make. The $18,995 model's 300 hp Continental I0-520-D engine takes off over a 50-foot obstacle in 970 feet, climbs at 940 feet per minute, has a top speed of 151 mph, travels at 141 mph on 75 percent power, and still has the same 56 mph stall speed. The

Cessna Agwagon's panel is typically simple

model 300 Agwagon just uses *its* 37 gallons of fuel a little faster (15.8 gallons per hour, compared to the 260's 14).

GRUMMAN. Like everything else Grumman builds, it tries to make its ag planes a little bit different and a little bit better than the competition. Naturally, the prices are usually a little bit higher, too.

The Ag Cat is the only high-wing plane built specifically for agricultural work. This, according to Grumman, is in the interests of pilot safety when he is clearing fences at an altitude of about five feet. The competition says that a low-wing ag plane provides for a better down-wash effect on the crops being dusted or sprayed. Grumman uses a big powerplant for the same effect.

The basic Ag Cat has a 300 hp Jacobs R-755-A2-M1 engine and carries a useful load of 1,550 pounds out of a 3,750-pound GW. It climbs at 700 feet per minute and has a top speed of 131 mph, 75 percent power speed of 100 mph, and 65 percent power speed of 80 mph. Stall speed is 55 mph, and the price is $21,065.

The Super Ag Cat has a 450 hp Pratt & Whitney R-985 engine, has a gross weight of 4,500 pounds, and carries 1,810 pounds in useful load. Top speed is 16 mph faster, and stall speed is also up by another 12 mph, but the operational speeds remain the same. The price is $27,830.

Users say it's worth it.

WEATHERLY AVIATION. Like many ag planes, a Weatherly is sometimes loaded beyond its legal limit in actual field use. Although the gross weight is certified at 4,350 pounds, a Weatherly has been known to climb at 800 feet per minute with a "ramp" weight of 4,800 pounds. The power for the 2,550-pound EW sprayer is a 450 hp Pratt & Whitney R-985 engine, and the $19,600 price beats the closest competition by $5,550 for that big a powerplant. Stall speed is also the most dangerous of any standard ag plane: 69 mph.

Top speed is 128 mph and speed on 65 percent power is 105 mph. The Weatherly uses gas normally at 20 gallons per hour, which doesn't last long from a 45-gallon tank.

But it's all competition. Ag planes are now selling at the rate of over 1,000 aircraft a year compared to only 75 a year just 10 years ago.

Rotorcraft

An ag operator makes or loses money on his turns when he gets past the end of the field he's working on and has to come back to make another pass for the next row of crops. If he's in a helicopter, all he has to do when he gets to the end of the field is turn the aircraft around like a barber's chair and come right back.

Can Bell 47-J make rooftop landings common?

Bell Helicopter even *looks* complicated

A helicopter can take off from the roof of a downtown sky-scraper and land on the roof of another office building across town before some of the tenants in the first building can get down to street level by elevator.

The helicopter pilot can literally take off from his backyard and may be at his destination halfway across the state before his neighbor can even drive his car to the home-town airport. And he can land in a parking lot across the street from his ultimate objective.

Why, then, are there still such old-fashioned contraptions around as the fixed-wing airplane (not to mention the automobile)?

The average wing pilot has a ready answer for this question. "Just looking at a helicopter is enough to show you that a thing like that could never fly," he is likely to say. "I will stick to a regular airplane for flying, like the good Lord intended."

In general, the more air time an amateur pilot has to his credit, the more afraid he is of a helicopter. He is full of stories about how things fall off in flight. He knows what would happen if *that* engine ever quit. And if that silly little tail rotor ever goes flooie, the whole business starts spinning around from the torque like a berserk barber chair. Helicopter pilots all have rabbit eyes and drink their whiskey straight by the shot glass, etc., etc.

Naturally, such opinions are the result of ignorance. It's widespread ignorance, though, and less than 2 percent of all licensed pilots hold a helicopter rating. Learning to fly one is expensive, and compared to flying a fixed-wing aircraft, the complexity of a helicopter demands a much higher standard of accuracy; helicoptering is even tougher than ag flying.

"The mosquito that carries a light bulb" is also expensive to buy, to operate, and to maintain. Costs for comparable performance are roughly three times the costs for a light single-engine fixed-wing plane. There is a serious shortage of instructors, mechanics, dealers, and—worst of all—places to land legally.

Numerous areas, whole towns, and even entire states have antihelicopter laws. In many cases, a helicopter can land and take off only from a regular airport—which rather defeats its whole purpose.

The best hope for the long-overdue popularity of the helicopter is the recent development of the light gas-turbine engine, which may well turn out to be more important to the industry than anything since turbocharging. Less than a yard long and a foot in diameter, the Allison T63 free turbine engine, for example, weighs less than 140 pounds and is certified at maximum power of 317 hp. This is the powerplant that enables choppers like the Hughes 500, the Bell Jet Ranger, and the Fairchild Hiller 1100 to cruise with five people at 150 mph for 400 or 500 miles.

These three white hopes are changing more minds about the future of helicoptering than all other models combined. The 500 costs $78,800 and carries a useful load of 1,328 pounds out of a 2,400-pound gross. The 2,900-pound GW Jet Ranger carries 1,540 pounds of useful load and costs $89,000, and $91,500 buys an FH 1100 with a 2,750-pound GW, of which 1,355 is useful load.

Model 1100 is such a strong contender that Fairchild Hiller is no longer pushing its 305 hp three- and four-seat $49,950 and $63,950 models, or the once-"best" 315 hp $69,000 four-seater.

Hughes 500-U

Bell has pulled back only on the 10-seat, $325,000 1,100 s-hp Lycoming-powered 204-B and still makes five other models. They range from $39,950 ag models with 265 hp Lycoming engines and 280 hp 3-seaters tagged at $44,950 to the 15-seat 205-A with a 1,250 hp engine that is still undergoing certification tests at this writing.

Hughes also offers a pair of conventionally powered helicopters with 180 hp Lycoming engines. The two-seater, with a useful load rating of 661 pounds, costs $33,500. A three-seat model, with 712 pounds in useful load, is $33,640.

So far, the only other manufacturer using the new Allison engines is Berlin Doman, which supersedes the Caribe Doman Company's $130,000 400 hp 10-seater. The Berlin Doman 10-seater is a twin using 370 s-hp engines, for a useful load limit of 2,750 pounds. Price is $290,000.

The only other twin-engine helicopters are Boeing's big $700,000 25-seater with 1,500 s-hp GE engines, which can carry 11,961 pounds in useful load; Sikorsky's same-powered 30-seater, which costs $913,150 and carries 6,744 pounds in useful load; and the Sikorsky "Flying Crane," with massive 4,500 s-hp Pratt & Whitney engines, which can carry up to 67 people in a removable pod, has a useful load certification of 22,890 pounds, and costs $2,100,000. Sikorsky's 13-seat model S-62-A gets along on one 1,250 s-hp GE engine, carries 2,967 pounds in useful load, and is priced at $317,825.

Twin rotors working in tandem from a single engine have the advantage of an extended center of gravity, and the Jovair four-seat Sedan is a good example of what can be done with a 235 hp Franklin 6A-350 engine. Priced at $49,750, the Jovair Sedan carries 850 pounds at 85 mph for a 210-mile range. The all-new Filper Beta 400 now uses a bigger 285 hp Continental engine, easily carries four people within the 1,100-pound useful load limit, can cruise at 130 mph, and costs $39,850 (the 210 hp version, with two seats and a 700-pound useful load for $19,850, didn't work out too well, even with the much-simplified blade articulation system).

Jovair also makes the newly redesigned two-seat 180 hp model J-2, which carries 550 pounds and which is not a helicopter at all, but an autogyro (a gyroplane depends on its movement through the air—rather than power—to keep its rotor blades turning, which simply act as a rotary wing; propulsion is provided by a conventional aircraft propeller system). The J-2's motor and prop are mounted aft of the little cabin. Price: $13,970.

The lowest-priced regular helicopter is Scheutzow's $12,000 two-seater with a 180 hp Lycoming engine and a 590-pound useful load limit, cruising at 80 mph in a bubble canopy under a flexhub rotor that eliminates bearings. Other lower-cost helicopters include the three-seat Enstrom, with a 205 hp Lycoming engine and a useful load limit of 720 pounds for a 95 mph speed at cruise ($35,960); and the new 235 hp Continental Tom Cat with a 1,180-pound load limit, cruising at 75 mph and costing $22,500 (upped from the 210 hp version priced at $18,500).

Although Bell has built and sold more helicopters than all other manufacturers combined, the strongest competition for the new gas-turbine choppers is from Brantly now that Lear Jet has taken over the operation. The Brantly design looks more like a

Filper Beta Tandem-Engine Model 200

regular airplane than other helicopters, and the full-fuselaged tricycle-gear model 305 cruises at 110 mph with five people aboard. It has a 305 hp Lycoming engine, carries up to 1,060 pounds, and costs $59,500. A smaller two-seater with 180 hp and a 650-pound useful load limit goes for $30,900.

Smallest of 'em all is the one-seat Bensen Gyrocopter, with a gross weight of 500 pounds and a useful load limit of 253

Igor Bensen at the Gyrocopter's controls

pounds. The powerplant is a 90 hp McCulloch engine (that's right . . . McCulloch is the company that makes chain saws). This vehicle is strictly for fresh-air buffs, and the pilot rides on a few pipes resembling a bicycle frame without so much as a windshield to protect him from the elements.

The Bensen is reputed to be capable of a 60 mph cruise speed, and for a man with steel nerves and a lot of faith in his safety belt, the service ceiling is 12,500 feet above the ground directly below his heels. The price is right, though: $1,195. However, the pilot has to put the thing together himself, inasmuch as Bensen does not have a type certificate for selling the ready-to-fly aircraft (the FAA objects to the single-ignition engine, for one thing). The Gyrocopter is thus usually flown as an "experimental" plane in the United States. Bensen has sold well over 600 kits to date.

Home-Builts

If a man doesn't have the requisite $1,195 for a Bensen Gyrocopter kit, Igor Bensen will sell him a set of plans for $30 so he can build the whole thing from scratch in his garage. Do-it-yourself airplane builders are increasing in numbers so fast that they support dozens of "manufacturers" who have nothing to sell but the plans, for which they charge from $10 to $125. Interest is so widespread that many such plans sellers have to charge a dollar or two even for their brochures to protect themselves from the idly curious.

There are more home-built planes flying today than all the aircraft operated by all the airlines. Of the 2,600 home-builts licensed by the FAA, fewer than 500 are "originals," but there are another 7,000 under construction . . . and who knows but what some incipient Orville Wright will come up with the ideas that will enable the industry to realize the dream of a light plane in every garage?

It is in this hope that the FAA will allow a do-it-yourselfer to build almost anything so long as it doesn't threaten the life and property of United States citizens other than the pilot. The

This is the Bensen B8M "Gyrocopter." This particular machine was originally built in Canada by Al Cudney, now of Raleigh, North Carolina. Mr. Cudney taught himself to fly in this machine. It is powered by a 72-hp McCulloch engine.

situation was not always so. Barnstorming and home-building were so chaotic in the 1920s and 1930s that federal legislation made licensing a home-built plane impossible. By 1934, most of the states had also put through state laws that grounded the home-builts, and by the start of World War II only Oregon remained free of such bureaucratic interference. It was not until 1948 that irate home-builders were successful in getting a new "amateur-built" aircraft category established.

But once this status was official, the home-built field began growing, to the point that the Experimental Aircraft Association now has over 45,000 members. Some 6,000 new members joined in 1967 alone, and the EAA is represented in all 50 states and in 51 foreign countries. For a week every July, the EAA's convention turns the relatively sleepy airport at Rockford, Illinois, into the busiest airport in the world. In 1967, this largest of all

Simplicity of construction and a ticket to pure fun is graphically illustrated in the RLU-1 "Breezy" designed and built by three Illinois engineers. "Breezy" uses Piper PA-12 wings, has a 90-hp Continental Engine, and cruises from 70 to 90 mph. It is very easy to fly, lands on a dime, and has unparalleled visibility.

aviation events was attended by more than half a million visitors, without the EAA having spent one cent in advertising.

The biggest hit of any EAA show is usually something like the Roloff-Unger-Liposky (the three Midwestern engineers who built it in their spare time with "eye-ball engineering") pusher with tandem seats named *Breezy*. Essentially, it is a Piper wing, a 90 hp Continental engine, and conventional tail surfaces tied together with uncovered steel tubing framework. Only a Bensen Gyrocopter can challenge it for pilot-visibility. Even the governor of the state took a ride around the field in the passenger seat.

Many home-builders like fanciful names for their aircraft.

One, patterned after a Beechcraft, is dubbed *Son of a Beech*. A two-place tandem is called *The Tuholer*. One of the most popular is called *The Mustang*, with no static to date from Mooney.

Aside from the swarms of "standard" home-builts constructed from store-bought plans (many with modifications according to the notions of the builders), every EAA convention attracts far-out innovations, too. They include delta wings built from $1,800 worth of parts; midgets that the pilot has to fly in a prone position; three-engine planes with a gross weight of 220 pounds; and planes built of fiberglassed cardboard to compete for attention with racers, aerobatic planes, helicopters and autogyros with up to six engines apiece, and gliders that weigh as little as 86 pounds.

Aside from standard aircraft engines (many salvaged from wrecks), powerplants include Volkswagen and Ford Model A and even T engines, motors originally designed for (and sometimes previously used in) power mowers, Go-Karts, motorcycles, outboard motorboats, and golf carts.

They are safer than they may sound. An FAA inspector keeps an eagle eye on every vital step in construction, and even after the plane flies he almost always puts restrictions as to how and where it can be flown. Night flying and instrument flying are almost always verboten. The biplanes are particularly safe to fly, and the EAA sells the plans for one of its own for $10 per set.

The EAA bipe, powered by an 85 hp Continental engine, is a one-seater with a 1,150-pound gross weight that can carry 440 pounds in useful load. It takes off in 500 feet, climbs at 1,000 feet per minute, has a service ceiling of 11,500 feet—where it can cruise at 110 mph—and has a range of 305 miles. Top speed is 125 mph, stall speed is 50 mph, and the EAA lands in 800 feet. Cost of the materials runs from $1,500 to $2,000, including a good used engine. The EAA has sold almost 4,000 sets of plans for this plane, and it is either flying or under construction in almost every part of the civilized world.

One of the most popular distributors of blueprints is Stits Aircraft, with plans available for four different models. The Stits Skycoupe is one of the few home-builts that is so good it has achieved type certification for manufacture. The Skycoupe named

Black Magic by builder Ed Fisher of Mentor, Ohio, has won numerous awards for excellence in performance as well as in construction. Many home-built flying machines cost less than a new compact car. Construction costs with new materials run from around $600 to $4,000, with an average of around $2,000, including a used engine. There is also a matter of about 2,000 hours of spare-time work for the average finished job. Thus, if the home-builders have anything to teach to the industry, it is not in the field of cost cutting.

If the do-it-yourselfer figures his time as worth only $3 an hour, his labor added to the material cost is around $8,000. If a manufacturer adds 50 percent for overhead and administration, he'd have a hardware cost of $12,000; add a profit and sell the product through a distributor and dealer, and you'd have a price tag of $20,000 or $25,000—and there are a lot of factory-built airplanes that sell for a whale of a lot less than that.

No home-builder who can count over 10 without taking his shoes off ever builds his own plane to save money, regardless of what he tells his wife. Besides the materials, he needs equipment, too. If he needs to learn a special skill such as welding, that also costs money. A riveting gun, plus a compressor to run it, is on the "must" list for metal fuselage and wing work, and the garage-turned-machine-shop can easily account for several thousand dollars worth of equipment.

The only real reason most men build their own planes is simply because they like to do it. David Long, for example, was Piper's chief engineer . . . and he designed the Midget Mustang purely as a hobby. This plane has since become one of the most popular "blueprint" single-seaters, and the all-metal racer cruises at 190 mph with only an 85 hp engine.

It has since been redesigned as a low-wing two-seater by Robert Bushby, who is "by day" a Chicago-area lab technician in the petroleum industry. He sells his 40 sheets of plans and drawings, plus a 60-page illustrated manual, for $125. Not counting the necessary 1,750 hours of work, the Mustang II costs around $2,300 to build. Gross weight is 1,250 pounds, it carries 500 pounds in useful load, and it cruises on 75 percent power at

Hugh Beckham of Wichita, Kansas, built this all-wood Taylor Mono-plane in three years' time for $550. The ship, painted in camouflage colors, cruises 105 mph on a Volkswagen engine.

167 mph. The cheapest factory-built plane that can do that is the Maule Strata Rocket, which sells for $15,498.

Hugh Beckham, of Wichita, Kansas, couldn't stand the sight of all those Cessna and Beech beauties coming off the production lines without having a plane of his own, so he built one of his own . . . for $550. It took him three years to do it, and piloting the midget monoplane is more like wearing it than riding in it, but the all-wood Taylor will cruise at 105 mph behind its 40 hp Volkswagen engine. The tight-fitting single-seater is of British design and bears a striking resemblance to a miniature Spitfire.

Pete Bowers' problem was getting his plane to and from the airport for flights, which were not frequent enough to warrant expensive hangaring, so he built a plane with wings that could fold flat against the fuselage so it could be towed on the highway and stored at home in the garage. After the all-wood one-seat tail-dragger won the 1962 EAA design contest, so many people were after him for plans that he went into the business at $15 per set. It can be built for $1,000 in materials and has a top speed of 120 mph.

Another folding-wing home-built is Robert Nesmith's popular Cougar, an easy-to-build boxlike high-winger that can cruise at 140 mph. Bob Campbell, a Phoenix, Arizona, auto-body repair-man, modified the Nesmith drawings to incorporate a T tail. After $2,000 and four years of spare-time work, he has a 1,300-pound GW plane that can carry 630 pounds in useful load and climbs at 1,400 feet per minute.

Mike Frey, 32-year-old Waco Texan, and John Astlund, of Gardena, California, both believe that Lou Stolp's Starduster plans are the best in the business. Frey used a 150 hp Lycoming engine in his version and can carry 520 pounds of useful load in the 1,350-pound GW one-seat biplane, with a top speed of 180 mph. Astlund has worked on F-106 jet fighters and has an

Robert A. Campbell of Phoenix, Arizona, modified his aircraft from the basic Nesmith "Cougar" drawings to incorporate a "T" tail. This "Cougar," one of many flying, is powered by a 108-hp Lycoming.

Beautiful workmanship and finish is apparent on the Stolp Adams SA-100 "Starduster," built by John Astlund of Gardena, California. The engine is a 125-hp Lycoming 0-290-G.

The first amphibious home-built to gain popularity is the Volmer VJ-22 "Sportsman." This "Sportsman" was built by Dr. Andrew Chapeskie of Barry's Bay, Ontario. The aircraft was modified from the original plans by mounting the engine in a tractor configuration instead of a pusher. The engine is a Lycoming 0-290-G of 125 hp.

This Nieuport 24BIC, World War I fighter, was built by Dr. Roy C. Wicker of Atlanta, Georgia. The aircraft is an exact duplicate of the famous fighter of the First World War and is powered by a 120-hp LeRhone rotary engine. Cruise is 110 mph, and the rate of climb is 750 fpm. The aircraft is on display at the EAA Air Education Museum in Franklin, Wisconsin. In this photo, EAA President Paul Poberezny is in the cockpit.

unusually fine cockpit layout accordingly, which won him an EAA award for outstanding workmanship. Stolp also sells plans for a bigger, two-seat Starduster with a 24-foot wing span ($50 per set) and is a full-time dealer in home-builder supplies as well.

Volmer Jensen's plans for the Sportsman, the first amphibious home-built to get a big play, call for a pusher-type engine. However, Dr. Andy Chapeskie of Barry's Bay, Ontario, Canada, modified the drawings by mounting the 125 hp engine he finally decided to use in a tractor configuration. The doctor spent two years and $8,000 building his Sportsman, which can cruise at

EAA Biplanes are under construction all over the world. This is one of the roomiest and most comfortable home-built biplanes available, and the aircraft performs well. It was designed for simplicity and ease of handling. Over 3,500 sets of plans for the EAA Biplane have been sold by EAA. This EAA Biplane was built by Louis Lasnier of Mayville, New York.

90 mph with a 515-pound payload in the 1,600-pound GW retrac amphib.

Dr. Roy Wicker indulged nostalgia when he decided to build his own plane and put together an exact duplicate of a Nieuport 24BIC World War I fighter plane, leaving off nothing but the machine guns. Snoopy would envy the 120 hp LeRhone rotary engine in going after the Red Baron. Rate of climb is 750 feet per minute and cruise speed is 110 mph. Even the "coffin and death's head" insignia on the fuselage is authentic.

Representative Home-Built Plans

Source	Price	Name	Comment
Standard Biplanes			
Experimental Aircraft Assn. PO Box 229 Hales Corners, Wisc. 53130	$15	EAA Biplane	roomier cockpit than most

Source	Price	Name	Comment
Meyer Aircraft 5706 Abby Dr. Corpus Christi, Texas 78413	$50	Little Toot	monocoque construction
Ralph Mung, Jr. 1218 N. 91 E. Avenue Tulsa, Okla. 74115	$39	Sport	one of the most popular

Aerobatic Biplanes

Source	Price	Name	Comment
C. H. Pitts Box 548 Homestead, Fla. 33030	$100	Pitts Special	THE aerobatic home-built
Dorothy Smith 1938 Jacaranda Pl. Fullerton, Calif.	$25	Miniplane	delicately responsive
Stolp Aircraft PO Box 461, Municipal Airport Corona, Calif.	$25	Stolp-Adams Starduster	bigger 2-seat model, $50

Parasol Wing, Open Cockpit

Source	Price	Name	Comment
Ace Aircraft Mfg. Co. 106 Arthur Rd. Ashville, N.C.	$29	Baby Ace	popular since 1931
Same	$29	Junior Ace	2-seat design
H. L. Woods 6544 Portsmouth Dr. Reynoldsburg, Ohio	$35	Woody Pusher	all-wood tandem 2-seater

Folding Wing

Source	Price	Name	Comment
Pete Bowers 13826 Des Moines Way Seattle, Wash.	$15	Fly Baby	tow behind car, store in garage
Len Eaves 3818 N.W. 36th St. Oklahoma City, Okla.	$20	Cougar	155 mph top speed
Stits Aircraft PO Box 3084 Riverside, Calif. 92509	$75	Playmate	Stits is also a dealer in supplies for home-builders

Source	Price	Name	Comment
High-Wing "Box" Construction			
S. J. Wittman PO Box 276 Oshkosh, Wisc.	$125	Tailwind	easy to build 2-seat classic with 165 mph top speed capability
Low-Wing Standards			
Robert Bushby 848 Westwood Dr. Glenwood, Ill. 60425	$125	Mustang II	2-seat design of classic Mustang I racer
Anton Cvjetkovic 8731 Nada St. Downey, Calif.	$25	MiniAce	all-wood construction, single-seat
Same	$10	MiniTwo	2-seat conversion plan with above
Same	$65	CA-65	top speed over 150 mph
Same	$15	retractable landing gear	for CA-65 and other low-wing planes to 1,500 lbs. GW
Falconar Aircraft Ltd. Edmonton Industrial Airport Edmonton, Alberta, Canada	$60	Piel Emeraude CP-30	2-seat, 65 hp 112 mph top speed French design
Same	$60	Piel Emeraude CP-300	2-seat, 90 hp 137 mph top speed
Same	$50	Druine Turbulent	Falconer is large-scale plans distributor
Stits Aircraft PO Box 3084 Riverside, Calif. 92509	$25	Playboy 3-A	aerobatic
Same	$35	Playboy 3-B	2-seater with dual controls
Mrs. F. J. Taylor 25 Chesterfield Crescent Leigh-on-Sea, Essex England	$25	Taylor Monoplane	midget "Spitfire"

Source	Price	Name	Comment
Thorp Engineering 909 E. Magnolia Burbank, Calif. 91501	$125	T-18	classic 2-seater, cranked wing
M. L. Turner 6842 Pine Park Dr. Ft. Worth, Tex. 76118	$65	T-40	for 1-seat version; 2-seat also available

Amphibian

Volmer Aircraft 104 E. Providence Ave. Burbank, Calif.	$125	Sportsman	uses a Champion wing

Racers*

Robert Bushby 848 Westwood Dr. Glenwood, Ill. 60425	$75	Mustang I	speed to 190 mph
Tom Cassutt 32 West Cliff Dr. Huntington Station, N.Y.	to specs	Racer II	to 230 mph, stressed to 12 G
G. F. Styles 22 Gosden Rd., West End Woking, Surrey England	$60	Luton Beta	150 mph tops, winner of British design competition
Mrs. F. J. Taylor 25 Chesterfield Crescent Leigh-on-Sea, Essex England	$33	Titch	to 170 mph, racing adaptation of regular low-wing design

* By definition in regulated racing competition, a midget racer must have fixed landing gear and at least 66 square feet of wing area and must be driven by an unmodified 90-cubic-inch engine (which means, in effect, a Continental C-85).

CHAPTER 12

Aero
economics

After a man makes up his mind about which make and model of airplane he wants, his decisions are only just beginning. He's got to decide what he wants to pay for it, who he wants to pay for it, when he wants to pay for it, and maybe even *if* he wants to pay for it.

"What" means "how much." Forget about "suggested list prices," which are illegal anyhow. Federal law prohibits the factory from pegging a hard-line price. Besides, this is the aviation industry, which still has a "silk scarf" aura to an amazing degree for economists.

Aircraft distribution is like automobile dealership only in that both operations are concerned with passenger vehicles. A car dealer might have to sell ten automobiles a week to stay in business, but many airplane dealers may only sell one a month. Competition keeps the car dealer's prices in line, but the airplane dealer's price structure is at the mercy of the merciless.

Such a prospective buyer may like a plane with, say, a "suggested list price" of $12,850. If he is privy to the fact that this particular factory sells to dealers at a 30 percent discount from "list price," he knows full well that the dealer's actual cost is $8,995. If he waves a $10,000 check at the dealer, what's the poor dealer going to do, say, "No"?

Airplane buyers are too few and far between. And as the man said, "You can't lose money by making money."

The man who said that, of course, is no longer in business. However, the average fixed-base operator runs his business like a golf pro runs the pro shop; he is an enthusiast first and a businessman second. If the dealer is typically one part mechanic and three parts aviator, he figures what the hell, he's making money on parts, maintenance, and tie-down fees. Lessons are picking up. The cola machine is paying off good. Besides, this guy will buy a lot of gas if he buys a plane. And the dealer craftily figures that he will "get" the customer when he gets around to avionics. So he takes the ten grand and the hell with the way the auditor is always whining about figuring in over-head as part of costs.

The airplane buyer who can't get a new plane for 15 per-cent to 20 percent less than the "suggested list price" just isn't trying if he shops around a little with a checkbook in his hand.

Unfortunately, a lot of prospective airplane buyers don't have anything *in* the checking account to speak of. Many com-panies, too, are loath to tie up sizable sums in company planes; the average company that buys executive aircraft is usually pretty progressive, and when progress means company growth, working capital is more valuable in fluid inventories than in frozen assets.

And that's what banks are for. However, only a handful of the 13,000 banks in the country will have anything to do with "dangerous" airplanes. When the aircraft itself is the collateral, the airplane buyer has to seek out a specialist. This is despite the fact that a good plane is a much better financing risk than the average automobile; most planes do not depreciate like auto-mobiles, and plenty of planes built in the 1950s and even in the 1940s are worth more today than when they were built . . . which should be enough to make a loan officer's mouth water when he considers the collateral.

One of the pioneers in aircraft financing is the Beverly Bank in Chicago. One reason is because the bank's president, Wes

Larson, is a pilot himself. Entering the then wide-open market in 1958, BevBank has since financed over $75 million worth of planes, and the bank's aviation department now operates in 42 states and several foreign countries.

The staff includes five licensed pilots, including two with jet ratings, and they aggressively go after the business. Frank Sinatra's Lear Jet, for example, was handled not through one of the giant West Coast or New York banks, but through the relatively small Beverly Bank deep in Chicago's South Side. The bank also handles financing for flying clubs, for the insurance requirements that sometimes surprise new owners, and even for flight training.

Beverly Bank's success has generated banking interest in many parts of the country, and perhaps a hundred banks are now feeling their way into the market. The Chicago bank is planning to offer a seminar for bankers who would like to learn the ins and outs of aircraft financing.

One of them that won't need it is the Michigan Bank of Detroit, where Bob Horder has long dominated Motown's financing of private planes. Another specialist in the field is the Pullman Group in Chicago, a working affiliation of the Pullman Bank & Trust Company, Standard Bank & Trust Company, and Country Bank & Trust Company of Blue Island; head of the Aviation Finance Department is Ernie Moritz, who finances used as well as new planes and works with dealers as well as with individuals and corporations. Pullman rates can dip as low as 5 percent and less, with down-payment requirements as little as a fifth of the purchase price, starting with a minimum of $5,000.

A newcomer to the field in the east is the National Community Bank of Rutherford, New Jersey, which has set up an aircraft loan division in the commercial loan department with James Peters (himself a pilot) at the controls. He started with a lot going for the operation, inasmuch as New Jersey leads the rest of the country in aircraft per square mile, with over 2,200 private planes flying out of the northern part of the state alone; the state has 81 public airfields and 70 private ones. Within a year, National Community Bank was also promoting its aviation financing service in nearby states such as New York, Pennsylvania, and Connecticut as well.

The Southwest National Bank of Wichita, Kansas, entered the field in 1962 because its management figured that its future was already closely tied into the light aircraft industry, what with Cessna, Beech, and Lear in town. W. A. Pivonka, senior vice-president in charge of consumer loans, was assigned the organization job and got himself a pilot's license, and business has since boomed to the point that the bank had to buy a company plane of its own to facilitate operations in the surrounding five-state area.

Typical of the smaller banks who are willing—nay, anxious —to handle aircraft financing is the Dania Bank, Dania, Florida, just below Ft. Lauderdale. Frank Peuser, vice-president, and Eugene Huguelet, head of the installment credit department, are so enthusiastic about promoting fly money that they recently moved a whole tricycle-geared plane into the bank for a lobby display complete with "you, too, can own" literature (a Wichita product, and with Riley such a nearby neighbor!).

Inasmuch as the general flying public sometimes has a hard time finding such banks, many brokers are entering the field as middle men to meet the demand for paper. One of them, Arthur Z. Brown, of Deerfield, Illinois, is so active in the aviation market that he has more planes registered in his name in the *Civil Aircraft Register* of national registration numbers than any of the banks that specialize in the aviation field.

The point is, there *is* financing around for the airplane buyer today through standard channels at bank rates. This is one reason why so many corporation officials are able to justify the ownership of company planes to their stockholders' satisfaction; a $50,000 investment (as in a typical twin) actually costs only $3,000 a year at standard bank rates—and a company plane can save that $250 a month in motel bills alone, not to mention increasing the productivity of the executives, expanding markets, and so on.

And that hypothetical case would apply only if the company wasn't making any money. Almost any company in business at all is in the 50 percent tax bracket, at least; that would mean that the interest cost of $3,000 a year, fully deductible, would actually be costing the stockholders only $125 per month.

"Fully deductible" is a big if, admittedly. IRS agents go over flight logs with particularly fine-toothed combs, and many seem to consider the mere fact of aircraft ownership a challenge. Flight logs must be meticulous in detail to thwart these eagle-eyes with the poised blue pencils, and every entry must have names, places, and *dates.*

The one method of acquisition that leaves the least room for argument with the tax people is finance-leasing. This tax dodge does not build up any equity, and the property is not kept on the books as a taxable asset. Title is not vested in the user, and aside from simplifying income-tax complications, finance-leasing also minimizes personal-property tax situations in many parts of the country. Some leases can even be carried as a liability.

Finance-leasing is widely used in the acquisition of everything from major investments in production machinery to real estate and buildings, but its use in aircraft acquisition is in its infancy. A usual lease covers total purchase price and finance charges in five years, when the lessee has the continuing option to renew the lease for as many years as he wants at 1 percent of the original equipment cost per year. And it's all legal.

The individual owner of a private plane can also take advantage of leasing, although in a somewhat reverse manner. Take, for example, a man who has saved up $3,000 toward the purchase of a $15,000 plane. If he pays it off in five years, his installment payments and insurance premiums will run around $300 a month. If this is liable to put a crimp in the family budget, he can often make a deal with a flight school or fixed-base rental operation to lease the plane from him—to the advantage of all parties concerned.

In the usual agreement, the fixed-base man puts the "leased" plane on the regular flight line, where it pays part of its keep in regular hourly rentals, with the owner getting 75 percent of the revenue. If the fee is $20 an hour, the owner thus gets $15 an hour . . . and if the "prostitute" is used 20 hours a month, the owner realizes an income of $300 a month—which covers what he's shelling out, and his own use of the plane is "free."

Furthermore, if the owner uses the plane 10 hours a month himself, he can deduct two-thirds of *all* expenses as business expenses, including the higher insurance premiums!

The advantage to the school or fixed-base operation is obvious; a fleet of a couple dozen single-engine planes would represent an investment of $300,000 or $400,000, but on lease-back arrangements there is no investment at all, and no overhead accordingly when planes stand idle. The owner takes care of all repairs, and usually in a shop operated by the lessor.

Whether an airplane owner can afford to keep a plane for his exclusive personal use depends as much on how often he uses it as on his income. As a rule of thumb, anybody who uses a plane less than 200 hours a year is better off renting it himself.

Many manufacturers (notably Piper) love to put out brochures showing how planes in the $15,000 class can be operated 200 hours a year for combined hourly direct costs plus annual indirect costs for around $12 an hour. All such manufacturers' figures leave out quite a bit.

In the first place, the biggest indirect cost of all—depreciation—has to be figured into any realistic cost figure. That 20 percent a year a corporation auditor can get away with on a finance-lease contract is not in itself realistic, though. The *Aircraft Bluebook*, published by the Aircraft Dealers Service Association, is a better guideline as to what used planes are really worth, which is what depreciation is all about.

Thus, according to recent issues, on the average for *most* single-engine planes, a plane depreciates 17 percent the first year, another 12 percent the second year, 9 percent the third year, 8 percent the fourth year, and 7 percent the fifth year—or a total of about 44 percent for the five-year period.

That hypothetical $15,000 plane, then, would run depreciation costs like so:

17% OF $15,000 THE FIRST YEAR—$2,550
12% OF $12,450 THE SECOND YEAR—$1,494

9% OF $10,956 THE THIRD YEAR—$986
8% OF $9,970 THE FOURTH YEAR—$798
7% OF $9,172 THE FIFTH YEAR—$642

There are plenty of exceptions. Some special-purpose models and makes not much in demand depreciate as much as 50 percent in the first year. Others will hold up amazingly well (for example, the *Bluebook* lists a 1948 Cessna 120 for $2,100, which cost $2,845 new; just try selling your car for 73 percent of its cost after 20 years of use).

In general, depreciation costs level out decreasingly after five years. Average single-engine planes retain 35 percent to 40 percent of their original value for a long, long time, with twins leveling out at about 30 percent of their original cost after perhaps the same 10- or 15-year period.

But for those first five years, depreciation is the biggest single indirect cost of owning a new plane.

The second biggest indirect cost is the value of the money itself. If the buyer of that new plane sells $15,000 worth of income-producing securities to do so—or refrains from buying such securities—he will sacrifice an annual income of, what, $900 a year? That, too, is a cost involved in owning an airplane.

A more obvious cost is insurance. This depends on the limitations on usage and even on the pilot's experience as well as on the value of coverage. A good VFR pilot might get hull insurance, with full coverage for ground and flight operations on a $250-deductible policy, for as little as 2 percent. Utility operation might cost 4 percent of the coverage (or 10 percent for a crop duster). Say our man with the $15,000 plane is a private pilot with 300 hours of air time and gets a 3.5 percent rate; his basic insurance will run $525 for the first year.

Single-limit liability insurance, for $250,000, will cost another $200 a year or so.

Hangaring costs will average $30 or $40 a month, although this can go up to $60 at some of the East Coast airports. Outside tie-down fees should run around $15 or $20, which is all that's needed in mild weather. A combined average might run about $325 a year.

Here's how those first year costs add up:

DEPRECIATION	$2,550
USE OF MONEY	900
HULL INSURANCE	525
LIABILITY INSURANCE	200
HOME-BASE FEES	325
	$4,500

This is all before the owner ever gets off the ground, which would come to $22.50 an hour for 200 hours of operation a year (but $11.25 an hour for 400 hours a year, $9 an hour for 500 hours a year, and so on). By the fifth year, with lower costs for depreciation and hull insurance, the indirect costs would still be $2,388 for the annual operation.

This is why there are so many flying clubs in general aviation, to share the indirect costs between the members. A multiple-ownership "club" can be anything from a two-man 50-50 partnership to big organizations like Sky Roamers, Inc., the Los Angeles co-op with more than 200 pilots. The author, for example, owns a one-fifth interest in a Cessna 172 (*The Flying Fifth*) with four other part owners: a dentist, who uses it on Wednesday; a salesman, who uses it to broaden his market; and a couple of week-end pilots, who argue over who gets it on Saturdays and Sundays.

Each member of such a club pays his own direct costs based on the number of hours he uses it. Direct costs include reserves for maintenance and inspections.

Annual inspection and licensing (or every 100 hours for the operator-for-hire, and a careful private pilot operates in this area the same way) are mandatory, with the inspection comparable to the tune-up on an automobile. Along with minor parts, fixing dents, and so on, this comes to around $1.25 per air hour for the average light plane.

A major overhaul of the engine and prop represent a big-ticket expense and run from $1,000 to $2,500 for a single-engine plane. If our friend with the $15,000 plane has a 180 hp engine, his engine and prop overhaul will cost around $1,500 and can be expected between 800 and 1,200 hours (tops) of air time. Figuring midpoint at 1,000 hours, this is a direct cost of another $1.50 per hour of flight.

Using about 9 gallons of gas an hour at sensible cruising speeds, his fuel consumption will be about $4.50 an hour, including oil with a 50-hour oil change.

Aviation gas (80 octane) is about 12 cents a gallon higher than the cost of premium grade (ethyl) gas for a car. However, the state taxes on automobile gas run from 5 cents to 8 cents a gallon, depending on the state, and they either do not apply to aviation gas or are refundable in full in 31 of the 50 states. The tax for avgas is less than the tax for auto gas in other states and is as high as auto gas tax in only two states (Alabama and Vermont).

Oil consumption can be figured at about one pint per 10 gallons of gas, and aviation oil is generally standard at 50 cents to 65 cents a quart.

The pilot of that 180 hp engine will probably be flying at about 145 mph, which means that he'll be getting about 14 miles to the gallon, or considerably better than he does with the family car if it is anything much bigger than a compact. In any case, adding his direct cost of inspections, maintenance, ordinary parts and labor, plus the gas and oil, produces a direct operating cost figure of $7.20 an hour—about 5 cents a mile.

Bigger airplanes cost more; smaller planes cost less. But that man with his middle-size $15,000 plane really can use it at a lower total cost than driving the company car—even for the first year if the plane is used enough—by him personally, in a lease-back arrangement, or as part of a club.

In temperate climates, logging 50 hours a month is no trick at all (many light planes are flown over 1,000 hours a year). That 600 hours a year will cost $7.50 an hour in indirect costs, for a total operating cost of $15.70 an hour. *That* figures out to be little more than 11 cents a mile . . . and, man, just mundanely driving a decent-size new car can cost more than that for depreciation and insurance alone!

So you *would* like to buy an airplane!

Summary
of makes
and models

This list covers private aircraft currently registered for flight in the United States, including planes built by manufacturers no longer in business. Active companies currently in production are designated with their addresses, and "new" listings are marked with an asterisk. Recently discontinued operations are marked with an X. Brand names of current models are capitalized.

Ace Aircraft
Admiral
Aero Commander—*see* North American Rockwell Corporation
Aeronca
AEROSTAR—Ted Smith Aircraft Company
Aetna
AG CAT—Grumman Aircraft Engineering Corporation
AGWAGON—Cessna Aircraft Company
Aircraft Builders
Aircraft Industries of Canada, Ltd., St. Johns, Quebec, Canada
    United States marketing agent: Dee Howard, 130 S. Terminal, San Antonio, Tex. 78205

Aircraft Manufacturing Company
Aircraft Mechanics
Air Products
Air & Space
Alaska Helicopters
All American
Alliance
Allied Aero Industries, Inc., Atlantic Aviation Division, Box 398, Pottstown, Pa. 19494
X Alon Aircraft, Inc.
Alsema
American Aeronaut
American Aircrafting
American Airplane
* American Aviation Corporation, 318 Bishop Rd., Cleveland, Ohio 44143
American Eagle
Anderson
APACHE—Piper Aircraft Corporation
Arlington
Arrow Aircraft
* ARROW—Piper Aircraft Corporation
Atlas Aviation, Inc., Houston, Tex.
AUTOGYRO—Jovair Corporation
Avionautica
AZTEC—Piper Aircraft Corporation
Baker
Barnes
BARON—Beech Aircraft Corporation
Bartlett
Baumann
Bay Aviation
Beachey Pusher
BEAGLE Aircraft, Ltd., 2 Buckingham Gate, London, SW 1, England
BEAVER—De Havilland Aircraft of Canada
Bede
Bee Aviation

Beech Aircraft Corporation, 9709 E. Central, Wichita, Kans. 67201

BELL Helicopter Company, Box 482, Ft. Worth, Tex. 76101

BELLANCA—International Aircraft Manufacturing Company

Bensen Aircraft Corporation, Box 2746, Raleigh, N.C. 27602

* BERLIN DOMAN Helicopters, Inc., PO Box 385, Tough-kenamon, Pa. 19374

Bernard

BOEING Company, Commercial Division, Box 707, Renton, Wash.

Bolkow GmbH, Nabern/Teck, Germany
United States Distributor: Pioneer Aviation Corporation, 923 S. San Fernando Rd., Burbank, Calif. 90500

BONANZA—Beech Aircraft Corporation

Borland

X BRANTLY Helicopter Corporation—see Lear Jet Industries

Breguet

Brewster

X BRIEGLEB Sailplane Corporation

BRITISH AIRCRAFT CORPORATION, 399 Jefferson Davis Hwy., Arlington, Va. 22202

* Britten-Norman, Ltd., Bembridge Airport, Isle of Wight, England
United States representatives: Jonas Aircraft & Arms Company, 120 Wall St., New York, N.Y. 10005

Budd

Buecker

BUFFALO—De Havilland Aircraft of Canada

Buhl

BURNS Aircraft, Starkville, Miss. 39759

Butler Aviation Corporation, 29 Broadway, New York, N.Y. 10006

* CADET—Mooney Aircraft

Canadair

Cancargo

CAPSTAN—Slingsby Sailplanes

* CARDINAL—Cessna Aircraft Company

X Caribe Doman Helicopters of Puerto Rico

CARIBOU—De Havilland Aircraft of Canada
* Carstedt Aviation, 3521 E. Spring, Long Beach, Calif. 90801
CENTENNIAL—Found Brothers Aviation
CENTURION—Cessna Aircraft Company
Cessna Aircraft Company, Box 1521, Wichita, Kans. 67201
CHAMPION Aircraft Corporation, Osceola, Wisc. 54020
CHEROKEE—Piper Aircraft Corporation
Clark
Columbia
COMANCHE—Piper Aircraft Corporation
Commandaire
COMMANDER—North American Rockwell Corporation
Commonwealth
Continental Copters, Inc., Box 13284, Ft. Worth, Tex. 76118
CONVAIR Division, General Dynamics Corporation, Box 1128,
    5001 Kearny Villa Rd., San Diego, Calif. 92112
Corcoran
COURIER—Helio Aircraft Corporation
* COURSER—North American Rockwell Corporation
CUB—Piper Aircraft Corporation
Cunningham
Curtiss Wright
Dart Aircraft
DART—Slingsby Sailplanes
* DARTER—North American Rockwell Corporation
Dassault—*see* Pan American Business Jets Division
Davis
X Debonair—Beech Aircraft Corporation
De Havilland Aircraft of Canada, Ltd., Downsview, Ont.,
    Canada
Delackner
DERRINGER—Wing Aircraft Corporation
Detroit
DIAMANT—Flum-Umb Fahrzeugwerke, A.G.
DORNIER GmbH, 800 Munich 60, Box 25, Germany
    United States agents: Butler Aviation, 29 Broadway, New
    York, N.Y. 10006

DOUGLAS Aircraft Company, Inc., 3855 Lakewood Blvd., Long Beach, Calif. 90801

Downer

Doyle

* DOYN Aircraft, Inc., Box 18130, Wichita, Kans. 67218

Driggs

Druine

DUKE—Beech Aircraft Corporation

X Dumod Corporation of Florida

Duramold

Emigh

ENSTROM Corporation, Menominee County Airport, Menominee, Mich. 49858

Evangel

EXCALIBUR—Swearingen Aircraft

EXECUTIVE 21—Mooney Aircraft

Fairchild Hiller, 605 Southlawn Lane, Rockville, Md. 20850

FALCON—Dassault; *see* Pan American Business Jets Division

Federal

Filper Research, Inc., Box 28, Old Crow Canyon Rd., San Ramon, Calif. 94583

Fleet, Ltd.

Fletcher

* Flum-Umb Fahrzeugwerke, A.G., 9422 Altenrhein, Schweiz, Switzerland

Fock Wulf

Foka

Fokker

Ford

Found Brothers Aviation, Ltd., 8 Brydon Dr., Rexdale, Ont., Canada

Franklin Aero Industries, Box 398, Pottstown, Pa. 19464

Funk

General Aircraft

General Airplane

* GERONIMO Conversion Corporation, San Antonio International Airport, San Antonio, Tex. 78205

* GLASFLUGEL Ing. (BS1-b), Schlattstall, Germany
Golden
GOOSE—McKinnon Enterprises
Granville
Great Lakes
Grumman Aircraft Engineering Corporation, Bethpage, Long
Island, N.Y. 11714
GULFSTREAM—Grumman Aircraft Engineering Corporation
GYROCOPTER—Bensen Aircraft Corporation
Hall
Hamburger Flugzeugbau GmbH, Postfach 109, 2103 Hamburg
95, Finkenwerder, Germany
Handley Page, Ltd., 40 Claremont Rd., London, NW, 2,
England
 Sales department: Radlett Airdrome, St. Albans, Hertford-
 shire, England
* United States agents: International Jetstream Corporation
 (Subsidiary of K. R. Cravens Corporation), 26 Mercury
 Blvd., Spirit of St. Louis Airport, Box 100, Chesterfield,
 Mo. 63017
HANSA—Hamburger Flugzeugbau GmbH
Harlow
Hartman
Hawker Siddeley Aviation, Ltd., Hatfield, Hertfordshire, Eng-
land
 Agents: Hawker Siddeley International, Inc., La Guardia
 Airport, Flushing, Long Island, N.Y. 11369
Heath
Helicopters, Inc.
Helio Aircraft Corporation, Hanscom Field, Bedford, Mass.
01730
HELI-PORTER—Fairchild Hiller
Helisoar
Helton Aircraft Corporation (Culver), Falcon Field, Mesa,
Ariz.
Dee Howard Company, 130 S. Terminal, San Antonio, Tex.
78205
Huff Deland

HUGHES Tool Company, Aircraft Division, Centinela and Teale Sts., Culver City, Calif. 90230

HUSKY—Beagle Aircraft

X IMCO, Inc. (Call-Air)

Inland Avco

International Aircraft Manufacturing Company, Inc., Box 624, Alexandria, Minn. 56308

    Distributors: Bellanca Sales Company, Box 776, Plainview, Tex.

ISLANDER—Britten-Norman

* Israel Aircraft Industries, Ltd., Tel Aviv, Israel

    United States office: 850 Third Ave., New York, N.Y. 10022

Jamieson

JETASEN—Maule Aircraft Corporation

* JETLINER—Carstedt Aviation

JET RANGER—Bell Helicopter Company

JETSTAR—Lockheed-Georgia Company

JETSTREAM—Handley Page

JOBMASTER—Aircraft Industries of Canada

JOVAIR Corporation, 11920 W. Jefferson Blvd., Culver City, Calif. 90230

JUPITER—Sud Aviation

Kaiser

Kaman

Kellet

Keystone

KING AIR—Beech Aircraft Corporation

Kinner

Knight

Laird

LAISTER Sailplane Products, 11516 S. Brookshire, Downey, Calif. 90241

LAKE Aircraft, 12801 Day Rd., Mishawaka, Ind. 48544

Langley

Lark Aviation

* LARK COMMANDER—North American Rockwell Corporation

LEAR JET Industries, Municipal Airport, Wichita, Kans. 67201

Levier
Lickman
Lockheed-Georgia Company, 86 S. Cobb Dr., Marietta, Ga.
    30061
Luscombe
Macchi
Mars
Martin
Maule Aircraft Corporation, 6780 Brooklyn Rd., Jackson, Mich.
    49201
McClish
McCulloch
McDonnell
McKinnon Enterprises, Inc., Rt. 1, Box 520, Sandy, Ore. 97055
Mercury
MERLIN—Swearingen Aircraft
* METEOR—Allied Aero Industries
Midwest
Miller, E. B.
* MINERVA—Allied Aero Industries
Minnesota
Mitsubishi Industries, Ltd., 10 2-Chomi-Marunouchi, Chiyoda-
    Ku, Tokyo, Japan
Monocoupe
Mooney Aircraft, Inc., Louis Schreiner Field, Kerrville, Tex.
    78028
        Alon Aircraft Division, Municipal Airport, McPherson,
        Kans. 67201
Morane
Morrisey
Moth
MUSKETEER—Beech Aircraft Corporation
MUSTANG—Mooney Aircraft
Nardi
NAVAJO—Piper Aircraft Corporation
NAVION Aircraft Corporation, Navion Field, Seguin, Tex.
    78155
Nelson

Nich Beazly
Nieuport
Noorduyn
NORD Aviation, 2/18 Rue Beranger, Chatillon-sous-Bagneus,
France
United States marketing agent: American Nord Aviation,
1145 19th St. NW, Washington, D.C. 20036
X North American Aviation—see North American Rockwell Cor-
poration
North American Rockwell Corporation, North American Avia-
tion Division, International Airport, Los Angeles, Calif.
Aero Commander Divisions: Administration, 300 Sixth
Ave., Pittsburgh, Pa. 15222; Box 1469, Albany, Ga.
31702; 5001 N. Rockwell Ave., Bethany, Okla. 73008;
Box 520, Olney, Tex. 76374
Northrop
North Star, Inc. (Siai-Marchetti), 304 Henry St, Brooklyn,
N.Y. 11201
Northwestern
Olympia
Omega
Orenco
OTTER—De Havilland Aircraft of Canada
Overland
Pacemaker
Pacific Airmotive Corporation, 2940 N. Hollywood Way, Bur-
bank, Calif. 91503
* PALOMINO—San Antonio Aviation
Pan American Business Jets Division, 200 Park Ave., New York,
N.Y. 10017
Parks
Parmount
Pasped
PAWNEE—Piper Aircraft Corporation
Perth Amboy
Pfalz
Rinaldo Piaggio S.p.A., Viale Brigata Bisago 14, Genoa, Italy

Piasecki
Pietenpol
Pigman Reed
Pilatus
Piper Aircraft Corporation, Lock Haven, Pa. 17745
Pirtle
Pitcairn
Platt
Wiley Post
Henry Potez, 46 Ave. Kleber, Paris 16E, France
Pratt Read
Procaer
QUAIL—North American Rockwell Corporation
QUEEN AIR—Beech Aircraft Corporation
Rand
RANGER—Mooney Aircraft
Raven
Rawdon
REIMS-ROCKET—Cessna Aircraft Company
Republic
Rhein-Flugz
Riley Aeronautics Corporation, Box 8576, 2100 N.W. 50th St.,
    Executive Airport, Ft. Lauderdale, Fla. 33307
Roberts
* Robertson Aircraft Corporation, Bellevue Airfield, 15400 Sun-
set Hwy., Bellevue, Wash. 98004
ROCKET—Maule Aircraft Corporation
X Rockwell Standard Corporation—*see* North American Aviation
Roe
Roose
Rose
Ross
Rowley
Ryan
SABRELINER—North American Rockwell Corporation
* Sailplane Associates, Inc., 1023 Kirkwall Rd., Azusa, Calif.
91702

St. Louis

* San Antonio Aviation, Inc., Stinson Field, Hangar 10, San Antonio, Tex. 78214

Saturn

Scheutzow Helicopter Corporation, Box 40, Berea, Ohio 44017

SCHWEIZER Aircraft Corporation, County Airport, Elmira, N.Y. 14902

* SCORPIO—Franklin Aero Industries

Short Brothers & Harland, Ltd., PO Box 241, Queens Island, Belfast, North Ireland

> United States marketing agent: Remmert-Werner, Inc., Lambert Field, St. Louis, Mo. 63145

SHRIKE COMMANDER—North American Rockwell Corporation

Siai-Marchetti—*see* North Star, Inc.

SIKORSKY Aircraft, Stratford, Conn. 06497

Simounavon

Sioux Aircraft

Simplex

SIREN, S.A. (Edelweiss), 13 Rue Ste-Honoré, Versailles, France

> United States marketing agent: Ken Lingstone, Box 9977, Washington, D. C. 20015

* SIRIUS—Allied Aero Industries

SKYHAWK—Cessna Aircraft Company

SKYKNIGHT—Cessna Aircraft Company

SKYLANE—Cessna Aircraft Company

SKYMASTER—Cessna Aircraft Company

SKYROCKET—Atlas Aviation

* SKYSERVANT—Dornier GmbH

SKYWAGON—Cessna Aircraft Company

Slingsby Sailplanes, Ltd., Kings Lane, Kirbymoorside, Yorkshire, England

> United States marketing agents: Western Soaring, 1234 Washoe Dr., San Jose, Calif. 95120; Clarance See, Ltd., 730 Cold Spring Rd., Baldwinsville, N.Y.

Smith, D. E.

Ted Smith Aircraft Company, 9016 Winnetka Ave., Northridge, Calif. 91324

SNIPE—North American Rockwell Corporation

Sopwith

Spad

SPARROW—North American Rockwell Corporation

Spartan

STALLION—Helio Aircraft Corporation

Standard

Star Aircraft

* STAR—Franklin Aero Industries

Stark

State

* STATESMAN—Mooney Aircraft

Stearman

Stinson

STRATA ROCKET—Maule Aircraft Corporation

Sud Aviation, 37 DeMontmorency, Paris 16E, France

Superior

Swallow

Swearingen Aircraft, Box 6904, San Antonio, Tex. 78209

Taylorcraft

Temco

THRUSH—North American Rockwell Corporation

Timm

TOM CAT—Continental Copters

TRADEWIND—Pacific Airmotive Corporation

Transworld

TRAVEL AIR—Beech Aircraft Corporation

TURBO COMMANDER—North American Rockwell Corporation

TURBO 18—Volpar

X Turbo-Porter—Fairchild Hiller

TURBOROCKET—Riley Aeronautics Corporation

TWIN BEE—United Consultants Corporation

TWIN BEECH (18)—Beech Aircraft Corporation

Umbaugh

U-C-C
United Consultants Corporation, Box 175, Norwood, Mass.
  02062
Universal
Universal Aircraft
VEGA—Allied Aero Industries
VELA—Allied Aero Industries
Verti-gyro
Vertol
Verville
Vickers
Viking Aviation
VIKING (Bellanca)—International Aircraft Manufacturing
  Company
Volaircraft
Volpar, Inc., 16300 Stagg St., Van Nuys, Calif. 91406
WACO—Allied Aero Industries ("private label" by Sud)
* WEATHERLY Aviation Company, 2304 San Felipe Rd.,
  Hollister, Calif. 95023
* Windecker Aviation, Midland-Odessa Air Terminal Industrial
  Park, Midland, Tex.
* Wing Aircraft Corporation, 2600 W. 247th St., Torrence, Calif.
  90509
Witt
X World Jet Aircraft, Inc.
WREN Aircraft Corporation, Box 4115, Meacham Field, Ft.
  Worth, Tex. 76106
* YANKEE—American Aviation Corporation
Zefir
Zenith

Index